# CYCLING THE EARTH

Also by Sean Conway:

*Hell and High Water*

# CYCLING THE EARTH

## A LIFE-CHANGING RACE
## AROUND THE WORLD

### SEAN CONWAY

EBURY
PRESS

1 3 5 7 9 10 8 6 4 2

Ebury Press, an imprint of Ebury Publishing
20 Vauxhall Bridge Road
London SW1V 2SA

Ebury Press is part of the Penguin Random House
group of companies whose addresses can be found at
global.penguinrandomhouse.com

First published by Ebury Press in 2016

www.eburypublishing.co.uk

A CIP catalogue record for this book is
available from the British Library

ISBN 9780091959760

Typeset in India by Thomson Digital Pvt Ltd, Noida, Delhi

Printed and bound in Great Britain by Clays Ltd, St Ives PLC

Penguin Random House is committed to
a sustainable future for our business, our
readers and our planet. This book is made from
Forest Stewardship Council® certified paper.

*For Martin and Missy Carey.*
*Without your selfless generosity I'd never have been*
*able to complete the once-in-a-lifetime opportunity to cycle*
*around the world. I'll be eternally grateful.*
*Thank you.*

# CONTENTS

# 1

# OUT OF FOCUS

When I was growing up, I wanted to be a photographer and see the world. I had visions that my life would be spent on assignment for *National Geographic*, catalogue shoots in the Peruvian jungle and high-end advertising campaigns in the deserts. Jungles and deserts, that's where I wanted to be. I remember vividly my first camera, which I swapped for a packet of sweets from Cameron Barnes, one of my best friends at school when I was ten. That may sound like a good deal, but the camera really was a piece of shit, and the sweets were a roll of Super-Cs and some biltong (my absolute favourite). The camera had no focusing option and just three exposure settings: sun, cloudy and night. But it looked cool and when I pressed the shutter for the first time a fire started to burn inside me to travel and capture the world.

I remember sending the first roll of film in to the local pharmacy to be developed. They had to send it to the big city to get it done, which would take a week. It was the most exciting week of my existence on this planet. Eventually

Monday came back round and I went to pick up the photos. I was so nervous: what if they were all blurred, over-exposed or just generally shit? I so wanted them to be good. But I was handed the prints and Janet, the elderly nurse who worked at the pharmacy, told me, 'You took some really great pictures there, you should be a photographer when you grow up.'

I was hooked. Throughout my teens, I became obsessed with photography. I spent hour upon hour in the darkroom, photographing the school prom, rugby and cricket matches and trying every sort of photography I could imagine, from wildlife to journalism, and I bloody loved it. Piles of *National Geographic* magazine were scattered all over my room, the best pictures carefully cut out and stuck to the wall as I imagined crawling through a crocodile-infested river to get that one shot of a nearly extinct and elusive sloth. God damn it. I was going to be the best photographer anyone had ever seen. I honestly and truly believed that by the time I was thirty years old that would be the case. I was going to see the world and my camera was going to be my ticket to adventure.

November 2010. I had done the journey from London to Birmingham three times this week and it was killing me. The 50 mph speed limit for non-existent road works was a joke, but nothing like as much as what my life had become.

I was in Birmingham to take family portraits at the Busy Bees Nursery. The glamorous *National Geographic* commissions hadn't come through. Instead, I was setting up my lights and background in the only room they had available at the nursery: the fucking toilet. As a summary of where my career had ended up, it couldn't have been more accurate. I spent the next ten minutes trying to fit two fairly large parents and their four kids on a background that was only two metres wide. The father stepped back at one point, putting a huge hole in the paper backdrop. I had no choice but to include the urinals on either side of the background to get everyone in. It was going to take me a hundred years to Photoshop this photo and I was £35 down already with the torn background. Even if they bought the full package at £25, I was still making a loss.

'Smile, who's the cheeky monkey?'

*Click. Click. Click!*

'Who's a silly sausage? You are!'

*Click!*

With each release of the shutter I could feel my soul slowly dying. I was in complete autopilot mode as child after child was brought to me and sat down on the white background, which was now covered in piss, vomit, snot and dog shit from someone's shoes.

'Waaaaaah!' The fifty-seventh baby of the morning started to cry profusely. I was lying on my side, camera in one hand, puppet in the other trying to make a clearly miserable child smile so their parents could get some sort of decent photo for that year's Christmas card.

'Thanks Sean,' one of the nursery staff said. 'Unfortunately there are a few babies sleeping and their nap time finishes in a couple of hours. Could you wait until they are up? Their parents really want some photos.'

'How many of them?' I asked, knowing full well, from experience, that it was likely to be four at the most.

'Two, but their parents are well off and always buy the full package.' I was losing more money but waited begrudgingly. When the kids eventually woke up, they cried their eyes out and I didn't get one decent pic to sell to the parents. I packed up the studio, threw my piss- and shit-covered background in the bin and headed back down the M1 towards London. I thought my life couldn't sink any lower. I was wrong.

February was always the most depressing time of year for a photographer. Everyone was feeling a bit fat so didn't want photos of themselves. It was cold, monotone and bleak outside and no matter how you looked at it there were only so many ways you could photograph that lonely leafless tree on the top of the hill on Hampstead Heath. The one thing I did have to look forward to this particular year was my thirtieth birthday. I had organised a big bash in Proud Galleries in Camden with the theme of Africa. I had made up a Zulu warrior costume.

'Caroline, what are you going dressed as for my birthday?' I asked my girlfriend as we lay in bed on one lazy Sunday morning.

'Mmmmm,' she replied with a worried look on her face.

I stayed silent. I had a bad feeling as to what was going on.

'I'm really not sure,' she eventually replied.

'About the costume?'

'About us,' she began to cry. 'I'm not sure it's working.'

I got up and put my clothes on.

'Aren't you going to say anything?' she asked.

'To be honest, I can't fucking believe you're doing this before my birthday,' was all I could think to say.

'I know, I'm sorry,' she continued.

'Whatever.' I got up and started packing my stuff. To really embarrass her at work, because I knew she hated it, I had sent her thirty valentine cards from different people including Michael Jackson, Mandela and Robert Mugabe, which she now had all over her bedroom. I started frantically taking them down.

'You don't want these anymore then,' I said angrily.

'No Sean, please leave them. I love them.'

'Like fuck, don't insult me please.'

I threw them all in my bag; all the while Caroline sat in the middle of her bed crying. Why the fuck was she crying and not me? I stormed out, slammed the door behind me and got in my car to drive all the way back to north London where I lived. Two hundred metres down the road I felt immediately guilty for storming out. I pulled over. Fuck. What's happening to me? Life shouldn't be this shit. I turned around and went back. I knocked on the door.

Caroline was there in her towel. She had just been in the shower. That annoyed me. I thought she would have at least been mourning in bed all day.

I don't have much memory about what followed as waves of nonsensical emotions came from both of us. None of it mattered or was even remotely relevant. I didn't really know why she wasn't happy until she said something that I'll never forget.

'Is there someone else?' I asked.

'Not someone in particular, just generally other people.'

That hit me hard. Basically, she was saying that she was meeting many other people that she deemed could be a better boyfriend for her. Not just one other person, but many, which meant I was now somewhere far down the list in potential partners, not even a close second.

Looking back now, that was the turning point at which I realised my life was truly and utterly shit. I was an unmotivated, uncreative miserable sod who was so unhappy the only positive thing in my life was my girlfriend, who I then chased away because I put too much pressure her. The following months were a whirlwind of emotions. My thirtieth birthday came and went and I got suitably drunk and emotional as I staggered home barefoot, alone in the dark at five in the morning, the empty streets overwhelmingly claustrophobic. Ahead of me was a chap standing under a streetlight having a cigarette. I got closer and realised it was a guy from my local pub. I didn't know his name, because I had forgotten years ago and was too embarrassed to ask again.

'Mate. What you doing under the lamppost at this time of the morning?' I asked

He looked up and nearly fell over. He seemed a bit drunk too as he tried to work out why there was a Zulu warrior coming through the darkness towards him.

'Just had my birthday. It was African themed,' I explained. 'How are you?'

'Not so good, mate. Girlfriend just dumped me and I'm a mess, if I'm honest.'

I could see he had been crying. We were about the same age and for some reason seeing him crying under a random lamppost really struck a chord. Something in my life needed to change. I didn't want to be that dude under the lamppost crying my eyes out. Surely there was more to life than this?

The following day, I went to see James, my business partner, with whom I had started the nursery photography business nearly eight years previously. I told him I wanted out: it made good money but I was just too depressed to carry on. I was now thirty years old and barely wanted to pick up a camera, and the thought of photographing another snotty child actually gave me panic attacks.

'Take the week off and then let's talk,' he said.

James was always the thoughtful and sensible one. I took him up on the offer. During that week James made the decision to stop nurseries all together as he too was hating it but was far better at dealing with it than I was. We got rid of all seven freelances we used, including other photographers, Photoshop assistants, sales agents and online ecommerce guys. We shut down the office, sold the desks and all other business supplies on eBay.

A few weeks later I sold my shares in Lifepix Photography for £1 (so as to not ruin a friendship) and walked away: James being the joker gave me a Jersey £1 note. I remember holding the note to the light like you do to check the watermark. The sun glimpsed through the leaves above me as I stared up into the trees. As my focus shifted between the pound note and the sky behind the leaves I felt a huge weight off my shoulders. I vowed from that day on never to make life decisions based solely on my financial gain but to base them on my happiness instead. I needed to save this pound note, so rushed to the local charity shop and found a frame for £4 that would fit the note, and immediately framed it. I was now technically £3 in the red after the sale of my business.

I had no idea what I was going to do but didn't care. I had no money, no proper education after high school and no employable skills. The only thing I knew was photography and I now hated it. But I wasn't photographing crying babies any more. That was all that mattered. I may have had nothing. But I also had nothing to lose either. A week passed as I decided on my options in life. I had enough money to continue to rent my flat and live in London for another three months and most of that was money available from credit cards. I had three more months to make a serious plan otherwise I'd likely have to move back in with Dad, in South Africa. It was that or get a job somehow, with no CV or any employable skill.

Maybe I should go travelling. That seemed to be the one answer that I always came back to. Maybe I would *find* myself or something and all that shite. I could go hide away in Tibet, or India or somewhere equally remote. Maybe then I'd fall back in love with photography again. The only problem was that I had no money. I was £3000 or so in debt and spending credit card cash on rent. Also, as much as I wanted to go travelling, it seemed a soft way out. I needed something bigger than just travelling.

What could I do that was challenging, travel-based, and didn't cost too much money? For the next week I scrounged ideas but everything I found was either prohibitively expensive or wasn't that exciting. One day, feeling typically depressed with life and starting to regret selling my business, I decided to have a bath. Too lazy to wait for the water to get warm I got in feeling numb, both physically and emotionally. What was I going to do for the rest of my life?

As the hot water started to overtake the cold, and warmth started coming up from my feet, I started to think about other people who'd gone off adventuring. The first person who came to my mind was Mark Beaumont. As soon as I thought of his name my heart jumped and started to race a bit. Mark Beaumont broke the world record for round the world cycling back in 2008. I remembered watching him on TV and thinking, 'Damn, that's awesome.' It's surprising I hadn't really thought of it since. I guess when you think it's out of your reach you push it out of your mind, much like going to the moon. I never thought it because, 'that'll never be me'. Cycling around the world, the fastest, was like being an astronaut. It was what other people did. Who are these other people, I asked myself for the first time. Why am I not one of them? Maybe I could be? Surely not!

By now the water had started to engulf my chest making my heart race even faster. I felt excited, even nervous, for the first time in a very long while. I jumped out of the bath and googled Mark. Fuck me. He was just an ordinary bloke with a big dream and the gumption to make it happen. He didn't have millions of pounds. He wasn't an Olympian. He wasn't ex-army. He wasn't from Chelsea and he didn't wear red trousers. He was a Scotsman who by all intents and purposes was quite similar to me, apart from the fact he's over six foot tall.

His record for cycling round the world stood at 197 days. That was 100 miles per day. Maybe I could do that. I closed my laptop and started pacing around my room. On the third or fourth lap I saw my reflection in the mirror. I had the biggest smile I had seen on myself in years. I felt alive. The speech Rocky gave his son came into my head: 'It ain't about how hard you hit, it's about how hard you can get hit and keep moving forward.'

I took a permanent marker and jumped on my bed and right above me, on the ceiling, I wrote it down. Life had hit me down but I was going to keep moving forward, all the way to Australia and back again. This ticked all the boxes for me. I could travel, push myself and also with some luck get a sponsor to fund it. The new Sean was born that night.

# 2
# LEARNING TO RIDE

It's amazing what a new lease of life does to you. I hadn't really noticed before, but I had awful skin, wasn't sleeping properly and was always anxious. These symptoms had been around for so long I just presumed that's what was normal. If I had known what real life was like, a life of challenge, being fit and having a huge goal, I would have quit years ago.

I felt I'd wasted my twenties and now was in a rush to make up for all the years of the bullshit rat race, chasing the wrong dreams. I felt good and when you feel good and positive, good things happen: I managed to secure a sponsor to fund my cycle and also found out that the world's first ever round the world bike race was due to start in February 2012. I entered it. Besides a few canoeing races as a kid and cross-country this was in fact the first official race I'd ever entered in my life. And what a way to start.

The rules of the competition were simple. You needed to cycle a minimum of 18,000 miles, go generally east or west, not go back on yourself (in other words, you couldn't do circles in a flat country to make up the mileage) and you also had to pass two antipodes on the earth. Besides that, you could skip countries that had bad roads or were dangerous and choose the best route. It really was quite a task to decide where to go. There are many things to think about but I loved this new challenging life I had made for myself. Photographing snotty kids seemed a hazy distant memory already.

Although the world record was the focus, I got a very interesting email from Nick Sanders. He had the record in the 1980s and he gave me two bits of advice. Firstly, records get broken or forgotten and most people only have one chance at cycling around the world so make it count. Secondly, take loads of pictures, as your memories, no matter how amazing you think the experience was, will fade. Because of his advice I decided to try and cycle a bit in each continent (except that icy one, of course). It was a bit of a risk adding Africa and South America, which are notoriously slow, but I didn't think you could call it round the world cycling without at least doing a bit of each.

Over the next few months I trained my arse off. Forty hours a week. Up at five, looking at the ceiling reading Rocky's speech first and then various other motivational quotes to spur me on. I'm a visual person so it really did help having them right above my head when I went to bed and got up every morning. My landlord, though, was going to be really pissed off when he found out. I'd hopefully be halfway to Australia by then!

My week was a combination of road cycling and gym days. Some were one or the other, both on a few, with Sunday my much-needed rest and laundry day. With this much exercise, you build up a pretty disgusting set of dirty clothes very quickly. I couldn't keep up with it all, so just used to get in the shower fully clothed to wash the salt off my clothes. I could go for three days of this before all the oil and grit from the roads had truly embedded themselves and they needed a proper wash.

My routes generally went north towards Cambridge and then on to Kings Lynn, before turning round to fight the headwind back to London. Saturday was the big day. I'd usually do around 220 miles from London to Lincolnshire or a round trip to Norfolk and back. If I was feeling particularly adventurous, I'd do London, Brighton, Portsmouth and back to London.

For every litre of sweat that dripped off the end of my nose, for every puncture I had to repair, for every godawful recovery shake I had to drink, the better I became at cycling. My confidence was high and I was feeling the happiest I had been in a long time. I had even stopped drinking, which was something I hadn't managed in years. I used to have two cans of beer when I got home almost every night. It wasn't good and only since stopping had I realised just how bad it was for my body and my mind. The less I drank now the less I wanted to drink. The only major downside was that I realised some of my friends really weren't as funny as I'd thought they were. That was quite disappointing actually.

By November I was in full swing. Although winter was setting in fast I felt a new man. This would be the first time I didn't have to photograph any crying babies in eight years. I can't tell you how that felt. To justify my decisions even more I didn't even have one nursery contact me saying how sorry they were we had stopped. At the end of the day no-one really gave a shit about what we were doing. It wasn't ground-breaking and with digital cameras getting better by the month, parents were taking just as good photos at home.

Three months to go before the start of the round the world bike race. I still had a lot more training to do. I was starting to feel the pressure, but it was time to step up my game even further.

This was my new Saturday routine. It would be about 9.30 pm by the time I got back to my cold and lonely flat in north London. I couldn't feel my feet, my legs felt like jelly and I had a rasping cough. I lived on the second floor and had to carry Maid Marian, my beloved bike, up about 17 stairs, which took up the very last bit of energy I had left. I had been out training for nearly sixteen hours and managed to cycle from north London to Norfolk and back again. I didn't seem to have any control of my body as I fumbled with the keys to get the front door open. After an eternity and dropping my keys on the floor twice I made it in. I checked my phone for messages. Only one. It was from my trainer, Steve: 'Hope the training is going well, mate. Make sure you eat properly. Steve.'

I knew a few of my mates were out for drinks yet I hadn't received a message from any of them. Who could blame them, really? I had said no to so many requests over the last three months that they'd all given up. That had been the hardest thing to manage since I started training. Six months ago I couldn't even cycle 40 miles without having to catch the train home. Today I managed 220 miles. Although a huge achievement I wasn't overly excited. I guess I was just way too tired.

Still in my dirty Lycra I turned on the shower and got straight in. The warm water helped in some way to make me feel better but all I could think of was bed. I then remembered Steve's text. Eating properly is the last thing I felt like doing. I could barely swallow the build-up of saliva in my mouth let alone chew on spaghetti. I'd just have to have another recovery shake instead of a proper meal.

After my shower and coffee-flavoured recovery shake I got straight into bed. I looked up at the ceiling above me. I had written in big red letters the phrase 'Mileage Makes Champions' and with today's 220-mile ride, my weekly total was up to 610 miles on the road. I kept staring at the ceiling wondering if 610 miles in a week was good mileage or not. It was impressive, but I would need to do nearly double that each week going round the world if I was going to break the record.

Mid-January: one month until the start. I had a few weeks left to sort out final logistics, move my life into storage, sell things that didn't fit into storage and slowly taper my training so that I hit the start line at full fitness. Annoyingly, I had been ill for three weeks over Christmas and New Year, which meant I was a little behind schedule. I realistically had two more full weeks of hard training before my taper started. I really needed to make them count.

The last six months had been a blur of training, being tired, wet, cold, fundraising, and eating for a family of four every day. Although it had been really tough, and I'd had to make many sacrifices, I felt I was doing the right thing. My parents were pretty worried about me, but at thirty years old I was still young enough to do this and for it not to have a negative impact on the rest of my life. In fact, it could only have a positive impact considering I was completely miserable before. I'd forever regret not at least trying to go for it. It was a lot harder for my father who lived in South Africa, because he couldn't see what it was all about. My mother lived in London so she could see the change in me and appreciate the effort I was making to follow in the footsteps (tyre tracks?) of my cycling heroes. I loved travel and exploration-based adventures and could easily have used my credit cards to wander around the world slowly, but that wasn't enough for me. I wanted to push myself, test myself, see what I was capable of, and to finally prove that I could be *'one of those other people'* whom I'd read about in the papers.

This year was host to the first ever World Cycle Race. It was the brainchild of round the world cyclist Vin Cox, who on returning home from his ride realised his record could easily be beaten and invited people to do so. The idea of racing against other adventure cyclists added a whole new aspect to my adventure. There were now ten of us all starting at the same time from the same place, all going for the world record. It was turning into a very interesting race with some strong competition. My advantage was ignorance. Because I had only started cycling properly six months previously I wouldn't know if my saddle was chaffing badly because I'd have nothing to compare it with. For all I knew that would be normal chafe. If you think it's normal you can forget about it and keep going. It's only when you have something else to compare it too that you decide it is in fact the worst chafe in the world, and that then plays on your mind.

Round the world cycling records are about a lot more than just being able to cycle fast for long periods of time.

They are self-supported. You get lost. You need to find your own place to sleep and your own food. Your choice of route is very important. A week of unexpected headwinds can ruin your chances completely. You need to concentrate on fast roads in flat countries where you might have a tailwind but still maintain a 'circumnavigation' feel without skipping large chunks of the world.

Up until January 2012, a month before my attempt was due to start, the official record was held by Vin Cox at 163 days. Alan Bate's record had been 'under review' for nearly two years as Guinness debated whether his semi-supported ride should be allowed. They finally decided that it was allowed and the record dropped dramatically to 106 days. I secretly always knew this might happen, but the reality was that my daily average to beat the record would have to go from a realistic 112 miles per day to a daunting 168 miles per day.

The other battle I had was balancing breaking a record and having the adventure of a lifetime. I was reminded again of what Nick Sanders had said when he emailed me: 'Records get broken or forgotten and today's newspaper is in tomorrow's recycling. Make sure you still have a proper good old adventure because you will most likely never be able to do it again.'

It was a fine balancing act coming up with a route that meant I had a shot at the record but also didn't sacrifice adventure. According to Guinness rules, you could legitimately zigzag through Europe to Turkey, fly all the way to Australia, cycle across it and a few days in New Zealand, zigzag across America and then cycle from Portugal back to England. You'd have followed their rules but missed out three continents and done more than 50% of your ride in two countries. Luckily most adventure cyclists still adhered to the ethos of round the world cycling, but it would be interesting to see what the other competitors did now that it was an official race.

From the start I decided to make one major rule for myself. Do a bit in each major continent, Antarctica excepted. This then meant I had to go through Africa and South America, which most round the world cyclists would miss out. My main route would be as follows:

I'd leave London and fly to Malaga in Spain, skipping France as I'd be doing it on the way back anyway so didn't want to do it twice, rather adding mileage to another country. I'd cycle from Malaga to Gibraltar and then across to Tangiers, Morocco where I'd do the 400-mile ride to Marrakesh.

From Marrakesh I'd fly to Santiago in Chile and cycle the iconic Pan-American Highway, making my way north through the Atacama Desert until I reached Lima.

From Lima I'd fly to Miami and cycle across America to LA.

From LA I would fly to Sydney and then head north along the coast for 1000 miles before heading inland and straight through the dreaded outback towards Darwin.

My next leg would be from Singapore through Malaysia to Bangkok, which would be pretty flat, and then on to India where I'd cycle from Kolkata to Mumbai.

I looked into cycling through Iran but the political situation meant I wasn't realistically going to be able to do it and cover the sorts of daily mileage I'd need too.

My final leg was from Istanbul, where I'd make my way through Eastern Europe and finally up through France and back to London, just in time for the London 2012 Olympics.

It wasn't ideal and I kind of felt like I was taking too many flights, but I was happy that it was the best I could do within the rules of the race, and I'd be visiting seventeen countries that I had never been to before. This really was going to be the adventure of a lifetime and I couldn't wait for 18 February to arrive.

# 3

# FINDING MY LEGS

'Ten . . . nine . . . eight . . .'

My heart was practically bouncing out of my chest with nervous excitement as the crowds started the slow countdown. The day had finally arrived. I had packed my entire life into thirty square feet of storage, said farewell to my friends and was just about to embark on what would turn out to be the most challenging experience of my life. The start to the world's first ever World Cycle Race was seconds away and I was one of twelve people lucky enough to be a part of it.

Greenwich Park was teeming with friends and family of the riders, general fans of adventure cycling and the media. It was all a bit overwhelming for someone who had only really started cycling properly six months earlier. My attempt to be the fastest person to cycle around the world wasn't my only challenge either. I had received a very nice email from a school in East London near the Olympic Park who wanted me to take their replica mini Olympic Torch around the world and back to London again in time for the Olympics. I had to say yes, even though it was 100g extra to carry: it was a cool idea and would give me added incentive to stick to my plan of getting back to London in time for the games. The media also thought this was a great story and I spent most of the morning in Greenwich getting interviewed and having photos taken of me with my little six-inch Olympic Torch.

Such were my nerves, I hadn't got more than three hours sleep the previous night and in my haste getting ready had decided not to put my thermal leggings on. As a result, I was freezing. I could barely move my lower jaw when Sky Sports News interviewed me: I must have sounded like a zombie. It wasn't just my legs that were cold either: someone had paid £100 at my charity fundraiser to shave off my huge afro. The idea was that I'd start today completely clean shaven and then see how long the beard and hair would grow by the time I returned. This seemed to be what all adventurers did. I had never grown a beard before. I very much doubted I'd enjoy having a huge ginger beard, but you have to try things at least once, don't you?

Most parks in winter are pretty sad places to look at. Disused playgrounds, lifeless trees and an empty eeriness make them rather depressing. Today, however, was different. The usual dull greyness of winter was consumed by the bright outdoor jackets, joyful smiles and nervous excitement overflowing around the Observatory. I found myself looking across the river to see the city of London below me. I loved London but the city itself had drained me of all creativity over the years. It wasn't London's fault; it was completely my own doing for chasing the wrong dream. Now, for the first time, I didn't feel suffocated by it. I was looking at London with a new perspective, with the knowledge that a brand new chapter in my life was just about to begin. The next time I'd see the city I'd have cycled the earth. That was a crazy notion that still hadn't quite sunk in. Hopefully, by the time I returned I'd have a new outlook on life, London and where my life was heading. For now though, I was heading to Australia. Shit! What a thought!

'Seven . . . six . . . five . . .'

My teeth started to chatter. I looked to my right to see Mike Hall, one of my fellow competitors, looking cool, calm and collected. Bastard! How did he do it? Mike was one of the main riders competing in this race and was probably my biggest rival. He had an impressive history of endurance cycling including a few 24-hour time-trial wins under his belt and best rookie rider in the 2011 Tour Divide, the world's toughest mountain bike race. He didn't give too much away about his preparation but every now and then he'd share what he was up to on Twitter or Facebook. It was pretty impressive. I also couldn't help thinking how sexy his bike looked. He was taking a bit of a risk going full carbon but then again his route was a lot flatter than mine and probably with less potholes.

I had decided to go for a full steel bike made by Thorn in Somerset. She was called Maid Marian and we had formed a special bond over the past few months. She may have been a little heavier but I knew, without fail, that she would work all the time, no matter what was thrown at her. I think Mike was surprised at how light my set-up looked. When he asked me if he could pick Maid Marian up, I said, 'Not a chance', with a huge grin on my face. I knew that my set-up was probably one or two kilos heavier than his but didn't want him to know that. Dirty race tactics or just playing the mind games everyone plays? This was a serious race after all.

Along with Mike at the start line in Greenwich were seven other riders: Jason Woodhouse, Kyle Hewitt, Martin Walker, Richard Dunnett, Simon Hutchinson, Stephen Phillips and Stuart Lansdale. There were also three other riders starting at different locations, as per the rules of the race: Kristina Stoney, Juliana Buhring, and Paul Ashley-Unett had decided on this strategy. Of these cyclists, only a few were actually racing: Jason Woodhouse, Martin Walker, Richard Dunnett and Juliana Buhring, who was going for the female world record. Mike still seemed my main rival but the others didn't give much away in the lead-up, which was always a concern. I had no idea how strong they were.

My set-up came in at around sixteen kilos excluding food and water. I was probably a little too concerned with keeping the weight down, to the point of sawing my toothbrush in half and cutting the pieces of material off the end of my zips. It was completely unnecessary but if it played on my mind, then it needed to go. In total, my list of equipment looked like this:

Thorn Mercury steel bike with Rohloff hub gearing and Brooks saddle
Yeti Passion One sleeping bag
Klymit X-Lite camping frame
Terra Nova Extreme 'bivi' (bivouac sack)
One set of cycle clothing (including: shorts, shirt, jersey, rainproof overcoat, socks, shoes, compression tights, helmet, cap, gloves and watch)

GoPro, iPhone, iPod and point-and-shoot camera with all charging cables (I had a built-in dynamo on the front wheel to give me power to charge everything while I was cycling)

Mike had a similar set-up but with heavier camping gear according to what I had read on Twitter. It was definitely going to be interesting to see the different problems we'd encounter along the way. He had the Ferrari and I had the Rolls-Royce: speed versus reliability! I was no betting man but it was a tough call as to which would win an 18,000-mile race.

'Four . . . three . . . two . . .'

I felt nauseous as it hit me what I was about to undertake. I was going to be spending just over three months sitting on a piece of leather the size of my hand while trying to push over 168 miles per day.

'Good luck, mate,' Mike said, looking across.

'You too, mate,' I said back, but I am not sure he heard me with the noise of the crowd counting down. My lips were so cold they hardly moved.

'One . . . go, go, go!'

Whistles and cheers erupted. Mike and a few of the others shot off as if it were a 100 m sprint. By contrast, I struggled to clip into my pedal and found myself lagging behind. The route leading south through Greenwich Park was lined with people waving and clapping. I was pleasantly surprised at how many of my friends had turned up, looking a bit hungover, on this cold Sunday morning. Such had been my training schedule, I hadn't seen many of them for months. There was even an ex-girlfriend there who I hadn't spoken to in about three years. Along with my mates, loads of my family were also there to see me off: my mum and sister, uncle, aunt, and first and second cousins from Zimbabwe. This was the first time we'd all been together in a long, long time and it was a shame I didn't have too much time to chat to them all. I felt emotional and guilty that all these people had come all this way, just to see me disappear for months. As I pedalled further and further away from the start line, the crowd gradually got quieter and quieter. Eventually, all I could hear was the sound of my heart. *Thump, thump, thump.* This was it: there was no turning back now. I was by far the most nervous I had ever been in my entire life.

My route from Greenwich was to head to Gatwick Airport where I would stop the clock and then get a flight to Spain where my adventure would officially start. I had managed to persuade seven other keen cyclists to join me for this opening 35-mile leg. It was great to have some company, and also have someone who knew the route through the busy network of roads heading out of London. The plan was to wait for them at the bottom of the park. Once the crowd had disappeared from sight I turned a corner and in a split second all my nerves went away. Standing together in a huddle were three of my fellow competitors, all with their maps sprawled out, trying to work out where they were going. From here it looked like Stuart, Kyle and Simon. I burst out laughing. They were lost within a mile of starting. At least I wasn't the only one who felt unprepared for this adventure. That made me feel so much better. Moments later, I met up with my entourage and we slowly worked our way through the barrage of traffic lights and busy south London roads towards Gatwick.

Although I had done nearly 10,000 miles in training I still somehow didn't feel as if I had worked out a system for where everything went. I had put my jacket at the bottom of my bag and had to stop and dig everything out to get at it. Lesson one: keep jackets near the top in case you need them. Although our pace was fast it took nearly three hours to do the 35-mile ride to Gatwick. Mike, by contrast, must have been halfway to Dover already, where he would take the ferry to France. He was going east around the world; I was going west. I wondered if we would meet half way?

I could only get a flight out of Gatwick first thing the next day, so booked a hotel at the airport for the night. My family and some friends decided to come and have dinner with me as a final goodbye and an attempt to fatten me up a little. Mum and my sister Kerry were there and suitably excited about my challenge: they took every opportunity to tell anyone and everyone what I was doing, shouting out at random people, 'He's cycling around the world.' Mum and Kerry have always been my biggest supporters. They saw how unhappy I had been and how happy I was now. It was great to have them there with me. I only wished Dad was there as well. But being in South Africa, he hadn't really been able to be as involved as I'd have liked.

'Come on Sean, eat this.' Russell, my cousin, shoved a second plate of pudding in front of me. 'You're looking a bit thin.'

Russell was right. I hadn't put on nearly as much weight as I was supposed to. I weighed 67 kg, which might have been the heaviest I had ever been, but I was still in the 'very lean' section on my body mass index. I was hoping to get up to 70 kg so that I had some fat to burn before my muscle tissue started to disintegrate. I'd just have to keep on top of my nutrition from day one.

Just before bed I went on Twitter to see how the other riders were doing. Mike and Martin were in France, which was expected. Jason had already broken his bike and was looking for new parts. Stuart had forgotten his passport in north London and had had to go back and fetch it. Kyle, meanwhile, had pulled out of the race stating he didn't want to leave his wife and their newborn. And that was just day one.

For the second night running, I didn't sleep well. I tried to get some sleep on the flight to Spain but had a crying baby next to me. That was probably karma getting back at me because apparently I used to cry as a baby on planes. I landed in Malaga at around 10.30 a.m and was pleased to discover that unlike the start in Greenwich, it was warm and bright: an ideal 18 degrees. These were perfect cycling conditions and one of the reasons I was heading west and towards South America – to chase the summer and the heat that went with it. I operate much better when it is warm and the idea of pushing east through northern Europe in mid-winter actually scared me. Chasing the summer meant I could carry less clothing, and lighter camping gear.

Having landed in Spain, the next task was to reassemble Maid Marian. Gatwick sold bike boxes which had allowed me to package Maid Marian up carefully. I spent the next hour putting my bike back together, which involved putting the handlebars, saddle, wheels and pedals back on. This should really have only taken twenty minutes but was the first time I had ever done it. It was something I should have practised beforehand as the race clock started the moment I cleared customs. The rules stated that time in transit – flights, ferries and so forth – didn't count towards your race time.

The thinking was that if there was a flight delay it wasn't your fault. Once you had your bike in your possession again, however, then the clock started and counted towards your race time. You had to prove it by getting signatures from people, taking photos of your watch, the location and flight arrival board times. This was all part of the application you had to submit to Guinness on returning to prove you did in fact have the world record. The reality was that the difference between first and second place could be as little as half a day, so every half hour mattered.

Eventually Maid Marian was back in one piece and I was ready to go. There was just one problem: I didn't know what to do with the box. There were no bins around, so I wandered over to two airport security guards to ask.

'Pardon *señor*, um, is it possible to throw my box away?' I realised I was doing the patronising slow talking you do when on holiday. The irony was that I had dated a Colombian for nearly two years and she didn't teach me a word of Spanish. Missed an opportunity there.

'Ah, no problem.' The security guard smiled and pointed to some stairs leading to the terminal building. I said thank you and walked over, but there was no sign of any bin anywhere. After searching around, I dragged the box back to the now confused-looking guards. They pointed towards the stairs again. Again I looked at them as if to say, I didn't know what they were talking about.

'*Señor*, come.' The older and grumpier of the two took the box out of my hands, dragged it towards the stairs and secretly hid it out of sight. Are you kidding? I thought. You could fit a bomb big enough to detach Spain in that box and you are hiding it under the stairs to the terminal building, the stairs that passengers use to get into the airport. To think that I had been made to take my shoes off before getting on the flight that morning.

I decided the best thing was to make a run for it. I didn't want to be around when the *policía* found it and searched through their CCTV for the culprit. So with that I jumped on Maid Marian and made a swift exit. Unfortunately, in my haste I forget to cycle on the 'wrong' side of the road and had a close shave with an angry looking taxi driver. I really needed to get into the swing of things. It'd be really embarrassing if I got run over before I even reached 100 miles.

I had no map for Spain but figured that if I kept the coast to my left I'd eventually reach Gibraltar. I had downloaded some Google maps onto my phone so could use them if I needed. Finding the coast was easy: it was next to that big blue thing. Trying to work out Spanish road systems, however, was a whole new experience. I'd be cycling along a perfectly good 'A' road, which would then turn itself into a motorway for about two miles and then back to an 'A' road again. Cycling on motorways is prohibited in Spain, so I spent most of the morning doubling back on myself and cycling along the beachfront path. This wasn't allowed either and I got shouted at a few times by the *policía*. When I eventually made it onto a long stretch of 'A' road, my speed was good. I had a small tailwind and was keeping a good average of 17 mph. But there were just so many diversions and stops that I wasn't doing much more than ten miles every hour – I had no chance of breaking the world record if I kept this up.

The sun was just about to set when I cycled over the last climb before descending into Gibraltar. It was beautiful and I stopped for a moment to take it all in. I couldn't see it but knew that on the other side of that golden expanse of water was Africa, and the next leg of my adventure. By the time I reached the port where I was to get a ferry to Tangiers in Morocco, it was getting dark. Having worked my way through the town and all the way to the end of the eastern peninsular of the port, I was surprised to learn that ferries stopped going from Gibraltar to Morocco a few years back. Great research there, Sean! I then had to make my way all the way round the port to Algeciras where I'd be able to get a ferry in the morning.

Algeciras was quite a rundown looking town – industrial and not very pretty. Everything looked closed, too. I was quite tired from a week of restless sleep so figured I'd find a hotel, get some dinner and go to bed. The only hotel around seemed decent enough and they even let me take Maid Marian into the room. This was very important – it was as if she was my partner and I didn't want us to be separated. We were a team, after all.

I checked in and made my way up to Room 13. Good thing I'm not superstitious. I must have been the only person in the hotel as all the lights were off and I had to rely on my bike light to find my way down the corridor. Over a dinner of Moroccan tagine at the restaurant over the road, I felt I was finally getting into the swing of things. Africa and my real adventure started the following day. I couldn't wait.

# 4

# GETTING SOME BIG MILES DOWN

I had no idea what time my ferry was so I got up at 6 a.m. and made my way to the port. I was in luck: the next ferry was due to leave an hour later. I was a little apprehensive about this boat ride because the last time I did it I'm sure we nearly sank. It was in 2006 and a few friends had decided to do a road trip around Morocco. In those days there were no cheap flights so the only way was to fly to Spain and then catch the ferry. About halfway into the crossing there was a huge storm that came out of nowhere. The ferry turned into a potential death trap: people were falling off their chairs, glasses were smashing, games machines were tumbling over and huge pot plants slid across the floor, smashing against walls. People were projectile vomiting over everything. Even some of the ferry staff were huddled together reading the Koran, and when the staff get stressed out, then you know it's bad. I get extremely seasick, so had spent most of the ride with my head in my lap praying that we would sink so that it would all be over.

Fortunately, this crossing was much smoother. The ninety-minute journey allowed me to think about the task that lay before me. Cycling around the world! What a phrase. Pedalling, with your own two legs, around the entire planet. To me, that seemed the most exciting thing anyone could do, short of going to the moon. Not that I was the first person to attempt it, far from it. As soon as someone made a bicycle that could withstand the task, someone was on the case. Thomas Stevens was the first person to cycle around the world from 1884 to 1886 and he'd done it on a Penny Farthing.

Thomas Stevens' attempt was just the first of many. Cycling in the early twentieth century was extremely popular and in Britain there seemed to be a real competition to see how far you could push yourself. Along with round the world cycling came the competition to see who could cover the furthest distance in one year. A fiercely competitive period of long-distance cycling ensued: Marcel Planes managed just shy of 35,000 miles in 1911; that record stood until 1932 when Arthur Humbles managed 36,000 miles. By 1937 the record stood at over 62,000 miles. Surely no one was going to break that.

Then on 1 January 1939, just before the war, Tommy Godwin started his attempt. The first few months were fast but just off the pace at around 160 miles per day. Three months in and Tommy knew he'd have to step it up a gear and in June, July and August of 1939 Tommy rode through the night averaging over 230 miles per day. By the end of the year, Tommy had achieved an incredible distance of 75,065 miles. That's averaging over 200 miles per day and in pre-war times when bikes were heavy and tyres unreliable. Guinness have regarded his record as too dangerous to attempt so have discontinued it. He is one of my biggest heroes.

Over the following years, cycling took a little bit of a hit as public transport got better and people started to buy their own cars. Cycling was for poor people and everyone seemed to forget all about those long-distance cycling heroes. With the most-miles-in-a-year competition no longer an option, the next challenge was the record for round the world cycling. Guinness seem to have the only guidelines on this attempt and in 1984 decided you had to cycle 13,000 miles and pass two antipodes for it to be considered a world circumnavigation record. Nick Sanders stepped up to the plate and managed the distance in 78 days including transfer time. He averaged 170 miles per day on the bike and did it completely self-supported.

Guinness then decided to change the rules again and increased the mileage to 18,000. Everyone seemed to forget about round the world cycling for a while. That was until in 2008, when Mark Beaumont came along and managed the feat in 196 days. All credit to Mark: although his average of 100 miles per day was far off previous long-distance record holders, his incredibly adventurous route and talent for documenting it caught everyone's imagination, including myself. The floodgates were open again. Attempting to be the fastest person to cycle the world was now 'the thing to do' much like the most mileage in a year had been in the 1930s. Within a few years another four people had attempted and succeeded in beating the record. Then the record was 163 days set by Vin Cox, while Guinness adjudicated Alan Bates semi-supported attempt. Guinness gave Alan the record a few months before my race started, meaning I would now have to average 168 miles per day.

\*

When I arrived in Tangier, it seemed unusually quiet and nothing like the Tangier I knew of. Tangier was a huge bustling city but here there wasn't a building in sight. I found someone who looked like a doctor in a white coat but was in fact a ferry worker.

'Um, is this Tangier?' I asked.

'Yes, Tangier Med.'

'So not the city?'

'No, the city is 40 km that way.' He pointed westwards down the coast.

Great, I thought. Yesterday I went to the wrong port and today I took the wrong ferry to the wrong part of Morocco. I was certain I knew this part of the journey but should probably have researched it a little more. It wasn't all bad: mileage was mileage and it all counted towards the 18,000. My tracker recorded my mileage and as long as I was going generally west I could take any road I wanted to. I hadn't really planned too much and liked it this way because it gave me some freedom to let the adventure tell me where to go rather than the other way round. I had booked my flights in and out of each leg and just needed to make the most of the in-between whilst pushing 168 miles per day. Although mileage was mileage, the Tangier balls-up meant an extra 25-odd miles that were incredibly hilly, but also that I probably wasn't going to make it to Casablanca that day, which was now a good 240 miles away. It was 8 a.m. by the time I was on the bike – a pretty late start for trying to do a big day. I'd probably have to stay in Rabat overnight, which looked to be 190 miles away.

It was great to be back in Morocco. The cloudless sky merged with the crystal blue ocean to my right. The road was fast and without potholes. Cycling conditions were fantastic:

I was feeling strong and kept a steady 15 mph pace. My target was to stay at around 14 mph, which meant I wouldn't fatigue as much. As both my trainer Steve and my mentor Mark kept telling me, it's the pace that kills, not the distance. Before I'd left Britain, Steve had put me through a heavy 35–40 hours per week training schedule which culminated in a 220-mile ride every Saturday. He was also my nutritionist and taught me all about getting the right sort of food in me and what to look for when dashing into a supermarket in a rush: 'High fat diet, mate. Fat has 9 kcal per gram. Carbs only have 4 kcal per gram. You get much more "bang for your buck" with fat and it's a better energy source.'

It was hard to find fatty food, so I generally went one third carbs, one third fat and one third protein. My mentor Mark, meanwhile, is an Ironman legend and has done over 450 triathlons. He taught me all about technique, saving energy for tomorrow and avoiding injury. Under their tutelage, I'd gone in six months from not being able to do 40 miles to being able to cover 220 in a day. It was tough but it's what I needed to do in order to have a fighting chance at the record.

I had managed to get a quick bite to eat on the ferry, so it wasn't until Tangier that I stopped for some food. Morocco makes the best coffee I have ever had so I tucked into a hug cup and ate two omelettes. My breakfast time was a little longer than planned as I rearranged a few things on Maid Marian for more comfortable riding because, as I was quickly learning, comfort equals speed. I was also learning that you can cycle as fast as you like but if you spend too much time off the bike you'll lose time, too. I would need to live fast if I were to break the record. Time to get back on the road.

After Tangier the road flattened out and turned south, following the Atlantic coast. I put my head down and managed to tune myself out as I put down the miles. I did all my training without listening to any music so that I'd be prepared for dealing with my own thoughts. It's one of the hardest parts to cope with when spending a lot of time on your own. Your mind can play games with you: it can trick you into feeling tired; it can tell you to give up when it's tough. As a result, it had been important to focus on the mental as well as the physical training in the lead-up to my journey. The idea had been to put myself through mental hardships in training so that during the race I didn't lose focus when times got tough. I would spend hours cycling on my own without listening to music or having any company and trying not to speak to people along the route: no asking for directions, no interaction, just me on my own making it happen. It was important to control my thoughts and use them to my advantage. I had my iPod with me now but only wanted to use it as a psychological boost for when I felt I needed it.

It was 4 p.m. when I decided to stop for more food. I came across a small Moroccan café complete with a dead cow's head on the wall. I was in luck. The cow's head looked fresh, which meant the meat in my beef and couscous tagine was going to be good. I thought of taking a selfie with my Olympic Torch in front of the dead cow but decided against it. I wanted to get as many pictures of me with the torch in interesting places around the world to send back to the school, but suspected that a dead cow probably wouldn't have gone down well with the teachers.

I had done 120 miles since getting off the ferry and it was time to look at the map to see where I would land up for the evening. The plan was to stay in hotels for this leg of the journey while I got used to everything and fell into a rhythm. Rabat looked like a good place to stay and was only 70 miles away. I reckoned I should make it there by 9 p.m. at the rate I was cycling, bringing my daily total to over 190 miles. Not quite the 200 miles I was hoping for but still way above record pace.

The road along the coast got smoother and less hilly, with a huge hard shoulder. The scenery wasn't spectacular but good enough to keep my mind busy as I made a healthy effort to look around and enjoy the ride rather than just keeping my head down. People seemed to be taking a great interest in me as I cycled past them, usually shouting or waving. I didn't feel at all threatened though and was glad to reciprocate. On the odd occasion someone on a bicycle would try to catch me and I would feel slightly bad seeing them get smaller and smaller in my mirror before turning around and heading back. I was feeling good and feeling fast.

I found myself surprised by the truck drivers too. They would give one hoot to say they were coming and two if they thought it might be tight due to oncoming traffic. I had put a small rear view mirror on my handlebars so could see any dangers that crept up on me. Getting run over was one of my biggest worries. James Cracknell and Mark Beaumont had both been run over during their big cycle rides, both in America: Mark was able to carry on but James to this day struggles with his head injury. I tried not to think about it as it's something that I couldn't really control. What I could control was how many times I could move my legs in circles in one day. That's what I needed to concentrate my energies on.

By 10 p.m. I had reached the coastal town of Rabat. It seemed picturesque with well-lit streets and tree-lined roads. I spent an hour and six hotels looking for a room where they would let me take Maid Marian inside. Eventually I succeeded and passed out on the bed. I was starving but too exhausted to go and find some food. In total I had managed 193 miles and although extremely tired, I was still feeling strong. However, my average was a little too fast at nearly 16 mph in the end. I knew I'd really have to slow it down otherwise I would crash heavily in a week or two. *It's the pace that kills, not the distance.* It was a fine balancing act: I knew I couldn't go too fast and yet I also knew that if Mike or the other riders just did one mile per day more than me, they'd beat me by about twenty-four hours. My coach Mark said it'd take a week or so before I found my rhythm. That time couldn't come fast enough for me.

I opened my eyes and a shaft of light beamed through the window. It seemed overly sunny for early morning, I thought. Then I looked at my clock. Shit! It was 8.30 a.m. I had overslept by two hours. I jumped out of bed and packed everything up. The day's plan was to get to Marrakesh by the evening, and starting later than I had expected, I knew it was going to be a real push.

It was nice to see Rabat in the daylight. It was a beautiful city with an ancient-looking medina alongside spectacular-looking mosques. There was an obvious wealth to the city. I also loved all the slightly old-school Moroccans who still wear their Jedi-looking *djellabas*. I almost expected to see Darth Vader appearing from a dusty alleyway to chase away all the Jedis! I was just falling into an imaginary world of

*Star Wars* when a huge 4 x 4 turned right in front of me and then hooted as though it was my fault. I screeched to a halt and had to jump up on the pavement to avoid hitting him. The traffic in Morocco is pretty bad at the best of times and trying to cycle through the city at rush hour was a whole new experience. I spent the next half hour courteously giving drivers the right of way and creeping up the edge of the road to avoid certain death.

My progress was mind-numbingly slow. I pictured Mike in the same situation bombing through the middle of traffic and overtaking me. Certainly, I couldn't carry on at this pace if I had any chance at reaching Marrakesh at a reasonable hour. I stopped on the side of the road to take off my jacket, look at the map and have a word with my mascot.

It had been a cold winter's day in late November 2007 when I first spotted Little Flying Cow. I had wandered into an overheated charity shop in north London for no other reason than to browse all things vintage. There wasn't much new to see because I had visited this particular charity shop only the week before, but as I was looking around something caught my eye. There he lay, all sad and lonely at the back of a pile of other discarded toys. A small brown cow sprawled out as if trying to fly out of the shop and into the world. How long had he been there? What kind of life had he lived up to that point? Who had given him away? His wide questioning eyes and slight grin reminded me of the excitement you felt when you first visit somewhere new. At the reasonable price of one pound, I had to have him. I would name him Little Flying Cow (even though technically he was a bull) and he would accompany me on all of my holidays from that day on. This was our first proper adventure together and he'd now been upgraded from holiday to *adventure* mascot. Tied to the top of my handlebars, he was going to travel the world with me.

'Right, mate. Time to take this seriously,' I said to Little Flying Cow.

It was then that I decided to, well, cycle like a complete idiot. I *was* in a race after all and couldn't afford to piss around unnecessarily giving taxi drivers right of way. I jumped back on Maid Marian and put my right arm out and turned into the middle of the road hoping that cars would just move out the way. One or two hooted and swerved around me, but everyone seemed to be hooting anyway so it didn't make much difference. In a strange way, being more confident meant drivers would give me more room. Also there seemed to be an unwritten rule that the person ahead has right of way no matter where they want to go. If you were behind, you had to move for them. Once you knew this and didn't mind being hooted at, you could weave your way through traffic. My pace shot up and although it was completely nerve-wracking, I managed to get out of Rabat and carry on along the coast towards Casablanca without incident.

The road and scenery was much like the day before but this time I had an even bigger tailwind. There were times when I was cruising along at 24 mph. There is no better feeling in the world, especially when you are against the clock. To improve matters further, I had also come up with a plan to cut down the time I spent off the bike eating. At my second coffee and food stop I bought a two-litre local soft drink bottle and cut it in half. I then cut holes in it and tied it on the front of Maid Marian, hanging it off the tri bars. I even burned the edges of the plastic where I had cut it so that it wouldn't cut me when I put my hand in. I then filled it up with mixed fruit and nuts. I managed to put over 1000 kcal in it and knew I could potentially eat two full baskets in a day. That's either 2000 kcal more food or two stops I wouldn't need to take. I even cut some drainage holes in the bottom in case it rained. I didn't want to carry more weight than I needed to now, did I?

Even with the tailwind and my eating-on-the-move system, I'd still only managed 120 miles by 6 p.m. I had cut inland before Casablanca as I knew the city would slow me down and take valuable time away from my day. By dark I had only done 150 miles and hit a huge wall. I was pushing nearly 16 mph again and could feel it in my legs. I needed to eat more so stopped, had another coffee, and took on some more food and a sugary injection of Coke. I didn't think I was drinking enough either: three litres in 150 miles wasn't nearly enough liquid.

I got back on the road and turned my brain off, trying not to focus on anything other than to 'keep moving forward', Rocky's speech on repeat in my head, drowning out all the other sounds.

It was getting a little colder, so I had to put all my layers on. This was a slight worry as I had no more winter gear and it couldn't have been more than eight degrees. Head down I carried on not really looking around. I hadn't felt threatened at all in Morocco but no matter how well travelled you are, the darkness does bring with it some nervous moments. A few people would whistle at me from the roadside. In the day it seemed friendly, but at night they seemed a little more sinister. I seemed to be climbing a lot and my watch showed I was at nearly 400 m above sea level. I had no idea how high Marrakesh was so didn't know what was ahead of me.

Every now and then I'd get a long downhill only to get to the bottom and see a five-mile dead straight road slowly climbing back up again. Eventually I made it to the top to see yet another long stretch. This one greeted me with a long downhill and halfway down a man came running from a building shouting and waving his arms. I didn't know what to do. I dare not stop. For all I knew he was a robber trying to take Maid Marian away from me. Luckily he didn't reach the road by the time I passed him and I flew by not even turning my head. I heard him shout after me but didn't look back. I was a little nervous now. This was the first time I'd seen someone go out of their way to stop me. I decided to step it up a gear. Twenty more miles to Marrakesh. If I pushed it, I could do that in just over an hour.

I hadn't gone more than a mile when I saw blue flashing lights come up behind me in my wing mirror. A large police van drove past, pulled ahead and stopped in front of me. My heart raced. In my mind the Spanish had worked out who left the 'bomb' at Malaga and sent someone to get me. This was obviously a ridiculous idea but I had done 180 miles by now and was pretty knackered. It turned out the man running into the road was a policeman wanting to tell me that it was dangerous to cycle at night. I spent a few minutes trying to explain that they were actually holding me up and it was affecting my race. I'm not sure they believed me, or cared! After they took my passport details, probably to help identify my body when I got murdered, I was allowed to set off again.

That little burst of adrenalin kicked me back into Bradley Wiggins mode and I sped up the next few hills as if they were vertical drops. Ten miles outside of Marrakesh I was then greeted with every cyclist's best friend: a long downhill all the way to the city below. The twinkling lights looked almost festive as I zoomed down the long final descent, the city like a huge Christmas tree, and my present was reaching the city centre and stopping the clock. It was nearly midnight. The roads were gloriously empty. All I could hear was the sound of the rubber on the road and the wind rushing passing my ears. I cruised down averaging over 30 mph and made my way to the city centre where I paused the timer.

I wish I could have done more in Africa. But cycling any further meant going south from the UK, which doesn't follow the general east or west guidelines that Guinness set for a circumnavigation attempt. Their rules state that firstly, the minimum distance ridden should be 18,000 miles, and that the total distance travelled by the bicycle and rider should exceed an equator's length, i.e. 24,900 miles. Secondly, the journey should be continuous and in one direction, east to west or west to east. Thirdly, you must ride through two approximate antipodal points. Finally, you can stop the clock whenever you reach an impassable barrier and need to take scheduled transport, i.e. flight to another continent. These rules make for a very adventurous competition. It allows riders to come up with their own route. It allows female cyclists to skip countries that aren't as friendly towards female cyclists. It allows you the freedom to have YOUR adventure rather than following someone else's.

That second day in Africa, I managed 205 miles in 15 hours. Far too fast but I now had a day's rest before my flight to Santiago. According to my official race time, because I stopped the clock at the ferry, my daily average was well over 200 miles per day. I was well ahead of the 168 miles a day needed to break the record. I was tired but felt good knowing that I could do two fast 200 mile days and not land up in hospital.

Reaching Marrakesh and stopping the clock also allowed me time to see the progress of the other riders. I didn't really have time to do this while cycling as that was time off the bike I couldn't afford. It seemed that Mike, Richard and Martin seemed to be the only real contenders now and were all pushing some pretty big days. Although they had covered more mileage they had spent more time doing so because they hadn't reached their 'clock stop' transits yet. According to my log my daily average was over 200, helped massively by my big day into Marrakesh. Feeling confident and happy with my start I passed out in the hotel.

One continent down. Five more to go!

# 5
## HILLS

I was dressed in full Lycra because I hadn't packed any casual clothes, and was staring longingly at the conveyor belt. Round and round I watched, for an hour, hoping she would mysteriously come through the black rubber doorway and back into my arms. But she didn't. I'd landed in Chile but Maid Marian hadn't. I was told that the system said she made it onto the flight to Santiago but somehow didn't come off the flight. This could only mean someone must have stolen her from the runway. I was told to go find a hotel and they'd call me when they knew of anything, but for a while I just couldn't tear myself away from that empty conveyer belt.

The airport was a good half-hour bus ride from the centre of Santiago but I didn't see any of it. I had my head in my hands wondering why this was happening to me. I saw at least seven other bikes come through, but not Maid Marian. I contemplated looking on eBay for the culprit who might sell her there, but it was too early. If I stole a bike I'd wait a week before I put it online anyway. Does Chile even have eBay?

There was nothing I could do except wait for the dreaded phone call. I had no idea what I'd do if they had lost her. No one would insure the actual bike for this race, so I'd be royally screwed.

Santiago was a beautiful city. Huge grand buildings with palm trees and brass statues give it a distinctly Spanish feel. Towering behind the city were the impressive Andes Mountains. It was a very dramatic starting point to my South American leg. If, that is, I was going to be able to start it.

I wandered the streets in search of some food and then just generally exploring. I didn't want to book a hotel just yet in case I got a call from the airport. I was surprised how little attention I was getting; apart from the fact I was in full Lycra and without a bike, I could easily have been in Barcelona. Everyone seemed really friendly and a stall owner even gave me a free Chilean flag to put on Maid Marian.

I was trying to be positive, but eventually at around 5 p.m. I figured that even if my bike arrived tonight I'd still stay in the city and leave the following day. I found a central hotel which cost $60 – a lot more expensive than I thought it might be considering I was in South America – but I had no choice so settled myself in, looked at a map of Chile I had bought and ran a warm bath. It wasn't as relaxing as I had hoped because my mind kept thinking about Maid Marian being either lost or held captive somewhere.

Just then I heard my phone ring. I jumped out of the bath and ran across the carpet and over the bed, leaving a long wet trail of soapy water behind me. I stared at the phone for a moment. Part of me didn't want to answer in case it was bad news. I thought I'd rather stay here for eternity being blissfully ignorant than hear she'd been stolen, effectively ending my world record attempt. I slowly brought the phone to my ear.

'*Hola señor*. Your bicycle we find. She come tomorrow same time.'

'Thank you, thank you, thank you! See you tomorrow!' I shouted and put down the phone. I was so happy I started to do a little naked dance and then realised my curtains were wide open. I couldn't tell if there was anyone in the building opposite because it had mirrored glass, but I didn't care. Maid Marian was on her way. My race was back on.

Twenty-four hours later, I stood for the second time looking nervously at the conveyor belt again. What had happened was they had put her on the flight and then too many heavy people had boarded, meaning they had to take off some luggage. Maid Marian was considered a heavy item, which was a little worrying: so much for cutting the fabric off my zips. It was a real case of déjà vu: I was still wearing the same clothes as the day before; the same security guards were still on duty. Although I was reassured that she was in fact on this flight, my heart was racing. The conveyor belt of luggage seemed to be going in slow motion but that must have just been me over-focusing on it.

'I see you're doing some cycling, dressed in Lycra and all.' A tall English chap tapped me on the shoulder.

'Hopefully,' I replied, not wanting to take my eyes off the little doorway where the bags came through.

'Where are you heading? I am just about to run across the Atacama.'

'Run it? That's amazing. How long is it going to take?'

'About two weeks I think.'

'That's bonkers.'

'Thanks. Are you just doing a bit of a holiday?' he asked

'Not really.' I explained about the round the world race and the wait for my bike.

'Wow. Does Mark Beaumont still have the record?'

I shook my head. 'A few people have broken it since, but my goal is to halve his record. I'm just above that pace with a 200-mile-a-day average so far, but we will see what South America throws at me.'

'Two hundred miles per day! That's incredible!'

I hadn't really thought about it properly because I was so focused with the task at hand, but I guessed 200 a day *was* quite good. As long as I was ahead of the 168 miles per day pace then I was happy.

We said our goodbyes and good lucks and I sat back down in my conveyor viewing position that gave me the best angle to the doorway. It wasn't more than five minutes before I saw the corner of a brown box coming through. There she was! The box was looking a little tattered and torn, but still in one piece. My South American adventure could finally begin.

In the end, the only casualty was that my iPhone mount on the handlebar had broken. That was probably a good thing, as I didn't want to have it on full show anyway. I was using my iPhone for a number of things like updating my blog, Twitter and Facebook, writing notes, navigation and most importantly, using the voice memo as a journal. I knew I'd be too tired to write my feelings down properly, so it worked a treat that I could cycle along and do a diary entry at the same time. It was also quite amusing listening back to my often nonsensical entries. I'd do an entry with complete urgency saying 'I MUST not forget' this or that detail, even though I had mentioned it only an hour before in the previous entry. Making any sense of it all when I got home would be a challenge on its own, but it was still better than writing things down because my written diary entries were often less than half the number of words than my verbal ones.

I was on the bike by midday and needed to head east towards the city before I could find the Pan-American Highway heading north. The Pan-American Highway is a famous route that barring the Darién Gap in Colombia and Panama, goes all the way from the bottom of South America through a series of roads all the way to Alaska. The section I was going to tackle was going to be one of the more adventurous parts of my ride, and most definitely the hardest section lay a week ahead of me in the form of the formidable Atacama Desert – the driest place on earth. There are parts of the Atacama where it hasn't rained for 400 years and there are no forms of life, even on a molecular level. Not the ideal place for a sun-sensitive ginger cyclist, then.

The Atacama could be the end of my race if things were too tough but equally, if I made it, it'd give me a lot of confidence for the rest of the ride. 'Get the tough sections out the way at the beginning when you are fit,' my trainer Steve had said. 'It's better than trying to deal with them when you are tired at the end.' Whichever way I looked at it, the Atacama was a make-or-break section of the whole ride.

It was already hitting 32°C as I reached the Pan-Am, only to discover a huge ten-foot wall running along its side. I had to continue past it for another mile before I could find another road heading north. I was surprised how big and busy the Pan-Am was, but I guess it was a highway after all. Luckily I didn't need to cycle on it just yet as there was a small side road running parallel. By one o'clock I realised I hadn't eaten so decided to get some food. At that exact moment those familiar golden arches decided to show themselves a few hundred metres ahead. Really? Was my first proper race meal in Chile going to be some American fast food? As I was in a pretty industrial area, I didn't have much of a choice.

Refuelled and rehydrated, I pushed on and found a gap to join the Pan-American Highway proper. To be on such an iconic road in a part of the world I had never been to before was a little overwhelming. The flat part of northern Santiago started to turn into nice rolling hills – perfect terrain for me. I felt strong on the climbs and then had a good few minutes to rest my legs on the downhills. Such was my focus on getting miles under my belt that I forget to put sun cream on. When I looked down at my arms, they didn't look too bad . . . until I pulled up my sleeve. I couldn't believe it: my arms were lobster red in comparison to my pasty white shoulders. I pushed my thumb against my forearm and saw the white fingerprint it left. And that was only two hours in the sun. How could I have been so stupid? I had no choice but to put my winter compression top on to stop it getting any worse.

The further north I rode, the hillier it got. By 9 p.m. I had only managed 110 miles but felt a bit too nervous to cycle in the dark. I hadn't seen a hotel for ages and figured I'd spend my first night camping. Then I saw an army camp just off the road, which I figured would be the best place to camp. I'd surely be safe there?

I made my way into the office where there were three scary-looking guards in camouflage. They looked up at me and didn't smile, or say anything at all. Eventually, with many hand signals, I managed to get my point across that I needed a place to camp.

'OK, come.' One of the younger officers signalled to meet him round the back. He wasn't smiling and looked grumpy. That made me nervous. I went around the rear of the building and followed the officer towards to the best-looking patch of grass I have ever seen. My eyes lit up as I knew I'd have a good night's sleep. I slowly walked towards the patch and gestured if that was where I should sleep.

'No, *señor.*' The guard signalled a fountain with his hands and made a water squirting sound.

Ah. 'Sprinkler?'

'*Sí.*'

Opposite the lush five-star grass field was a more rustic patch of gravel outside one of the residential compounds. The guard pointed and asked if it was OK. I went over to examine the ground. It was hard but dry. I was under a tree and next to a flowerbed.

'*Gracias señor,*' I said thankfully and started to unpack my kit.

'Is OK? I make food.'

Was he offering me food or was it just a statement of what he was going to do? I wasn't sure so said yes, thank you. He'd either come back with food or not. I thought I'd played that well.

I put all my kit out on the floor. This was the first time I'd ever opened my sleeping bag and mattress: I should have probably done a test run back home but had never got round to it. My sleeping bag and mattress were both the lightest in the world. The sleeping bag weighed 275 g and was good for temperatures down to five degrees; seeing as my entire route was summer-based I should be fine. My 172 g mat was a Klymit X-Lite camping frame: they called it a frame because calling it a mat or mattress was a bit of a stretch as it was a frame that had padding for your butt, shoulders and head. There was no padding in between those areas, just a frame connecting them. It was only half-length, which meant my feet were in the dirt below the frame. It didn't look comfortable at all but was surprisingly good. It folded up into the size of an energy drink can, which saved me a lot of space. I had also decided against a tent, which saved me nearly 1 kg as well as a lot of space: instead, I had a small bivi bag which weighed just 50 g. I was hoping that with a summer route it wouldn't rain on me too much.

Setting up camp was pretty quick. I realised I'd probably need some water for the morning so went over to the guard's house. I knocked nervously three times and he came to the door. I managed to get the point across that I needed water across pretty easily, but I had a little more trouble asking for salt. I needed some sodium (electrolytes) as I was sweating quite a lot in the Chilean heat. I did the universal (or so I thought) sign for salt, which was mimicking using a shaker, not the grinder. He had no idea. I tried guessing what salt might be in Spanish but he just looked even more confused. Eventually he asked me to follow him. I walked into the kitchen, where on the shelf was a pot of salt.

'Ah, *sal*.' He did the pinching action to show me what I should have signed. Why didn't I think of that?

'*Té?*' he asked. He was not one for many words.

'*Si señor, gracias.*' I could murder a tea.

'OK,' he said, still a little grumpy.

He then signalled that I should go and he'd bring it to me. What a friendly looking grumpy fellow he was. After my lovely cup of tea I realised his food comment was a statement and not an offer. I went back to my camp, opened a tin of tuna and had some nuts before falling asleep. My first night camping and I was a civilian on an army base in Chile.

It was around 2 a.m. when I was awoken by some scuffling next to me. There was someone in the bush. My heart was in my mouth: I hadn't chained Maid Marian up. Was someone here to steal her? I peered out the small hole in my sleeping bag. It was hard to focus, and as my eyes were adjusting something darted across my view. My heart jumped again but then settled as I realised it wasn't a person, but a dog. I looked out to see a whole gang of dogs around me, inquisitively coming over and sniffing the end of my sleeping bag. I froze so as not to disturb them. All I could think of was one of them taking a pee on me. I would not be best impressed. Thankfully, they soon lost interest and wandered off around the corner. I settled back down to try and sleep, my heart still racing a little.

It was a short night. My alarm went off at 4.20 a.m. and I hadn't slept well: partly because of the dog invasion and partly because I kept knocking my feet on rocks through the night. Getting up was painfully slow as I was pretty tired but I managed to be on the bike by 5 a.m. Breakfast was another can of tinned tuna and some water with salt in it. Luckily it wasn't very cold and by the time the sun was up the temperature was well into the twenties. Although the day was hot it wasn't nearly as hot as the previous day. My arms now covered by the compression top had started to blister and felt fragile to touch. My calves and knees started to burn too, so eventually at midday I gave in and put on my thermal leggings. I was dreading the heat that I thought might result but was surprised to feel a little cooler, now that the sun wasn't hitting my skin directly. 'Good job Sean,' I said to myself, knowing full well that it was a complete fluke, something I had not planned, or researched at all.

Along with the midday heat came the hills and the mountains. I knew I'd be cycling along the Andes but thought I'd be following the coastline. This turned out not to be the case at all. I would take a good hour to climb up each slope and then take less than ten minutes to descend. One hour up, ten minutes down . . . all day. Normally I like the hills but this was getting quite tedious and by 3 p.m. my right knee started to feel a little sore.

'Stretch Sean, must stretch,' I said to Little Flying Cow.

The plan was to get to the 200 miles mark, but by 6 p.m. I had only done 150 miles and knew it would be a push. It was getting dark by around 7 p.m. and I didn't really want to do much more mileage after 9. I figured I'd get my dark hours done in the morning. By 8 p.m. I decided that enough was enough at 170 miles. I was over the record pace for the day and the hills had really taken a toll on my knees; I didn't want to risk injury so early on. With no army base about, I started to look for a different place to camp. Just then I came across a timber yard full of cabins on stilts. There were loads of different cabins dotted all over the yard, about fifteen. Some were small garden shed types and others large enough to be someone's home. Around each cabin were piles of wood which looked big enough to build another cabin next to it. It looked like you bought a cabin from these guys and then they built it for you. It would be ideal if I could sleep in one of them. I had my eye on the bigger one off to my left: it had a large cabin with an attached porch off to the side.

'Please don't have any dogs,' I said to Little Flying Cow as I nervously went through the open gate. In amongst all the cabins and hidden by some trees was a house with some lights on. I leant Maid Marian up against one of the cabins and walked over. I'd never asked to sleep in someone's garden before and even though many travellers do, I was still nervous. I knocked, waited, and was just about to give up when a young chap in his early twenties came to the door. His name was Benito and thankfully he could speak a little English. After realising I wasn't going to rob him he warmed up and showed me to the big hut towering above the rest on six-foot stilts and an equally large porch off the side. It was the one I wanted for no other reason than it looked the prettiest, and felt the safest, being high off the ground. Result.

I thanked him and went off to my palace. It was amazing: Three bedrooms, a living room and a porch on stilts. There was no furniture or anything but it was mine, all mine. I loved it. Moments later Benito came back and walked up the stairs. He had an iPhone in his hand. I was quite shocked. I hadn't expected anyone to have an iPhone in Chile but judging by the quality of these huts I assumed they sell them to upmarket clients. These weren't any old shacks, and exquisitely crafted.

'*Señor*, you angry?'

Angry? God, no. Why did he think I was angry? I started to get nervous again. I hated conflict. Had I not showed my appreciation enough?

'No, not angry at all. I love this, thank you so much.' I tried to sound overly grateful.

'Sorry, sorry, hungry, eat for food?' he asked as he looked at his phone again. He had a Spanish to English app. Why hadn't I thought of that?

Dinner? Yes *please*. With that he said I should come to the house in fifteen minutes and then also showed me where the toilets were. Free bed, dinner and running water to wash my face. What an evening.

I washed but didn't change clothes – as I didn't have any – and went over to the house. I was greeted by Benito's mum with a huge smile, a bowl of soup, some bread and an avocado salad. She didn't speak at all and just smiled and went back into the kitchen. She had a warm homely demeanour about her that I liked. I wished I could speak Spanish. She looked like she had some good stories to tell. Benito was already at the table with his MacBook Pro out and was looking at my website which he had seen on my jersey. I had a live tracker that updated every ten minutes and he was really proud that the final dot for the day was at his house.

Everything in the house was made of wood. This family were obviously very passionate about the stuff. Not only did they build amazing cabins but also beautifully crafted furniture. I spent a good half an hour chatting and showing them photos on my website and Facebook, which they loved to see. By 10 p.m. I was knackered and retired to my mansion on stilts. I was a little short on the day's mileage but still ahead of the record, so felt good.

The new morning brought with it more sunshine. It was pretty predictable around here and the closer I got to the Atacama the more certain I became that it would be dry and camping out without a tent would be safe. I'd just have to deal with the rain if it came but it was unlikely. That said, it would be just my luck if it rained for the first time in 400 years while I was passing through.

Getting through La Serena, the first major town since leaving Santiago, was stressfully slow. The smooth dual carriageway turned into a bumpy single-track road. Cars and drivers were a lot less patient in the cities, as you can imagine, and it took a lot of effort and concentration not to be run over. Luckily I had my Morocco practice session to fall back on, which helped a little. Given the bumps, I was glad I had gone with 25 c tyres, though. I had been planning on slightly thinner 23 c tyres but the extra comfort you get with the wider 25 c far outweighed the 20 g extra weight.

The Pan-American headed inland from La Serena, which probably meant more hills to come. My right knee was quite sore when I awoke but got better within a few minutes of cycling. After I had been on the bike for ten minutes and had warmed up I stopped and managed a good ten-minute stretch. I liked this system. It gave me a chance to take off my jacket too, which I usually had to wear in the slightly colder mornings before my body warmed up.

My speculation was correct. As soon as the road started inland so did the start of the longest hill I had ever been on. It wasn't steep by any means but it just went on and on and on. It took me nearly three hours to do the fifteen-mile climb up to 1000 m. By the time I reached the top, my heart was racing and my legs burning. I was exhausted but happy that I was almost certain to have a long downhill ahead of me. As I lay in the baking heat my stomach started to rumble. I must have eaten something dodgy for in no time at all I really needed the toilet. Where was my emergency toilet paper? Right at the bottom of my bag, of course it was. Damn it. I cursed as I frantically unpacked everything and threw it on the ground in search of my toilet paper. Eventually I got it and ran for the nearest big rock. I tried to pull my tights down but realised I had bought bib shorts (cycle shorts that go over the shoulder – much like a wrestler's outfit). Fail! I hastily took off my jersey and then compression top, which by now was so tight with sweat I nearly couldn't get it over my shoulders. Eventually, and a little too close to a serious disaster, I managed to get my tights off my shoulders and did my business.

Within minutes of getting back on the bike I was greeted with the longest downhill of the race so far. What a psychological boost and a much-needed increase to the day's average speed: I zoomed down the ten-mile hill at 30 mph. Even with the hills I was keeping a fairly good average speed of 13.5 mph, which was not far off my ideal pace. It meant I could do 200 miles a day in fifteen hours on the bike: three hours rest, six hours sleep and off I'd go again.

The rest of the day followed a similar pattern as I climbed up to 1000 m again twice, with my knees hurting more and more. I needed to rest a few times along the way at truck stops. The Pan-Am was scattered with such places: they looked like most of the houses along the route, quite dirty and rustic, with the only way you could tell they were actually truck stops being the number of flags, usually Pepsi or Coke, outside them. There was at least one every 60 miles, though I worried how many there would be when I entered the heart of the Atacama in a few days' time

As the day went on, my right knee was starting to get a little worse and at 3 p.m. I had to take a good hour's rest to stretch it out. I really hoped I wasn't pushing it too much as there was no way I could afford to get injured. By now, I was a little behind schedule and knew I had another big climb ahead before the next town of Vallenar. I was hoping to push on past Vallenar that evening but after analysing my current average speed I figured I might have to stay there the night. My clothes were really starting to get baked in sweat so a night in a hotel was definitely in order.

I made the final climb back up to 1000 m as the sun was setting, casting my shadow onto the banks beside me. I fell into a trance watching my legs spinning over and over again as my elongated shadow danced back and forth following the terrain next to the road. I reached the final ascent just after the sun disappeared behind the horizon and the landscape turned from a magical orange to a mystical purple. I stopped for a moment, balanced Maid Marian on a rock and took a photo of her silhouette. She really was a beautiful machine and so far hadn't let me down one bit.

The final decent into Vallenar was fast and winding. The only traffic I saw was a tour bus that had broken down, and the guests looked on in shock as a hairy ginger guy zoomed past them. No matter how bad you feel a good downhill always lifts your spirits: '*HOLAAAAAA!!*' I shouted as I tucked into tri position. I had put tri-bars on Maid Marian, which are bars attached to the middle of the handlebars and that go forward with pads for your elbows. They allow you lean forward, put your elbows on the pads and hold onto the forward facing bars, becoming more streamlined in the process. It takes a while to get used to because you have no brakes on the tri-bars: if you need to brake quickly it means jumping up from tri position and finding your brakes on the handlebars.

I zoomed down towards Vallenar with a huge smile on my face, feeling good even though I was slightly behind mileage for the day. In fact I had only managed 150 miles. It was my shortest day so far and the only day below the magic 168-mile mark. Although annoying, I always knew my South American leg would be the hardest of all so some short days were to be expected.

Vallenar was quite a large city and built in complete grid format. I struggled to find a hotel again as they all seemed fully booked, but eventually one kind lady gave me a triple room for the price of a single. It still cost $60 though. Bed sorted, my attention turned to food. I had completely run out of supplies. The plan was to keep at least a day's worth of food at any one time in case I couldn't find anything. There was no point in carrying more as I couldn't really even carry a day's worth of water. I found a local supermarket and wandered around in a daze deciding what to buy. I bought some apple juice, tinned tuna, cheese, chorizo, cake and a chicken and rice meal from the deli counter. It was probably the best meal I'd found so far, and eventually tucked into bed full, showered and happy – even though my mileage was down.

My throbbing right knee was so excruciatingly painful that it woke me up. It was 3 a.m. and I couldn't move. When I got up I nearly fell over hobbling across to find some painkillers. I took one, washed it down with some apple juice and flopped back into bed. I must have pushed it too hard. I was annoyed with myself and my choice of route. I just hoped it wasn't a serious injury and only some swelling. I was planning to get up at 3.30 a.m. but pushed it back to 4.30 a.m. as there was no way I'd be able to get on the bike in the next half an hour. I fell back asleep praying my knee injury wasn't permanent. If it were that would be the end of my race. I wondered what injuries Mike, Martin or Richard were having? I hadn't been able to see their progress for a while and had no idea what sort of mileage they were doing.

By 4.30 the painkillers had started to work and I got out of bed slowly. My knee still felt fragile but I knew it always felt worse in the morning and would get better within ten minutes of warming up. As long as there wasn't any long-term injury. I decided not to think about that possibility. I left Vallenar in the eeriness of darkness. The town had been bustling the previous night and felt a totally different place. Not having a map of the town I just had to guess where I was going. Obviously I got this wrong and started the day with a long climb that I didn't need to do at all. I eventually made it back onto the Pan-Am and started north again.

The long downhill from the previous night opened into a flat plane. Within half an hour I found a little roadside coffee shop so decided to stop and stretch my now slightly warm knee. Coffee is great for a pick me up and also helps metabolise carbohydrate. The sun was just rising through the mist. As it got brighter and brighter I could see that it was a lot drier. There weren't many shrubs at all and the terrain was quite rocky and not sandy as I'd pictured the Atacama to be. I still had no idea if I was in it or not.

Unlike the day before, the road was really flat for most of the morning and I had a very welcoming tailwind. Trucks, although big, were pretty good at giving me a wide berth when passing and more often than not I would get a nice hoot and someone would shout something in Spanish out of the window. I took it as a sign of affection but they were probably saying, 'You stupid gringo, why you cycling in the desert. You going to die!'

The problem with flat tailwind-driven days is that you don't want to get off the bike. If you are pushing 4 mph into a headwind and take 10 minutes rest you only lose a mile or less in distance. If you are pushing 20 mph with a tailwind, that 10-minute break becomes a whole lot further. On and on I pushed. I started to climb again, but very slowly, my knees killing me, until I was nearly at 700 m again. Then all of a sudden there it was. About five miles ahead of me stood the towering sand dunes of the Atacama Desert. It looked vast and unforgiving: not a bush or tree in sight, just huge sand dunes going off into the distance and beyond the curvature of the earth. I could hardly contain my nerves. In a weird way I forgot the pain in my knees as my mind started to think about the next few days trying to cycle across the harshest place on the planet.

The closer I got to the towering dunes, the more ill I started to feel. Had I eaten something bad again? No, it wasn't that type of ill; it was more feeling dizzy and nauseous. I took my water bottle out of the cage and realised it still had some water in it and the second one was full. I had done 110 miles and only drunk one litre of water. That's the problem when you try to make the most of a tailwind: you forget to drink. I was massively dehydrated and possibly suffering from a little sunstroke too. I stopped immediately and finished the one bottle in one go. I still felt ill. My body needed some sugar but I wasn't anywhere near anything but sand.

After a short rest I got back on Maid Marian and in a fragile state carried on at a much slower pace. An hour later I came to a truck stop and saw a sign for a shower. It was 42 degrees and I needed to wash the salt out of my clothes. I parked up Maid Marian and got into the shower fully clothed to the questioning eyes of another truck driver. I could taste the sweat as the cold water ran down my face. It was glorious. Ten minutes later I was satisfied I was as clean as I could be and any longer would be wasting water, which I was sure was quite a luxury in the driest place on earth. As I stepped out of the cubicle I nearly fell over as both my knees had seized up from the cold water. I quickly sat down and started to massage them, giving each leg a series of sports massage judo chops to my thighs. This really helped and on my second attempt at walking I felt no pain at all. Maybe it wasn't my knees at all but my really tight quads that were putting extra tension on the knee ligaments. Either way I really need to do more stretching.

Having hit the dunes, the road then ran west towards the coast again. The coastal route was spectacular as I made my way to Chanaral: I had the Pacific to my left and the huge sand dunes of the Atacama to my right. Every now and then I'd see a small gap in the dunes which gave me a view a few miles into the desert. I was half expecting to see that runner from the airport. I couldn't imagine what it must be like to run in that heat. A death wish if you ask me.

Although I now had a slight headwind, I was still managing a good pace and felt a new man after being cleaned and rehydrated. The coastal road got rockier and rockier and a lot more dramatic as it carved its way through a range of windswept outcrops. By 7 p.m. I had managed 175 miles. I was tired but needed to make up for the short day the day before, so planned to push on a further twenty miles or so. Every bone in my body wanted to stop and find a quiet place to camp in this picturesque landscape. I was seeing incredible potential camp spots every mile but knew I had to push on.

It was long after dark by the time I reached Chanaral, with my daily total hitting 195 miles. I was stopped by the police asking where I was going to stay. I told them a hotel and thankfully they seemed happy with my answer and let me go. After finding accommodation, it was time for supper. There was a brilliant little burger van just outside the hotel and it seemed busy, so I went over and ordered a burger by pointing at someone else's meal as I had no idea what anything meant on the menu. I waited patiently for a solid twenty minutes, my mouth watering every time the lady would pass someone else their burger though the rustic hatch.

Eventually a burger the size of Russia came through and the lady pointed at me. Thank goodness! I was so excited. I took the burger and sat down on a nearby bench. As I got up to get a napkin, I heard loads of shouting and nearly jumped out my skin. I turned around to see what had happened: a dog had stolen my supper! I couldn't believe it; I was so angry. I was too tired to wait another twenty minutes so just ordered a portion of chips and sulked my way back to the hotel.

Normally food wins in the classic endurance conundrum of *food versus sleep*. Sleep this time, however, was making a good comeback. I sat on my bed, eating my chips and looking at the route for the morning. The map suggested I'd go inland into the actual Atacama Desert. That focus and the vast expanse of 'brown' on the map took my mind away from the fact that possibly the best burger in the world had been stolen from me.

# 6

# SAND, SAND AND MORE SAND!

Thump! I rolled over in bed, hit my knee on the wall and let out a scream. Thud, thud, thud! Shafts of pain surged into my knees with each heartbeat. The hills, it seemed, were taking their toll. Entering the Atacama not in full fitness was not a good idea, but I had little choice. I hobbled over to my bag and took more painkillers. My only reassurance was that the pain was coming at night and once I was on the bike my knees seemed to feel a lot better. Once again I pushed my alarm back, from 4.20 a.m. to 5.30 a.m. to let the painkillers kick in. Losing an hour each day was the equivalent of about ten miles in distance, which at this rate would put me a week behind Mike.

As it was, I was glad I slept in a bit. The route out of Chanaral was slow due to the bad road conditions and I had an hour less of night-time cycling, which minimised the risk of hitting a huge pothole and potentially buckling a wheel. It was still dark so I couldn't see what was around me. I was literally going blind into the Atacama, with dodgy knees.

With no trees or even rocks for guidance it was hard to work out whether I was going uphill or downhill at times, especially if there was a slight headwind giving me the feeling of going downhill.

By 7 a.m. the sun started to come up over the huge dunes inland of me and the golden sand of the Atacama started to show itself. There was a slight misty haze all around and the sight was breathtaking. I was already at 300 m above sea level and I had no idea how much higher I'd go, but for a brief moment I didn't care. This was the beginning of my Atacama adventure. I sat there basking in the warmth of the early morning sunshine before carrying on into the mist above. I felt part of the Pan-Am now and just hoped I had enough water to see me through. I had 2.7 litres, the maximum I could carry on the bike. Running out of water was not an option out here and I suddenly wished I had taken another bottle, just in case.

I carried on climbing all morning and by lunchtime I was at 1200 m above sea level. It was still really misty. I must have been in the clouds but felt like I was on the moon. Visibility wasn't more than 50 m at times and because I had a slight tailwind I couldn't hear the oncoming trucks until they appeared mystically out of the fog like a pirate ship on the Atlantic. The desert brought with it daunting reminders that this was a harsh part of the world to navigate. I had seen quite a few memorial shrines along the entire Pan-Am but they seemed a lot more frequent here. Some were really elaborate while others simply a tin box with a burned-out candle in it. I knew that these were mostly dedicated to truck drivers who'd had accidents but my mind tried to make me believe they were for travellers who had lost their way.

By mid-afternoon I had reached 1600 m and was above the clouds. The road was dead straight at times although at a slight upward gradient. It looked like they had just completed resurfacing this part of the Pan-Am, something that I was very grateful for. It allowed me to put my head down and switch off without risk of hitting a pothole.

The hills didn't stop all day. Just when I thought I was high enough I'd see another towering dune ahead. My right knee was starting to feel pretty buggered so I took another painkiller. I also got my first puncture. I'd become a bit over-confident in my tyres and went over some big potholes and got a 'pinch flat', which is when the inner-tube gets caught between the edge of the pothole and the rim. It's almost impossible to fix the inner properly as you always get two splits a centimetre apart from each other. I decided to just put a fresh inner in instead of trying to fix it. Still, given how far I'd cycled, it was pretty impressive to not have had a puncture until now. Those Conti GP4000s were great pieces of rubber.

By 6 p.m. I had only done 110 miles and was up at 2000 m above sea level. To put that in some perspective, the highest ski resort in the Alps is only 2300 m. It actually felt a lot like the Alps in a weird way except that instead of everything being white with snow, it was orange with sand. There was also the small difference in temperature: minus twelve degrees in France and forty degrees plus here. There were quite a few sand dunes I could have skied down though. I promised myself I would do that one day.

I knew that this would be the shortest day I'd cycle. By dark I had only managed 125 miles. I knew I was over the worst of the hills and that I'd get a nice downhill into Antofagasta in the morning. I decided to call it a day at the next truck stop. I walked into an empty restaurant, where there was a grubby looking man in his late thirties at the counter.

'*Hola, señor*. Do you have a bed to sleep?' I asked, using my hands as a pillow to portray what I wanted.

'No,' is all he said while writing something in a book.

'Is it OK if I sleep behind?' I tried to sign that I wanted to sleep outside behind the truck stop.

'OK.' I'm not sure if he actually knew what I meant but at least I asked.

I went outside and found a place to put my bivi between the wall of the truck stop and an old sign that was leant up against the wall. It made a perfect shelter. Just as I was unpacking the café owner came out and saw me.

'No, *señor*! Brrrrrr!' he said while rubbing his arms. '*Señor*, come.' I followed him through the café and out the other side. Attached to the café was a small cabin and inside were two single beds.

'You sleep. 10,000 pesos.'

'Is this your bed?' I asked with enough sign language for him to understand me.

'*Si*, me sleep!' he pointed to his car in the garage.

I didn't really know what to make of the guy. He hadn't been that friendly to start with and I wasn't sure what his intentions were. Part of me felt it'd be rude to say no, but I really just wanted to go somewhere quiet. Eventually I said yes and went and got Maid Marian. He followed me to get her and then back into the cabin.

'Food?' he asked, this time with a sinister smile on his face. It was the look of, 'Ha ha, you tourist shmuck. I've just ripped you off.'

'*Si, señor,* I'll come over in ten minutes,' I said while unpacking my kit.

With that he left the room and closed the door behind him. I then heard what sounded like a lock bolting! My heart started to pound and I froze to see if I could hear anything. Nothing! It was silent. I walked over to the door slowly and tried to open it. It was locked from the outside. Oh shit! This can't be happening. Why has he done that? My mind started to race in all directions. It started to make sense now. It was as soon as he came outside and saw Maid Marian that he then all of a sudden had a place for me under the pretence that it was cold. My fatigued mind had affected my judgement badly on this one.

'Think Sean, think!' I said out loud. Did I have anything in my bag to act as a weapon? No, I had decided against a Leatherman or Swiss Army Knife as they were too heavy. Shit, shit, shit. I started to bang on the door. Nothing! I went and sat back down on the bed. How could I have let myself get into this situation? Just then I heard the door unbolting slowly. My heart nearly jumped out my body as jumped up and braced myself. The door opened slowly and the café owner popped his head through the gap. This was it. Here's Johnny!

'Pardon *señor,* me forget,' he said and closed the door again without bolting it.

That night when I woke up, the pain in both my knees was the worst I'd ever felt. It didn't make sense: I felt numb and in pain at the same time. Surely I couldn't carry on. I hobbled over to Maid Marian and had two painkillers before collapsing back into bed. It was a difficult situation: I was pushing it way too much, yet I couldn't afford any more low-mileage days. Just one day sub 150 meant doing a 200 miler to make up for it. I was never good at maths but knew this 125-mile day was going to take some serious work to claw back. I just hoped there wouldn't be any more hills like the past few days.

I managed to get on the road by 4.15 a.m. The roads were a lot quieter and even though there was a slight climb to begin with, I eventually started the long descent towards Antofagasta. Annoyingly, the downhill came with a headwind coming in from the coast, meaning I was still having to pedal to keep a steady 13 mph. But at least there weren't any hills and I could kind of rest my knees a little. The salt build up on my shirt was getting bad to the point it was actually completely hard in places. I was convinced that if I swam in the sea I'd come out less salty than I went in. That thought made me smile, something I hadn't done in a few days. I guess I was just so stressed about the desert and my knees I forgot to enjoy it. I reminded myself that one of the main reasons for doing this ride was for the adventure.

At that moment I looked up to my left to see something I'd only ever seen in magazines and books – the *Mano del Desierto*, that famous statue of five fingers coming out of the ground. I had no idea I'd be passing it, my lack of planning skills rearing its ugly head again. I was surprised at how low key the whole place was. There was no sign, no road to it, just a small dirt track leading about 100 m to the base. It was lunchtime, so I figured I'd make the small detour off the road to go and check it out. From the road it looked little more than 20 ft high but the closer and closer I got the more it seemed to grow in front of me. I got out the Olympic Torch and took a selfie: the kids would like this one for sure. It's just a pity people had put loads of shit graffiti around the base and scratched their names in it. I guess they will soon put a huge fence around it and ruin the whole experience of discovering it. That would be sad. But for now it was my little discovery on my little adventure through the desert.

I was just about to get back on Maid Marian when I noticed that my Brooks saddle was sagging quite a lot. I couldn't remember if it was always like this, so looked at my phone for photos I had taken before. To my horror I noticed that the saddle was sagging about a centimetre lower in the middle than when I first got it. Could that be the reason my knees were in pain? You tend to always get sore knees if your seat is too low and a sore lower back if it is too high. I lifted the saddle, too high at first, so dropped it a millimetre or so until it felt right. I got back on and noticed straight away that it felt better. It was still all downhill to Antofagasta so I wouldn't really know if it helped till after, but for now I was happier.

I had two roads to choose from for this section of the ride: I could stay on the Pan-Am in the desert, which might be less windy and have more truck stops but would be a lot hotter, or I could head down to the coast where it might be windier but a little cooler. I figured the coast road would be more exciting and it also gave me another ten-mile downhill, which was always a good idea. But as I turned west, the wind coming off the coast hit me straight in the face. It was so demoralising. I had a section of road where I could have easily cruised down at 30 mph but was stuck at 9 mph and pedalling hard. On and on I fought. The wind gusted through the valley and even pushed me into the road at times. Eventually I reached the open hill leading into the city.

I had no idea Antofagasta was this large. It was by far the biggest city I had seen since Santiago. Cities take up a lot of time. In Antofagasta I needed to do four things: draw money, eat lunch, oil my chain, and stock up on food and water. Although these were four fairly simple tasks it still took me two hours to do them, except for oiling the chain. I couldn't find a bike shop but figured I'd pass a garage sooner or later. The city sprawled for miles and miles north along the coast with pretty bad roads and equally bad drivers. It felt very South America. A lot more of what you imagine South America to be – a coastal city with kids playing football on gravel patches. I liked it.

Once you have it in your mind that you need oil for your chain, you can't but notice the board-scratching noise it makes. I really needed something soon. I couldn't handle another two days with a noisy chain. Luckily it wasn't long before I came across some road works and the digger man said I could have some grease from his truck. Brilliant. I laid it on thick, every dollop bringing me a calm sense of happiness. After I had smoothed it out and given Maid Marian a once-over with a dirt rag I jumped back on and hit the road. I was instantly made aware of my mistake. The grease was so thick and gloopy it actually made it harder to pedal.

In the back of my mind I could hear Phil at my local bike shop: 'Never, ever grease a chain and even when you put oil on it make sure it's only a very, very little, unless the chain is completely buggered of course.' Damn it. It felt like I was cycling through cold syrup. I stopped and found a rag on the side of the road and tried as hard as I could to get the grease off. I took as much off as possible and although it made a small difference, it still felt sticky.

Antofagasta soon fell out of sight as one of the best roads I had seen all race opened up in front of me. The hard shoulder was wider than the actual road and it looked like it had only been completed the day before. The tar was pitch black and glass smooth without a hill in sight. Time to make up for the lost two hours at lunch. I stepped it up a gear and went into tri position. Amazingly my knees didn't hurt at all even when I powered down. I couldn't believe it. Did the last few days of excruciating pain happen just because my saddle had sagged? Such a small and stupid thing could have ended my attempt. I was annoyed that all that pain and sleepless nights could have been avoided if I had just realised it earlier.

I pushed on along the coast and although the good road ended, it remained flat and I had a small tailwind. The scenery was once again out of this world: the huge smooth sand dunes to my right balancing the rough ocean to my left. The sand seemed a little darker down here, which made it a little spooky. Although there were not nearly as many shrines as earlier, there were still quite a few dotted along the coastline. I even passed some sort of graveyard. The shrines and what would have been stones were all made of wood and had broken or faded. If a graveyard had a skeleton, this is what it would look like.

The next major town before I'd have to head inland again was Iquique, which was 230 miles away. I figured I'd have to stay there tomorrow night whatever, so I decided to try and divide my mileage accordingly. There was no point in killing myself today only to have a short day tomorrow. If I did 170 miles today I'd only need to do 190 miles tomorrow, which seemed very doable if I got up early and didn't stop much.

It was 8 p.m. by the time I had reached my 170-mile marker. It was dark, which meant I could duck off the road without anyone seeing me. The sky was clear so I could still kind of see where I was going. I found a little rocky outcrop and made camp in a little cove where all the really fine sand had built up. I decided to make use of my bivi because I didn't want to ruin my sleeping bag in the dirt. Within seconds of lying down I was fast asleep all wrapped up on my fine sand mattress.

For the first time in a long while, I had an amazing sleep. My knees didn't hurt at all. I did, however, feel a little sticky when the alarm went off at 3.50 a.m. and soon realised I was soaking wet. Had it rained in the night? I felt the sand around me, which was dry as a bone. In the dark, I looked for the label on the bivi. In small writing near the bottom it read: 'Non Breathable'. Are you kidding? This was the world's lightest bivi and cost more than my sleeping bag and it wasn't breathable. What was the point? There wasn't a scenario where you'd stay dry. You might as well sleep in the rain. You might actually not get as wet. I was annoyed with my bivi and myself for not looking into that, or testing the bag before I left. I decided against putting the sleeping bag back in the sack and bungee corded it behind the saddle to dry. At least in the heat it would dry quickly.

My first stop was to be 70 miles further up the coast in a town called Tocopilla. The route carried on along the coast and wound its way up and down through huge boulder fields. Even in the dark I could just about make out the landscape. By sunrise I had done 35 miles and eaten all my food for the day, which included more tined tuna, some nuts and cheese. I definitely hadn't eat enough the previous night, which meant

I'd probably been burning body fat and because I didn't have a lot of that I was probably breaking down muscle tissue. Nutrition was so important but I somehow always seemed to get it wrong.

The light brown sand made way for a dark grey rocky area the closer I got to breakfast. My body seemed to be in quite a routine and I almost always needed the toilet at around 9 a.m. That morning was no different. Bang on nine, my tummy started to rumble. Toilet time. I stopped and went to the bottom of my bag to get my toilet paper. Where had I put it? I took my sleeping bag off the back and looked in my main bag. It wasn't there either. This couldn't be happening: I still had two hours before the next town. I repacked everything, got back on the road but only managed another twenty minutes before realising that I wouldn't be able to hold it much longer. There was nothing but rocks around: could I use a rock as toilet paper? I guess if I found a smooth one then I could! I got off Maid Marian again and went behind a clump of boulders to see what I could find. Nothing but sharp shale everywhere. Then off to my right I saw something white. Hoping it was some newspaper, and with bum pinched, I hobbled over only to realise that the white thing was a small pile of bleached smooth white rib bones from an animal that had died, probably a stray dog. That would have to do. I still had bib shorts so took everything off in haste just in time. Using a four canine rib bones as toilet paper was definitely one of the weirdest things I've ever done but I was surprised at how well it worked.

By 11 a.m. I had managed 75 miles, which meant it was looking good for me to get to Iquique by nightfall. Although the route was now slightly hilly my knees seemed to be completely fixed. I couldn't believe such a small change had made such a big difference. Hills were actually fun again: well, not 'fun' but at least they weren't a killer like before.

By 1 p.m. the road seemed to get a lot flatter even though the terrain hadn't changed. They obviously changed engineer for this section, this guy having a soft spot for dynamite as the road cut through boulder outcrops that would have gone over or around before. This part of the Atacama was still very dry and hot and at one point I even got a nose-bleed. I tried not to get any on my shirt as I carried on cycling with my head held back. Some people say head forward, some say back, some say hold your nose, some say don't. I honestly never know which to do and usually end up doing all of them until it stops. It took a good twenty minutes this time. I even had a slightly sore neck after the bloody ordeal was over.

The afternoon got better and faster as the terrain got flatter and a nice tailwind picked up. By 6 p.m. I had done 175 miles. I felt good although a little tired. I still had 30 miles to cycle by the time it got dark but I could see the lights of Iquique ahead of me. I was still a hundred metres above sea level on the dunes, so knew I'd have a nice downhill at some point. I reached the city by 10 p.m. and I was right. It was at sea level and I did get a great downhill into the twinkling lights.

Within a few minutes of arriving in the city I saw a motel. Perfect. It looked a bit cheap but would certainly do. I knocked on the office door, which was answered by a slightly overweight lady who had the lowest-cut top I had ever seen. She stood up to show her equally skimpy red hot pants. When she said the room cost was 2000 pesos for one hour, it hit me: the red lights, the inappropriate receptionist and the conveniently placed car space right next to each room's doorway suggested this was where business men come to consort with ladies of the night.

'How much for eight hours?' I asked.

'No, *señor*, four only maximum.'

I was briefly annoyed because surely business was business and what difference did it make? But then I thought that I'd probably not get a very good sleep considering what would most definitely be happening in the rooms either side of me. With that thought I carried on into the city to find a more suitable hotel. After a bit of a search I came across The Radisson. I knew it would be expensive but I really needed some sleep. I had pushed 210 miles and needed a good bed, a warm shower and some decent food. Sure enough, the room was $100, which was a huge chunk out of my budget, but it provided me with everything I needed, including Wi-Fi which meant I could send a tweet. The first thing I noticed once I got to my room was how huge the bed was. The second thing I noticed was my reflection in the mirror. I had a huge grease smudge on my cheek that had probably been there for two days. No wonder people were looking at me weirdly in the truck stops. I was also looking extremely thin. I took my clothes off and took a photo. I had no body fat left. I'd need to start eating more if I was going to stop my muscles breaking down.

The Radisson started serving breakfast at 5 a.m and I was there as they opened. I didn't feel hungry at all but I forced down some cereal, chorizo, cheese and orange juice. My route for the day was to head back up into the desert and rejoin the Pan-Am. The first section was a ten-mile stretch of switchback as I made my way back up to 700 m above sea level. In the darkness all I could see were street-lights leading up into the starlit sky above. The highest ones seemed so far ahead I couldn't quite tell if they were stars or not. Slowly, I climbed, up and up. I got a few jeers as I passed some youths in their pimped-out cars but didn't acknowledge them as I made my way higher and higher into the night. Although high it wasn't very steep and I went into tri position and kept my head down. Switchback one, two, three, they kept on coming. On switchback five I heard what sounded like a small crying sound. I looked around but didn't see anything so carried on. I then heard it again, turned around and saw a tiny kitten. It was wet and very thin, meowing as it ran after me. It looked so sad. I couldn't cycle away from it as the road was too steep. I didn't know what to do as I had no food. The crying and the following carried on for another ten minutes until eventually, and a long way from where the kitten started, it gave up. It stopped in the middle of the road and carried on crying, getting softer and softer the further away I cycled. I felt awful, guilty even for spending so much on a hotel when that money could have probably saved that kitten's life. I hoped someone would find it and take it in.

It took me nearly three hours to do the first fifteen miles before I stopped for a second breakfast. I was now heading east and reckoned I would reach the Pan-Am heading north by midday. I was hoping to get to Arica by the evening, which would bring my daily total to around 190 miles. I carried on towards the Pan-Am enjoying the benefits of a nice tailwind. I knew though that as soon as I turned north it would become a heavy side wind. This happened every day here as the sun heated up the desert inland, the warm air rising and sucking in the coastal air. This lasted normally from 11 a.m. to around 4 p.m. – a large chunk of the day.

Sure enough, as soon as I turned north my pace dropped to around 9 mph as I battled with a mixture of side and headwinds. I pushed on and on but with each glance at my speedometer, I became more and more annoyed. I rode on thinking that somewhere else in the world Mike had a huge tailwind and was flying away from me. I decided it was time to listen to some music for the first time to take my mind away from the slow speed. I took out my iPod and turned it on shuffle: the first song that came on was Foo Fighters – 'The Pretender'. I started to feel teary. I wasn't crying but my eyes started to well up. The desert was just so unforgiving. I stopped for a few moments to compose myself. This was ridiculous. I was meant to be this hardcore endurance cyclist but was on the verge of tears for no real reason whatsoever. The desert, the heat, the race, the fatigue, the knee, the headwinds: it was all a little overwhelming.

After ten minutes fighting away tears I carried on along the top plateau of the desert. It was really flat, probably the flattest part of the ride so far, but that didn't help because my pace was still quite slow. At mile 130 I came to a huge gigantic valley. I was at 1300 m above sea level and the map suggested I would go all the way to the coast: downhill that was somewhere around 25 miles long. This was the longest downhill I'd ever been on and all my sadness from earlier turned to excitement. I'd surely be able to reach an average of around 25 mph, so would have an hour or so with no pedalling at all. I jumped back on Maid Marian and started down the valley. My excitement however was very short-lived as the road turned westwards and straight into the headwind coming off the sea. My pace dropped down to around 9 mph with pedalling. Even in tri position I couldn't freewheel without coming to a stop. It was demoralising. On and on I pushed down the valley, head hung low trying to submerse myself in music to take my mind off the slow pace. In the end it took me two hours to do the 25-mile downhill and it was 8 p.m. by the time I reached the coast. My total mileage for the day was so far only 155 miles. That wasn't enough so I decided to try and do as much of the uphill as possible. It looked like it was only fifteen miles long, so it would be good to make it near the top and sleep there.

The climb up wasn't steep at all and I managed an average of 8 mph, which was only 1 mph slower than the downhill section! Because it was now evening I wasn't getting the benefit of a tailwind as I headed inland up the valley wall. The road was quite narrow with crash barriers on each side, which meant every time two trucks came by I'd have to get off the road and wait for them to pass. The higher and higher I got the less rocky it became. I decided that instead of trying to find a place to sleep out in the open I'd sleep just off the road. I had cycled 165 miles, which was way off what I wanted to do, but the headwinds and long hill made going further impossible. It was nearly 10 p.m. when I jumped over the crash barrier and made my way down the sandy slope and out of the way of passing headlights. I put Maid Marian on her side, wedged my helmet and gloves under her so they wouldn't fall down the hill and began digging a bed into the side of the valley. Luckily it was really soft sand and it wasn't long before I managed to dig a torso-length platform to sleep on. While digging I found myself smiling. I loved finding weird places to camp. It added to the adventure of it all.

It turned out I had made a good choice in sleeping on the edge of the hillside as the plateau further up the road was bare and a little windswept: I would have found no shelter at all up there. I was now 40 miles from the Chile/ Peru border and found myself in a whole new level of nothingness. Sand, sand, sand, that's all there was. Sand. In my mind I imagine rainforests and Inca trails when I think of Peru but that's probably a lot further inland: the coast was still quite dry and arid. The climb out of the valley took me back up to 1000 m above sea level. It then flattened out, dropped back down to sea level before another heavy two-hour climb leading to a final descent into Arica, my last stop in Chile. The first thing I needed to find was a new chain so that I could get rid of this sticky greased-up one that was now covered in sand making it even more heavy and hard to push. Unfortunately, nothing seemed open. I thought that a bit strange but then on asking was told it was Sunday. I had no idea. I had lost count of the days awhile back. With no way of changing my chain I filled up on food and carried on towards Peru!

I was slightly nervous about my first land border crossing. I didn't have a visa for Peru but gathered I could get one at the border. I was worried about Peru as it was a much poorer country and the risks of having things stolen were a lot greater: I had been warned by a few people to keep my wits about me. I knew my life wouldn't be at risk but I figured I'd be seen more as a walking (cycling?) wallet. I also didn't know what to expect from the landscape. The Atacama had broken me and I was hoping for less sand, though figured the route ahead was probably the same.

The border between Chile and Peru consisted of many people sitting around, busloads of travellers with huge cases, army soldiers with massive guns and the odd stray dog looking for titbits. The whole process was pretty simple and after standing in various queues I was through in about an hour. Result!

Once over the border, I was right: Peru didn't change into a rainforest and was in fact drier in appearance than the last part of Chile. My initial route was slightly north to a town called Tacna before I carried on along the coast of Peru in a north westerly direction. I was right in the bend of South America which looked a million miles away from where I had started. That was quite exciting. My first major milestone.

The route to Tacna was a long, slow and steady climb to 600 m again. It was so slight a slope that without my altimeter I'd have thought it was downhill. I reached Tacna by mid-afternoon and spent a good two hours trying to do Peru admin, which included getting money, stocking up on food and water and getting some lunch. I also needed to decide on whether to go inland and follow the Pan-American or head along the coast. Ordinarily, I'd have followed the coast but there was about a forty-mile section of the coast road that was white on the map when everything else was yellow. Instinct told me that this might possibly be a dirt road. I couldn't afford to do a long section off road: that would take about twenty miles off my target daily total, something I couldn't afford at this stage. I worked out that I was possibly already a day behind what I should have been due to my knees debacle and needed to make up for it. With that I decided to keep on the Pan-Am.

That decision did mean a big climb back to 1000 m to get out of Tacna. By now it was 40 degrees and very dry as I made my way out of the town and up. The road finally flattened out and together with a pretty good tailwind brought a huge smile to my face. Since I had started using my iPod I hadn't turned it off. It really did help take my mind off the heat and the nothingness.

The change in wealth was pretty obvious in Peru. I made this conclusion by the number of horse and carts I saw taking up the road, which certainly gave a sense of poverty. I don't know why because my friend has a horse and they are bloody expensive! The Peruvians also seemed a lot friendlier, too. Chileans weren't necessarily unfriendly by any means, but didn't really acknowledge I existed as I cycled past. Peru was a different story. Everyone waved and gave me a huge smile as I went past. I felt less alone, which was a good feeling and helped me with my mental state.

I pushed on with my tailwind, only stopping a few times in small roadside stalls to try and get some food. It seemed a lot harder to find any actual food that wasn't biscuits and sweets. By nightfall, I had only managed 145 miles, which was my second or third shortest day. This had a little to do with the hills but mostly because of the time I'd spent off the bike in Arica and at the border post: without that I'd have done at least 170. I was still trying to offset my $100 bill from the Radisson so decided to sleep in the desert again. My knees no longer hurt so I didn't need a bed as much as before. The problem was that again there was nothing but sand and nowhere to find a shelter from the bright truck lights and the wind. On and on I cycled trying to find anything that I could sleep under or behind. Eventually I saw two fairly big rocks about 50 m off the road. They were by far the best camping option I'd seen all day. I waited for a truck to fly past as it hooted a greeting and then ducked off the road and through the soft sand towards my boulder hotel. As I approached the two-foot high rocks I saw what looked like a reed fence lying against them. My mind immediately started to think of ways I could make a shelter. After some small home improvements to the edge of the fence I managed to bend it into a little cove type shelter with the opening facing downwind. I felt like I was progressing as a human. Today I had managed to build myself a house. That excited me. It was great to be in Peru.

# 7

## *BANDITOS*

Day two in Peru. I woke up at 3.20 a.m., the excitement of being in a new country still fresh in my mind. My knee was a little sore again as I had neglected my stretching over the past few days: stretching always seemed to be the last thing on my mind when I was tired.

As I continued my journey, the Atacama gave way to another desert I hadn't researched. I pushed on through the golden sandy terrain until about 10 a.m. when I thought I saw a cyclist ahead of me. There was something dark just off the side of the road about half a mile ahead. I picked up my pace and raced ahead, excited at the prospect of seeing another cyclist who might actually speak English. It was only when I was 100 m away that I realised it wasn't a cyclist at all. It was just a tree. Initially, I was really disappointed that it wasn't a cyclist, but my mind then focused on the fact that this was a tree. I hadn't seen any vegetation for days and here, right next to the road, was a green and perfectly healthy tree. That seemed a little strange: I was 1000 m above sea level and there was nothing but huge sandy mountains around me.

I carried on up a small climb and when I finally reached the top I thought I was in a dream. Located in a natural crater flanked by desert mountains on each side was an oasis: green fields, trees and water. Actual water! It was a far cry from the harsh desert I was in only ten minutes ago. As I cycled through, I realised this was not just a simple oasis, but in fact a small wine region. Incredible. The contrast between rows and rows of green vines, juxtaposed against huge, stark, sand-covered mountains in the distance was surprising. The road went right through the middle of this little oasis as small dogs barked at me from a distance and farmers tended their crops. I pictured myself buying a farm and retiring to a place like this. Might have to work on my Spanish a bit though.

With the next town came the opportunity to have breakfast. I soon found a restaurant but it wasn't open even though it was 10.30 a.m. and the sign on the door said it opened at 9 a.m. I really needed to swap my front and back tyres around so there I sat, outside a small roadside café, swapping my tyres and waiting for breakfast number two. Eventually at 11 a.m. they opened the doors and I ordered some spaghetti and chicken.

'You not open at 9 a.m.?' I asked the waitress jokingly. She didn't understand. I looked around the room to see if I could find a clock to point at. There was one above the till. Strangely it read 9 a.m.! Mmmmm?

'Pardon. Is that clock *correcto*?' I felt like such a tit. Not sure *correcto* was even a word but it sounded Spanish.

'*Si, señor, nueve!*' The waitress said, touching her watch.

I knew *nueve* was nine in Spanish and I suddenly realised that there might have been a time difference between Chile and Peru. Turns out there was, and a whole two hours too. I guess Peru does go quite far to the west, so that would make sense. This also meant that when I woke up at 3.20 a.m. it was in fact 1.20 a.m. I laughed out loud at that thought. Who gets up at 1.20 a.m. to go cycling? There were a few trucks that must have thought I was crazy. Seems they had a point.

I was chased by a few dogs as I was leaving the village which really annoyed me at first but then when the third dog started to run across the field for me, it gave me an idea. If his owner was happy to let his dog run and potentially bite me, then I was going to see how far I could get his dog to run away from him: if I cycled too quickly then the dog would give up; if I cycled too slowly I'd probably get bitten. And so 'Chasing Dogs' was born, my new game which meant I no longer got annoyed with dogs barking at me.

Just as soon as the wine oasis appeared so it disappeared as if swallowed up by the desert again. The sand, hills and heat continued as I made my way towards Arequipa. I could feel my body wasting away. I just needed to make it to Lima. I had three more days and even if I dropped 20 miles a day I'd still be able to make up for it in America. By 9 p.m. I was in Arequipa and decided to stay there for the night. My daily total was only 150 miles, which was an embarrassingly short day again. I was putting a lot of pressure on my America leg to make up the miles.

I woke up with a fine case of the shakes. It was very slight. Almost like the feeling you get when you are in a building above the London Underground and it vibrates every time the

Tube goes under it. This feeling lasted about ten minutes and then disappeared. It must be something to do with trying to survive on less than six hours sleep each night. I hope I hadn't fallen into long-term fatigue. I got up slowly and started to organise myself for the day ahead, getting the next leg of map on top of my tri-bars.

'So where's today's section, Little Flying Cow?' But it wasn't there. Shit. I'd somehow managed to lose the next 150 miles of map: it must have fallen out at some point. The good news was that there is only one main road here, the Pan-Am, and as long as I kept the coast on the left I'd eventually reach Lima. The bad news was that I now had no idea how far it was between each town where I could get food and water. I'd have to stock up on everything as soon as I could in case there were any long stretches.

I left Arequipa before sunrise and was greeted with a really long downhill, which always lifted my spirits. Unfortunately, the road wasn't in good condition: I was told that the roads got worse and worse the further north you went and today was the first time their lack in quality affected my speed. Your uphill speed is always about the same pace no matter what the road is like, but it's the downhill where you can go from 30 mph down to 12 mph if it is bumpy, even slower on some of the corners which seem to be a lot worse. The only one benefit was that there was a nice tailwind pushing me along the flat bits. Even this had a downside, the wind bringing with it a sandstorm, covering most of the road in fine sand.

The closer I got to Lima the more populated the route became, and along with that people seemed to be giving me more stick as I cycled past. There were a few rude gestures and one kid even gave the finger gun treatment. I knew that most of it was harmless banter but it was the first time I'd felt at all threatened since I started my adventure. I eventually resorted to pulling my neck scarf over my face in an effort to look a little 'hard'. As soon as I did it I burst out laughing. Who was I kidding? I was a now-very-skinny, short ginger dude in a country where most of the people look like Pablo Escobar. I'd never in a million years be able to pull off the 'hard' look. At least I was quite fit so if they ran or cycled after me I'd probably win.

My Chasing Dogs game was becoming more frequent too. Most of the time it was only one dog here and there but then at around 2 p.m. I hit the jackpot of all games. I was coming up to a roadside truck stop when not one, not two, but five dogs started running from the small house next to the restaurant. The lady outside said nothing to stop them and was happy to see them attack a poor skinny cyclist. Time to break my now 200 m record. The dogs reached the road just as I passed them and started to run alongside me. I slowed down my pace a little as they barked and snarled at me; 50 m, 100 m they carried on. They were getting quite confident the longer we cycled together and I had to really pick up the pace a few times to stop them biting me. On and on we played: 200 m then 300 m. I looked behind me to see if anyone was calling after them but there was nobody. This was a record for me at 350 m or so. I was feeling happy and was just about to pick up the pace again so that they would give up when one of the smaller dogs dashed from behind me and went straight for my ankles. I was clipped in so couldn't move my foot out the way in time before he took a snarling bite into my right lower calf. Ouch! I shouted and unclipped, lifting my foot in the air. The dog carried on barking and running next to me. His mouth was foaming at the edges, which likely meant he had rabies. After another bout of shouting I was confident enough to re-clip into my pedals and speed off, leaving the dogs behind.

Once I was happy that they had all turned around to go back to their home, I stopped and looked down at my ankle. My heart was bouncing out of my chest: a little from the extra exertion getting away but mostly because if I had in fact been bitten by a rabid dog I was in for trouble. I was still wearing my compression tights to avoid sunburn and they had two little holes in them. My leg felt like it had been scratched but wasn't that sore at all. I nervously untucked my tights from my sock to examine the damage. I rolled it up to where the bite marks were and let out a huge sigh. His teeth hadn't drawn blood. That was a close one. I decided I might have to rethink my Chasing Dogs game strategy. I obviously wasn't very good at it. Also the name sounded like I was doing the chasing. All in all not well thought through.

Dodging dogs wasn't my only challenge that day. The roads got progressively worse and I could just about deal with the bumps and the heat, and finally my knees were better. But the one thing that made my blood boil were the peanuts I would lose from my front food container whenever I went over a bump. I wasn't eating enough as it was and every time I went over a bump I would lose at least 30 kcal of peanuts. If this happened twenty times a day that was 600 kcal that I couldn't afford to lose. It was so frustrating and made me cycle even slower. 'This is so *annooooooying*!' I shouted as another bunch of peanuts fell to the floor. I was leaving a trail of peanuts across Peru. At least if I got lost I'd be able to find my way back, unless an evil crow was following me and eating them all up.

In light of getting some grief from people earlier in the day I decided to cut my day short at 160 miles and not do any night cycling. I also needed to find somewhere to get some cream as my arms had started to blister and peel from that first day I got sunburned coming out of Santiago. The curse of ginger fair skin. You'd have thought I'd have worked it out by now.

The next day I continued along the coast, which every now and then would send me about five miles inland along a river before crossing where it was cheaper to build a short bridge and sending me all the way back to the coast again. These bridges were generally where little settlements formed as farmers made use of the river to grow crops. I was still trying my 'gangsta' face mask technique in each town just so that I might not be seen. In my mind that made sense anyway. By early afternoon I was off the coast and into the desert again. The road was flat and long and the sun harsh and dry. I had been getting my fair share of trucks hooting and big smiles along the route, which was nice, and I always made an effort to look into each driver's window as they drove past as 99% of the time they would be smiling and waving and I wanted to return the favour.

Then on one long stretch of nothingness, two guys who looked like cliché gangster types from any film depicting a South American drug dealer drove past and didn't look at me. They had vests, backwards baseball caps and drove a piece-of-shit car that was falling apart. I didn't think anything of it until I saw them pulled over a few miles ahead.

I moved out into the middle of the road and as I passed them I looked into their window and again they didn't even notice me. That was strange: here was a skinny European ginger guy in the middle of the South American desert and they didn't even look at me. I carried on pondering why, when ten minutes later they drove past slowly again. Now my heart started to race. They then parked ahead off to the edge of the road. This time, however, they pulled off just as I was getting near them.

I carried on and again they let me pass. I pushed on, checking my rear-view mirror to see what they were doing. Once more they pulled out, overtook me and went ahead and out of sight. Something in my stomach told me they were up to no good. I was in the middle of nowhere and no one would know if I disappeared. I made the decision to stop and wait to see what happened. If I saw them come back then I'd surely know they were up to something. I waited for another ten minutes and then carried on cycling. It wasn't for another ten more miles that I saw the car once more, parked on the side of the road again. I stopped straight away and went behind a bush near the edge of the road. I stood there wondering what to do. I was still 250 or so miles from Lima and couldn't afford to cut any more days off my target.

As I sat there I remembered someone once getting a police escort somewhere. I knew it was a long shot but because I was born in Zimbabwe, grew up in South Africa, lived in England and had an Irish passport I had four embassies I could potentially call for help. It was certainly worth a try. I didn't have the details so thought of the one person to call – my father. He is very practical and level headed and I knew he wouldn't stress out as much as Mum would: Dad thinks with his head, Mum her heart. I figured head was a better choice in this matter.

Luckily I had signal. I called him and he picked up straight away. It was great to hear his voice, a comforting sense of familiarity. I told him my slight predicament and although he was concerned, was straight on the case trying to get hold of the embassies. I was lucky to have phone reception and a full battery. Those two things often didn't coincide.

We started off with the Zimbabwean Embassy but had no luck. Second on the list was the Irish embassy but they weren't answering either. My dad then called the British embassy and was surprised that they had a team dedicated to helping people abroad. They were incredibly helpful and called me back within ten minutes with a number for a private security firm. It was $100 per day for a guy with a gun to follow me. I was very tempted but that seemed a lot of money. Lastly was the South Africa Embassy. They were incredibly friendly and it just so happened that the lady I spoke to had a son who was very keen on cycling. I told her my dilemma and the fact I was in a race. She took my details and said she would see what she could do but said it might take a few hours. I couldn't afford to wait a few hours as I needed to get to Pisco before dark. I decided to carry on cycling in any case. It was the most nervous I had been since I began. My pace slowed right down and every time I went over a rise in the road I'd expect to see the gangster guys waiting with baseball bats. My mind was going crazy. About an hour later I was going up a hill when I heard a siren behind me. I nearly fell over as I looked over my shoulder to see the Peru police hot on my tail. I started to pull over and they came alongside me.

'*Señor*, go, go, we follow. Race.'

'*Gracias, señors, gracias.*' I couldn't believe it. The South Africa Embassy had completely come through for me. I now had some police following me with lights on and everything. I felt bad that they were going so slowly so stepped it up a gear. I pushed on for nearly two hours when they eventually pulled alongside me, waved goodbye and turned off down a side road. I felt bad as I didn't even know their names. Within a few minutes I saw another police car ahead and when I passed it too turned its lights on and signalled they were going to follow me. Wow. Really? This was incredible. On and on I pushed with the police changing every few hours. At food stops I'd buy them a meal and we would chat in sign language as they didn't understand English and I still didn't understand Spanish.

By mid-afternoon I passed a stall selling bananas. I hadn't had fresh fruit in ages so decided to stop off.

'*Hola señor. Uno banana por favour.*' My lack of Spanish was becoming an embarrassment. The stall owner just laughed at me and pointed at a bunch hanging from the rafters. I pointed at the biggest banana, which cost all of 5p, and offered the police chaps one to which they agreed. I figured this would be a great time to do a short video of me and my police escorts. I peeled the banana and started filming a diary entry. As I turned to film the police chaps my banana broke and fell on the sandy floor. The police guys laughed and I laughed back. I turned back around to buy another one but the storeowner had gone round the back. One of the policemen then came up to me, grabbed another banana from the rafters, gave it to me, and said 'Shhhhh!' with his finger to his lips while smiling cheekily. Seriously? Was the policeman telling me to steal a banana? For another

5p I think I could afford it. I just laughed and put some coins on the table. They laughed too. Even though neither of us could understand each other it was fun to have hand-signing banter.

I soon worked out that I'd have someone to follow me all the way to Pisco, which was a huge relief. Even though I was making up for lost time I was still an hour behind schedule with all the waiting around and embassy calling. We pushed on together and soon became a well-oiled team. The police were pulling over trucks that were overtaking too close to me, and giving their sirens and lights a good workout in towns when people cut me up. I think they enjoyed it too because it was probably a whole lot better than sitting under a tree all day, which is the only other place I'd seen any police in Peru.

Having the security of the police behind me made me completely turn off for a while as I put my head down to get the miles in. I was riding faster than usual but I felt good. I'd sometimes look ahead for anything in the road and if it was clear I would then put my head directly down in tri-position and cycle just by looking down keeping my wheel perfectly in the middle of the white line. I called it White Line Chicken. The line would obviously always win this game but I'd see how long my nerves would last before I had to look up. Ninety-nine per cent of the time I could have carried on for another 200 m and was annoyed for giving in, but there was once or twice when a dog or chicken or pothole would appear out of nowhere. I was getting more and more confident with the police behind as generally everything moved out the way. Most of the time I'd look up for a split second, scan the road, see nothing new and carry on looking down.

At one point when I looked up I saw what looked like a European chap walking in the road. The nearer and nearer I got to him the more I realised he wasn't South American. I pulled up alongside him.

'Hey, sorry, you scared me,' he said as he stepped back slowly. He was also ginger, very burned and had a distinctly South African accent.

'Are you all right, mate? Where are you heading to?' I asked.

'Lima, bro.'

He wasn't carrying anything. No rucksack, no bag, nothing: just the tatty looking clothes he was wearing.

'Shit man, that's a long way, are you walking?'

'*Ya*, but there is a truck stop up ahead and I will probably get a lift and some food there.'

'I've got a few nuts for you if you're hungry? What happened man?'

'I've landed up in a bit of trouble and need to get to the embassy.'

By now my police friends had stopped right behind us and he looked slightly nervous when he saw them. He then looked at me with a 'who the hell are you with this escort' look on his face.

'Man, is there anything I can do?'

'No, honestly. I'll be in Lima tomorrow so it's all good.'

I could see he was tired and needed help but what could I do? He needed to get to the embassy, the embassy that was using their resources to help a cyclist rather than helping this guy who looked like he needed it a lot more than I did. I cycled off slowly and looked back to see the police stop and talk to him for no more than five seconds before carrying on following me. I kind of wished they had decided to leave me and look after him instead. I felt awfully guilty. At least I knew the South Africa Embassy were really helpful and he'd be in good hands when he eventually got there.

Pisco was about three miles off the Pan-Am towards the coast. The last bunch of police said I should go into the centre and make myself known to the police at the station. I'm not really sure why, but I said my goodbyes, gave them huge thanks and started the long, dead-straight road into Pisco. It took a while to find the police station and when I arrived and said I was told to go there, thinking they knew, I got some really blank stares as if they were saying, 'Yeah, you are here, so what?'

I did however need a hotel and they pointed me in the direction of one near the centre of town. I wasn't sure what day it was but the centre was buzzing with stalls and street food. It was so busy that it was hard to walk down the street without bumping into people. I was getting the most attention I had got so far as there weren't too many hairy ginger people in Peru. My beard was almost at an all-time record length. I came around a corner to the distinct smell of jerk chicken. Straight away I knew that's what I wanted, so followed my nose to a large open-plan restaurant with plastic chairs and foldaway tables. There were three huge BBQs laden with succulent flattened-out chickens. My mouth started to water. I ordered a full chicken and rice. It was glorious, far superseding anything I'd had at the Notting Hill Carnival. The quite typically South American waitress/bar-lady/cook, who wore slightly inappropriate clothing showing off her slightly large belly, kept trying to get me to stay longer because apparently after they stop serving jerk chicken the disco starts. As tempting as that sound I was pretty tired. By 11 p.m. I was in bed after I'd bought some cake in the market, which I was planning on having for breakfast. Yes, cake for breakfast. I felt so rock and roll.

There is a reason people don't have cake for breakfast. It doesn't go down well. The one I'd bought was way too sweet and dry and I had to wash it down with warm water. Not a great combination.

I left Pisco at 5 a.m. so that I could get a few hours in the morning darkness and wouldn't have to cycle in the dark through Lima. Lima was only 140 miles away and I hoped to be there by 5 p.m. I didn't have my police escorts today but that didn't matter. Besides this little morning session I had no more night shifts to do. By 9 a.m. I had covered 40 miles and passed a toll bridge. I saw a toilet sign so thought I take the opportunity as trying to find a place on the side of the road was getting a lot harder. I couldn't have been more than five minutes, but when I returned to Maid Marian there was a group of police standing around.

'Ah, Mr South Africa, yes?'

'Yes, that's me, I guess?'

'Ah, *cyclista, cyclista*, ha-ha, we photo.'

One of them took out his small camera phone and the others joined me. I barely had time to think as I stood smiling while they crowded around Maid Marian and me. They were really friendly and smiling and laughing. I had no idea what they were saying but they seemed in a good mood.

'OK OK, come, go, we follow.' One of them signalled to his car.

"Oh, OK, *gracias señor.*'

'Go, Go, Go!' another one shouted and laughed.

I pushed on as the houses got closer together and there were more and more people around. On one occasion a beach buggy drove the wrong way along my hard shoulder towards me. I quickly moved out the way and he gave a *'Sorry, but what you gonna do about it?'* gesture with his hands in the air to the police. He had balls. Fair play.

By 3 p.m. I was finally in downtown Lima. The Pan-Am was now a huge busy four-lane highway. Cars were cutting me up all over the shop. The police took me as far along the Pan-Am as I needed and then I had to make my own way into the centre of the city. It was 4 p.m. by the time I finished my South American leg. I put Maid Marian up against a wall and sat on the floor. I saw my reflection in a shop window. I was dirty, smelly and very thin. South America had thrown everything at me. The heat, pain, dehydration, *banditos*, police and fatigue shakes. I had cycled 2500 miles in fourteen days, which was about a day and a half behind schedule, but I was happy that I was ahead of the world record. That and the fact my next stop was America, the land of fatty fast food. Exactly what I needed.

# 8

# STEPPING UP A GEAR

I had quite an interesting flight to Miami via Colombia, the highlight (if that is the word) being going to the loo seven times and vomiting in one of those sick bags you get. Luckily I grabbed it when running down the aisle as both loos were occupied and I had that embarrassing moment of throwing up in the bag between two seats on row 48. I apologised to the two passengers who seemed less than impressed. I had no idea what caused it but felt a lot better afterwards. It might have been the malaria tablets I had been taking, as I didn't have anything to eat before I took the pill. Now I know why they always tell you to do that. Always thought that was an old wives' tale.

The American border control is notoriously cold and stern and they'd certainly give you the old rubber glove treatment at the first opportunity. I didn't really get any saddle sores but I am sure my backside had seen better times. I was nervous that my new look as a dirty bearded homeless person would push me a lot higher up the list of potential threats than I deserved. Luckily, the gentleman at Miami Airport Control was more interested in my little cycle adventure. This may have been helped by the fact I was laying on the heavy Hugh Grant accent. Americans love that stuff. To keep up my good luck, Maid Marian didn't get lost this time and everything landed up in one piece. The whole luggage system was so good that I barely had the agonising wait for her to arrive at the oversized excess baggage section of the airport.

It was 6 p.m. by the time I managed to leave Miami. My route was to head north out of Florida. I could now at least cycle safely at night so decided to push 75 miles up to a place called South Bay. Compared to Peru, the roads were incredible: flat and with a wide hard shoulder. The eating options were different too and I found myself stopping off for a Subway 'Footlong'. I needed fatty and salty food and the Italian BMT was around 1200 kcal with South Western Sauce. It was also fast food, so my time off the bike was greatly diminished. By nightfall I had done 45 miles and was going along at a steady 16 mph. The areas on each side of the road looked like classic alligator territory, swampy with loads of reed beds, and I figured it might be better to stay in a motel. Americans love their motels and they are usually in the region of $30–50 for the night.

Things were going well until at around 10 p.m. when I came to what looked like a very long section of roadworks. The orange cones had merged the two lanes down to one small lane that included the hard shoulder I was cycling on. There was no way one of the many absurdly huge American pick-up trucks and I would be able to both be there. I'd have to cycle in the sectioned-off section, which was wide and I'd at least be safe. I moved over and weaved in and out of the first few cones, just for fun, before settling into cycling in the middle of the coned-off lane. It was smooth and fast and was clearly new as I could smell that distinct smell of tar.

It was only after a mile that I realised something was wrong. Something seemed heavy and almost sticky. I took my headphones out and realised there was a weird sound coming from my rolling wheels on the new road surface. I stopped and felt my front tyre and was shocked to discover it covered in a fine layer of tar. The road hadn't dried yet. Great! I pictured a long thin line my tyres might have created over the last mile or so. I looked back nervously and waited for a car's lights to show me the damage. None. Which made sense when I thought about it: the steamroller weighs a few tonnes; if my little bike and I made a dent then they'd need to rethink their engineering. Even so, I was forced to move into the main road and move over whenever a car came. Luckily it was night so it remained fairly quiet. The pick-up trucks in America have lights as bright as the sun, which meant I had plenty of warning when they were approaching.

The next few days through Florida were pretty uneventful. The roads were a joy and I was making decent mileage and feeling strong. It was clear that my new diet which was a lot fattier and saltier was doing me the world of good. I struggled to find places to camp, though, so one night I snuck into a campsite and slept under someone's caravan, while they were in it. It wasn't a great sleep as the ground was full of ants that decided to use my face as a playground all night. It was too hot to completely go inside my sleeping bag so I didn't fall asleep till around 3 a.m. when I was eventually too tired to care anymore. Lucky the ants didn't bite, or so I thought. They did of course and it was very itchy all the next day.

Florida carried on getting better and better when it came to putting in big miles. The hard shoulder was clean, smooth and wide. The terrain was perfectly undulating too, which suited my style of cycling – it's a few minutes up the hill then thirty seconds down to recover. If you get enough pace on the downhill you can almost make it halfway up the other side. The weather was excellent too. Not nearly as hot as the 40 degrees I'd had to deal with in South America, staying a steady 25 degrees most of the day. I was averaging 180-plus miles per day. Sometimes I didn't believe that: maybe I had got my cycle computers wrong and was only doing 180 km per day? But I knew this wasn't the case as all the road signs matched my distance. All the while, I was keeping to a steady 13.5 mph, which meant doing 180 miles day after day didn't put you in hospital.

The southern part of Florida was quite spooky to cycle through at night at no fault of its own. About a year earlier I got the flu and watched season one and two of the vampire based TV show, *True Blood*. The programme looked like it was filmed in this part of the world and as the night drew in I became more nervous with every sound and cracking in the swamps. Every time I heard something in the bush I'd look around fully expecting an alligator to jump out being chased by a gaunt-looking vampire. I really do have a wild imagination.

I kept to fairly main roads through Florida but once over the state border it was a different story. Georgia decided that it would put huge one-foot wide rumble strips across the entire hard shoulder on all the main roads. It seemed senseless. They turned a perfectly good and safe cycling road into something you could barely walk on without twisting your ankle, let alone cycle on. No wonder I hadn't seen another cyclist yet. I therefore decided to do some back roads. It was great to be able to pick and choose my route through America. Up to now I pretty much only had one road to take: for Spain and Morocco the main road along the coast; for Chile and Peru the Pan-American. But now, in America, I could literally go where the wind wanted to take me (as long as I wasn't going back on myself). The one big problem I had with the Guinness rules was the idea of zigzagging in 'easy' countries purely to make up the required mileage. This was a strategy that some riders might take advantage of purely to make up fast miles. Although completely allowed it wasn't in keeping with the ethos of round the world cycling. I wasn't going to plan any zigzagging, but if the wind decided to push me north then I'd go with it. I liked that the weather was deciding my adventure for me. Who knew where I'd go and what I would discover?

The back roads through Georgia didn't disappoint. They were traffic-free and meandered through small homesteads and farms, each with a huge American flag on their gates or sticking out the side of their buildings. Americans love their flags and I wasn't complaining: it meant I knew exactly which direction the wind was going. It was a real treat to be able to look and enjoy the scenery for the first time in weeks. Yes the South American desert was scenic, but there are only so many times you can look at sand before it gets repetitive. The Georgian scenery seemed to be changing every half an hour, which helped pass the time. Before I knew it, it was 1 p.m. and I had managed 100 miles. I stopped for some spaghetti

Bolognese: this was the sort of meal that worked the best for me, with good fat, carbs and protein.

When I got back to Maid Marian I saw a small spot of oil on the floor below her Rohloff hub. I put my thumb near the rear cog and found it was covered in oil. I know Rohloffs have a tendency to leak if the rubber seals perish, but three or four drops in half an hour was way too much. I had no idea how long it had been leaking but they only took 50 ml of oil, and even if it started today I'd be out of oil in a few days. Thankfully, the other great thing about America was 3G availability. I had bought a SIM card in Miami, which meant I could Google a bike shop. I found a shop in Atlanta which was 200 miles north of where I was: they were an 'Official Rohloff Dealer' and when I phoned them were really helpful. The only problem was I really needed to get to them before 2 p.m. the following day because their main mechanic went home at 3 p.m. That meant I had 24 hours to do 200 miles and get some sleep sometime in the middle.

Not an *easy* task but doable. I pushed on through the green pastures of Georgia until at 6 p.m. it started to rain. This was the first time it had rained at all since I started my adventure. It was a nice change and in my mind Maid Marian was getting her first shower, which got rid of some of the dust covering her. By midnight I had done 205 miles and was pretty exhausted. I hadn't seen any motels for a while and Google told me the nearest one was still about two hours away. I decided I should just camp up somewhere and came across a church. I'd heard of many people sleeping in church grounds, so went around the back and made camp in between some bushes and the church wall.

\*

I was up at 5 a.m. and realised how lucky I was it hadn't rained in the night. I had no shelter and it had rained the evening before. My fatigued mind obviously decided to overlook that fact. Atlanta was still 100 miles away so I pushed north as the hills got bigger and the rumble strips got worse. The bike shop was quite far in the northwest part of Atlanta, which meant going through almost all of the different suburbs. Towards the south were the typical wooden houses with a central doorway and steps leading to the porch. They all had porches. Flags and porches. I liked it. More houses need porches. It's basically an extra room.

I arrived at what seemed like the centre of Atlanta and was faced with hill after hill. How could a city be this hilly? The northwest part of the city was obviously more affluent as the properties got bigger and were situated further from the road with huge electric gates and fences. These properties would be in the £20 million range in parts of north London. I had no idea how much they were here but I was guessing a lot cheaper. By 2 p.m. I had made it to the shop to the smiles of the manager and staff who were all expecting my arrival.

'Howdy, I thought you were going to be here by lunchtime.'

'Yeah, sorry,' I replied. 'I had no idea Atlanta was so hilly.'

'It sure is. Come on bring us your Rohloff, we don't get many of them in here.'

What? They were an official dealer on the Rohloff website. This wasn't a good start. Fifteen minutes went by when Chad – I love such American names – came out the workshop.

'Hey Sean,' he said. 'I'm really sorry but it looks like you can only put Rohloff oil in that hub.'

Are you kidding? Even I knew that. The manager overheard him.

'You mean you can't just put any grade 2 oil in?' he shouted from the till

'No you can't. Only Rohloff oil and we ain't got any here.'

Great. I'd busted my ass getting here, way off course, only to find they didn't have any oil. To make matters worse, it was Saturday and I couldn't get to the next Rohloff supplier before they closed. And then the following day was Sunday and everything was probably closed.

'Any chance I can use your computer and call some other shops?' I asked.

What the bike shop lacked in Rohloff knowledge they made up for in phone calls and research. Twenty minutes later they found a shop about sixty miles away that had oil. I'd never make it there before they closed but Frank, the kind owner, lived in Rome, which was thirty miles northwest of Atlanta. He said I could meet him on the highway there at around 7 p.m. Result. Americans in general had so far been the friendliest people I had ever met.

It was now 3 p.m. which meant I had an hour to kill before I needed to leave for Rome. I made the most of this time by eating two lunches, changing my tyres to GP4000s and doing some stretching. I had again neglected my stretching routine and my knees felt it. I was excited to be going to Rome as I had never been to the real Rome. I doubt this one had a Colosseum though, but who knows, maybe a millionaire got bored once and built a mini replica.

I met Frank at 7 p.m. and he had exactly what I needed. He was very friendly and a keen touring cyclist too. He didn't even charge me extra to bring it to me. We chatted a bit before we parted ways and I went off to find a motel. My daily total was only a feeble 130 miles, but I didn't feel too bad as it wasn't due to my fitness and I knew I could push harder. It was a little earlier than I would have wanted to stop but I needed to do a service on the hub. I found the cheapest motel, which came complete with cockroaches and graffiti on the mirrors and looked like one of many that you see in horror films. I should have guessed it would be bad when the check-in desk had bulletproof glass.

I took everything off Maid Marian and turned her upside down. I had done an oil change before so knew the drill. I got out my tool kit which had the Allen key on it and put it between the spokes. It fitted perfectly. I tried to unscrew the nut but the tool kept getting caught on the spokes. I couldn't even get the screw to move at all. There wasn't any space. I tried from every which way but nothing worked. I couldn't get the screw out. I sat back down dejected and annoyed that I had cut my day short to do an oil change and now couldn't do it. Also I would now have to leave later than normal so that I would be in Rome when the shops opened to buy another Allen key. If I left too early nothing would be open. That's if they opened at all on a Sunday.

It was still dark the following morning when I pushed on to Rome. It didn't have a Colosseum but it did have a Home Depot store open at 9 a.m. on a Sunday. Pretty impressive. They didn't sell just one Allen key, so I had to buy the entire pack. At the till I took off the one I needed and gave the rest to the cashier as a gift. She looked very confused. I spent the next half an hour doing a roadside Rohloff hub oil change, which involved putting in some cleaner while turning the hub through gears three and five, which utilise all the cogs. Do this for fifteen minutes then suck out the old oil. Turns out I literally had no oil left at all. You then leave the hub to let the last of the old oil drain out before putting in the new oil and a new screw provided. It wasn't long before she was ready to go. I jumped back on and straight away felt how easy it was to pedal. I felt like I was cycling on a cloud, she was so smooth. I immediately felt my spirits lift and my speed increase a mile or so an hour. It's amazing how such a little thing can make such a difference.

The original plan was to head towards Birmingham, for no other reason than seeing as I was in Rome I should probably visit another 'European' city. The wind had other ideas for me though and I decided to follow it north-westwards towards Alabama. I took advantage of the tailwind and used as many back roads as possible. This part of the world was very scenic and on one occasion I felt like I was in the Lake District, except with white wooden houses instead of stone ones. The back roads might be ever so slightly slower, but keeping a healthy and active mind though good scenery more than made up for it with the extra energy you get being in a good mood.

The full-fingered gloves I had used in South America were a little tatty by the end, so I bought fingerless ones for my USA leg. Unfortunately I forgot that the ends of my fingers needed sun cream and by mid-afternoon my knuckles were red and burned. I had no idea your knuckles could burn but mine were and they hurt like hell. I lost an hour with the hub oil malarkey but gained an hour because of the time difference as I crossed into Alabama. Even though technically it made no difference because my plan was to sleep five to six hours a night and cycle the rest, it still felt good to have done

140 miles by 6 p.m. My new oil, great scenery and better food meant I was able to push through to 181 miles before deciding to rest for the night.

After a good five hours sleep I carried on heading north-westwards making the most of the slight tailwind. Annoyingly, I left too early to make use of the free breakfast in the motel so had to find something early on. Even more annoying was that it was McDonald's. They do a huge cup of coffee for $1 though, which helped in a small way to make me feel better about having fast food for breakfast. Calories are calories and there is no room for being a food snob in the adventure racing game. If you need nutrition eating the wrong thing is better than nothing.

I was heading towards the iconic Mississippi river. There weren't too many places to cross it, so I had to decide on a general route for the day. I could either cycle directly west through Memphis and see where Elvis grew up, which would be very cool but also meant I'd lose time trying to navigate my way through a big city. Alternatively, I could head a little further north to bypass the city and head towards Missouri. Unfortunately, my dislike for cycling in cities outweighed my love for Elvis so I carried on towards Tennessee and Missouri. This also meant I could go through Florence, another 'European City' I hadn't ever been to. I was racking them up.

I made Florence in time for late breakfast and settled into a quaint little coffee shop. It felt very European and nothing like any of the other breakfast monstrosities I had seen up till now. The lady who owned the café was really excited about my ride and told me about various places I should visit.

She even overlooked the fact that in a moment of stupidity I pronounced Arkansas like it was spelled – *Ar-kan-sas*! I realised straight away and felt like such a dumb tourist. It's like when Americans come to London and ask where *Ly-ces-ter* Square is. How I've judged them in the past. I now have no leg to stand on.

When it came to paying, the lady insisted it was on the house and offered me a free coffee refill, which I accepted. But as I picked up my helmet from the seat next to me I knocked the entire cup all over her quaint white table cloth. Being an American coffee meant that it was nearly a litre, too. There was soon a double coffee waterfall going off the edge of the table and onto the quaint seat and then the floor. I felt so guilty. I eventually said my sincere apologies and was back on the road again feeling really embarrassed.

The route was still quite flat as I headed between Memphis and Nashville. I saw Paris on the map and was very tempted to cycle there too, but it was a little too far north for my general direction. And seeing as Rome didn't have a Colosseum, Paris definitely wouldn't have an Eiffel Tower. By 9 p.m. I had reached Jackson and had done 180 miles. I planned to cycle till midnight each day, so knew I'd hit the 200 mile mark. I was feeling surprisingly good. I refuelled on a burger that would feed a family of four before heading off into the night. Looking at the map I figured I'd be able to make it nearly all the way to where I'd need to cross the Mississippi. The wind picked up nicely and the road was good as I pushed on. By 1 a.m. I'd reached Dyersburg and had done 215 miles.

In my motel I decided to give my clothes a wash. I jumped into the shower and my right calf started to burn. I looked down and realised it was red and sunburned. Damn it! I obviously didn't put enough sun cream on, or it had sweated off. I thought that it was only the hot water that was making it sting and it would be better when I got into bed. But the burning didn't stop, to the point of not being able to fall asleep. My calf felt as though it was on fire. I hobbled over to the bathroom, took a towel and soaked it under the cold tap. I then wrapped my calf in the cool wet towel and climbed back into bed. It worked a treat. My calf no longer hurt. Impressed with my ingenuity I fell asleep with a smile on my face.

The only way to cross the Mississippi was to do a five-mile stretch on an Interstate Highway. I was under the impression you couldn't cycle on them, but one policeman I asked said he wasn't sure but it should be fine. The other option was to do a 160-mile route north and use a small ferry crossing. That wasn't really a viable option even though according to Guinness I could have gone there, stopped the clock at the ferry and had a day's rest. Technically, I could take two weeks rest there and still fall within the rules. Again, a stupid idea Guinness came up with. I decided that I'd chance the Highway Bridge, and a potential telling off if I get caught, instead.

I pushed as far west as I could on a small back road that followed the highway. There was quite a southerly wind that kept my pace slow as I leant slightly into the road to keep balanced. It was quite a strong wind but nothing compared to that one day in the desert, so it didn't affect my mood as much. In fact I'm pretty sure no matter what I came across, I'd probably had worse in the desert. Everything else now seemed easy in comparison. The only condition I hadn't really felt was hard rain.

I reached a T-junction and turned north towards the highway. My pace increased immediately from 9 mph to 17 mph as I made use of the tailwind. I knew it would be short-lived as the highway section was running east to west. I reached the highway and my heart started to flutter. I wasn't sure if I was allowed on it and what would happen but I made a dash for it. I was surprised at how big the Mississippi was this far north. I daren't stop in case I got caught but managed to take a photo with my phone as I zoomed past. The going was pretty slow, though, as I battled a heavy side wind, all the while stressing about getting caught by the Sheriff of Mississippi. I didn't even know if that position existed but if it did then I'd like to be him. It sounded cool.

I later found out that it was in fact legal to cycle on motorways where there is no other option. So all the stress was for nothing. On the other side of the river, I was back on the side roads heading west, still trying to fight the wind, which seemed to be getting worse and worse as the day grew longer. I must have passed four or five dead-straight side roads heading north, the exact direction the wind was going, before I eventually gave in to the wind and decided to let it decide my route for the day. It was the best decision I made all day, as I zoomed along at a steady 19 mph along the flat farmlands of Tennessee, only slowing down now and then to try and take a photo while still cycling. I knew I didn't want to go too much further north than Missouri but couldn't afford to miss the opportunity for a big tailwind and some easy miles. I put my head down and didn't stop till I reached Dexter, which was on the main road heading west towards Poplar Bluff. The wind had died down a little but I really needed to bite the bullet and carry on westwards instead of heading any further north. As much as I loved the tailwind, I hated the idea of zigzagging to make up miles for the sake of it. Also, I had looked on the map and seen Springfield. I knew there were quite a few Springfields in the USA, and wasn't even sure this was the one that *The Simpsons* was based around, but I didn't care. I just wanted a photo outside the sign.

I turned west and again my pace dropped to around 12 mph: not the worst but quite disheartening after my 19 mph session. I reached Poplar Bluff and decided to get more money, some nuts for my front food bag, and sun cream that actually worked on ginger people. I was directed to a pharmacy and after browsing the aisles for a while, I eventually hit the jackpot. SPF 100+ sun cream. I had no idea factor 100+ even existed. They might as well have a vampire as their logo. My legs were still quite red from the day before but at least I felt a lot better now. My route had been fairly flat all day but the farther west I went the hillier it became. The side wind was getting stronger too. At the top of each hill I looked into the distance and could see a huge storm brewing. It was in the exact direction I was going. I hadn't really asked anyone about the terrain so far but figured a bit of local knowledge might be useful. The first place I found to ask someone was a warehouse $1 store in the middle of nowhere on the side of the main road.

'We don't get many cyclists round here. Where you heading?' asked the friendly teller. I didn't want to say 'The World' as I knew I'd be stuck there for hours with questions, so decided to go with Springfield.

'Wow. Springfield. That's so far away, man. You must be really fit.'

'What's the terrain like there? Is it hilly?' I said, while failing to put on my Hugh Grant accent again.

'Yeah, it's real hilly, and it's also been raining for days.'

'Is it hillier than what I've just done?'

'Yeah, a lot hillier. Missouri is known for its hills. You want to be heading to Arkansas. It's super flat down there like.'

'So, not a good idea to go to Springfield.' My heart sank a little. I really wanted a photo in front of the sign.

'Not unless you want them hills.'

'OK. So what's the best and flattest route to get to Arkansas?'

'Well, you best go along for another few miles then take the road south to Pocahontas.'

'Excuse me. Pocahontas? Is that an actual place?'

'It sure is.'

Who knew? My disappointment about not making it to not-the-real Springfield was now completely overtaken by my excitement to go to Pocahontas. It seems Tennessee was full of European towns and Missouri was full of cartoon ones. It was decided: I'd head back south towards Arkansas. This did mean I needed to fight a headwind as I turned south, but it was a small price to pay for getting out of the hills and rain.

By 10 p.m. I made it to Doniphan with the idea of getting to Pocahontas for breakfast in the morning. My daily total of 170 miles was a little short due to my faffing around trying to get sun cream in Poplar Bluff, but it was still not a bad effort. As I lay in my hotel room I started to feel a little glow of confidence in my world-record attempt. I didn't know what Mike Hall was doing but I was way ahead of the 168-mile-per-day average. The big miles in America were certainly going to continue. I was finally starting to enjoy this ride. South America had tested me and strengthened me. Nothing that America threw at me would be as bad, which made me feel good.

The following morning I reached Pocahontas in time for breakfast. I'd wondered if they sold loads of Disney merchandise to try and capitalise on the cartoon success. I was disappointed not to find any but was told there was a statue of Pocahontas in the town: the real one, not the Disney cartoon. The actual Pocahontas died in Gravesend in Kent, which was another fact I hadn't known.

# 9

# MARTIN AND MISSY

'Sir, sir, you've been in an accident. Can you hear me?'

All I could see were blue and red flashing lights all around. I was confused. Why wasn't I in my motel? I felt the hard stony floor underneath me. Where was I? Did someone say accident . . .

'Sir, can you tell us your name . . . ?'

. . . How did I get on this bed being wheeled down a fluorescent corridor? This must be a hospital? How did I get here? What happened to the ambulance? Did I go in one? Where was I?

'Right sir, we are going to have to cut your clothes off.'

'Um, not the jersey if possible.' That was the first thing I said and I have no idea why. I guess subconsciously my cycle jersey had seen so much I couldn't bear to lose it.

'OK, we'll try . . .'

The room was dark. I was lying on my side on a bed. Was it a dream? Maybe I was back in my motel. I tried to move but couldn't. I had no energy at all. I was still in the hospital but couldn't remember much. I hoped they hadn't cut off my shirt. Where was Maid Marian? What about my tracker? My family would know it had stopped . . .

I was in a house, I think. It looked like a boy's room. I really needed the toilet. I was bursting. I tried to get up but my back and neck really hurt. I fell back down onto the pillow in pain. I lay there for a moment wondering if the toilet was absolutely necessary. It was. I then sort of rolled out of bed and held onto the side table for support. The room had an ensuite to the right of the bed. As I took my first step my right leg gave way and I nearly fell over. I couldn't really move my right knee joint. I hobbled over to the toilet and leaned against the wall very out of breath and dizzy. The room was spinning. After releasing what seemed like ten litres of liquid I hobbled back to as close as I needed to fall into bed without landing up on the floor. I still didn't know where I was but felt extremely tired and dizzy so fell asleep again.

I had no idea how long I had slept, but before I knew it I was bursting for the loo again. I repeated the same procedure as before. Holding onto the bedside table. Hobbling on my left leg. Leaning against the wall to pee and then falling back on the bed, this time from even further away.

The third time this happened there was a glass of milk and a smoothie on the side table with a bendy straw coming out of it. My mouth was extremely dry but I needed the loo again. I didn't know what I looked like. Surely with so much pain I must be pretty cut up. I held myself on the basin, too nervous to look at my reflection. Slowly I lifted my head and let out a huge sigh. There was nothing at all. I looked like, well, myself. No scars, cuts or black eyes. I smiled slightly, which hurt my neck and also my lower lip. I pulled it down to examine my mouth and then realised the cause of my pain. One of my lower teeth had chipped almost in half down the middle and was now acting like broken glass on my lip. I still had no idea what had really happened but to come out of it with no external injuries felt good.

I needed the toilet twice more within the following hour even though I hadn't drank that much. It was a real struggle. My back, neck and right leg hurt and I felt so dizzy I even had to sit and pee. It was dark outside, which meant I must have been in bed all day. I was almost certain it had only been one day. Just then I heard a knock on the door and a face appeared. A man who looked in his late forties wearing scrubs stood there, smiling. Somewhere in the back of my mind a memory came back from the hospital. I remembered being wheeled to a car in a wheelchair and getting into it. I remember one of the doctors at the driver's wheel. This must be where I was?

'Hey, Sean. My name is Martin. How are you feeling?'

He had a kind face and talked with an accent I couldn't quite place. He sounded almost British but with an American twang.

'I'm good, thanks. Thank you so much for this, all of this. Is this your home?'

'Yes, it's better than staying in the hospital. Can I get you another smoothie or more milk? You seem to like it.'

I looked over at the two plastic bottles now half-empty.

'I think I'm OK for now, thank you.'

'Can I get you some dinner? I'm making salmon if you want some.'

I must have fallen asleep again because when I woke up I was lying on my side with a plate of cold salmon and green beans next to me. I hadn't even touched it. I didn't remember Martin bringing it either and was worried because I must have been awake when he did. No one leaves a plate of hot food on a bed next to a sleeping person. I tried to eat some but couldn't chew at all. My jaw was too sore and I didn't have the energy either. After hobbling to the toilet again, I flopped back into bed and passed out exhausted.

'Knock, knock. Hey Sean. I'm Missy, Martin's wife. Martin is off to work but if you need anything, anything at all, just shout OK.'

It was light again. Morning. I didn't go to the toilet during the night, which was a pleasant change. I then suddenly thought that maybe I had wet the bed. Please god, no. Surely I hadn't. I felt around my body while trying to sit up slowly to greet Missy.

'Hi Missy. Thanks for everything.' I felt so useless and helpless sitting in a bed that wasn't mine, in some kind strangers' house on the other side of the world.

Missy had a huge smile which made me feel at home. My neck and head really hurt, even more than before, but I didn't feel as dizzy while lying down anymore.

'Here are some meds for you. Take one from the white bottle and one from orange one, three times a day. Then take one of these green pills once at night. That will help you sleep and relax your muscles.'

130

'OK, thanks, I just need the loo again. I've been about eight times in the last however many hours I've been here.'

'Oh yeah, sorry. You had quite low blood pressure when you came in so we pumped you with four litres of I.V. It's probably that you're just quite fit, I told them, but we didn't want to take any chances.'

I smiled for the first time. In trying to help me they had inadvertently caused me more pain every time I needed to get in and out of bed to rid myself of the four litres of I.V.

'Ha-ha, That's funny! Did you cut my shirt off?'

'No, you asked us not to so we kept it. We had to cut your shorts though.'

I laughed a little, which hurt my head, but was happy that my shirt had been saved and my stupid bib shorts, which nearly caused me a few ablution disasters, were now gone and I had an excuse to buy another pair that didn't include me getting naked to go to the loo.

'Ah thanks. I didn't like those ones anyway.'

I spent the next few days pretty much in bed drinking smoothies and milk. Martin and Missy would come in and check on me all the time and offer to get me anything I needed. Turned out all I wanted was smoothies and milk. I don't drink milk or smoothies in real life so I have no idea why I craved those two things so much. They even went out and bought me some clothes to wear. I didn't really understand it all but felt hugely comforted by their presence, and it was nice to see their heads poke through the door to check up on me every now and then. I also found out that Martin was actually Welsh but had lived in America for some time.

They also filled me in on what happened. On the morning of 22 March 2012 at 5.50 a.m. I was cycling towards Searcy from Bald Knob when a guy in a huge American-style pick-up truck hit me from behind doing 50 mph. I was flung onto the bonnet of the car, hit my head on the windscreen and was then thrown forward onto the road. Doctors tell me my helmet saved my life and the section at the back that is usually two inches thick had compressed or deformed, as they're meant to, down to a few millimetres. I was incredibly lucky as an impact like that can often just break apart a helmet, rendering it useless. My right leg hadn't clipped out of the pedal properly, so I sprained my ankle and tore the ligaments behind my knee. I had also suffered severe whiplash and concussion, which is why I felt so dizzy all the time. Thankfully, the driver stopped and called 911. I was completely unconscious for about half an hour until I remember the blue and red lights when the ambulance arrived. I was then taken to White County Hospital where Martin, the doctor on duty, and Missy, the nurse, happened to be on call. After a series of CT scans and MRIs they thought it best if they took me home and looked after me. I was also surprised that the hospital cared for me so well considering they didn't know if I had insurance or anything. You hear all the awful stories of people being left on the street without insurance. The hospital did $15,000 worth of treatment on me before they even knew my name. They also said they'd try to get payment from the driver and if they couldn't they'd not pursue me and write it off as bad debt. They felt bad that I got run over in their county.

It didn't make sense to me: I was insured to the hilt and they could get their money. It was just another thing to add to the list making Americans the friendliest and most helpful people I've ever met.

I was worried about my family. Did they know what was going on? Missy told me that in my semi-conscious state I had in fact dictated a message that went on Facebook saying I had been in an accident but was in fact all right. This was very strange, finding out that I was consciously making decisions but had no recollection of doing so. I'd also spoken to my parents on the phone at one point but couldn't remember it at all. That must have worried them but apparently I made sense and didn't sound that out of it.

Martin and Missy lived in a lovely suburb of Searcy in a beautiful home at the end of a quiet street. It was really peaceful, which was exactly what I needed. They had three kids: Matthew, the oldest, was as school most of the time, but I did get to hang around with Garret and Wyatt a lot. They were very well-behaved and great kids. Garret beat me at pool a few times and Wyatt would call me Mr Sean.

The local media in Arkansas decided they wanted to cover my accident, so I landed up doing a radio interview, a couple of newspapers and two TV shows. Poor Missy was carting me around here and there while I told my story to whoever would listen. My memory was still not completely altogether back and I would often forget things I'd done the previous day. This may have been to do with the painkillers but it was all quite disorientating nonetheless.

Only after about a week did I realise the real impact the accident would have on my race. In blind stubbornness I thought I'd manage to get Maid Marian welded and be back on the road within a few days and carry on in my world-record attempt. I was run over on the Thursday and apparently I was telling Martin I'd be back on the bike by Saturday.

As Saturday came and went, and I wasn't seeing any signs of getting better, I started to think about the reality of the situation. Not only would my back and neck take weeks to heal, Maid Marian was also unfixable. I felt sick when I heard the news that I'd have to get a new bike to carry on. Including training, Maid Marian and I had done about 10,000 miles together. I had settled into her perfectly and the idea of continuing my ride on a different bike made me very sad. Guinness had a rule that said you could stop the clock for no longer than two weeks when you reach a point of transit or an impassable barrier. I called Guinness to find out where I stood and although 'getting hit by a truck' counted as an 'impassable barrier' in their books, it didn't in mine. Even if I was allowed to stop the clock, the whole idea of cycling around the world non-stop as a feat of human endurance had gone. It felt like I was using a stupid loophole to get the record. Even if I miraculously was able to carry on in under two weeks, it wouldn't be right that I should be allowed the record, even if my actual cycle time was the fastest. No matter what angle I looked at it, I had no bike, and no way of being able to afford a new one as no one would insure my bike to start with. Oh, and I had a fractured spine.

As I lay in bed I realised the harsh reality was that my world-record attempt, the thing I had trained forty hours a week for, given up a social life for and spent all my savings on, had now ended. I sank into my pillow and started to cry. I couldn't stop. All my months of training, the pressures, the sacrifices, the big days in South America, the busting my knees to stay ahead of the record, all for nothing, came blundering out in tears as I wept into my pillow. Was there even any point in carrying on at all? Every time I closed my eyes, I wished I had just woken up a few minutes later, or taken a different road, or actually carried on west towards Springfield as I had planned. There were so many variables that could have changed the outcome of that Thursday morning. Why me? I stayed in my room over the next few days, not wanting to face reality. My dizziness wasn't getting better and I felt sick every time I tried to eat. I just wanted to give up and go home. I couldn't see a way out. Mum and Dad didn't want me to carry on either. They were obviously worried. In any case, I had no bike so might have no option but to go home anyway. This was not how this adventure was meant to pan out.

'Sean, Martin and I have already decided. We'd like to buy you a new bike so you can carry on your ride.'

I couldn't believe what they were saying. I burst out crying. I had no idea why they were being so generous. I didn't know what to say. I was lost for words. If I had a bike I could carry on cycling.

'But why, why me?' I cried, not knowing what to do or say and still a little confused, as in my mind it was all over.

'It's something we just want to do, it's done, we admire what you have done and want you to be able to carry on.'

'Thank you so so much. I don't know what to say.' Tears were still running down my face.

It turned out that they had already seen my bike was made by Thorn in Somerset and had called and asked them to build me another one and DHL it over. It would arrive in a week. There was a small flame at the end of the tunnel. My world record might have been over but at least I now had a bike to continue the trip.

It was at the end of the second week when Thorn delivered my new bike. As soon as I saw the box, the butterflies started to flutter in my stomach. Here she was: my new bike for a new adventure. Thorn had sent me the exact same bike. Straightaway I needed to name her and knew exactly what she'd be called; Maid Marian the Second. I couldn't let Maid Marian die. Hopefully her spirit would carry on in this new bike. I had spent two weeks pretty tired, confused, dizzy and in pain and hadn't really thought about getting back on the road. I didn't want to face the fact that my world-record attempt was over. I couldn't just carry on slowly. I would be letting everyone down, mainly my sponsors who took a big punt at me, funding the entire race hoping I'd win. Although I had received an email from them saying they didn't want me to worry and just do my best, I felt my best was not good enough. Martin and Missy had given me the means to continue, now I needed to find a new personal reason to keep pedalling, a new goal that wasn't just a holiday ride. I had so many mixed endows.

As I built Maid Marian II, I started taking things out of bags and rearranging them on the floor. I saw Little Flying Cow lying there still with his quirky smile. I felt bad I hadn't thought of him earlier and examined to see if he had any broken bones. Nothing at all. He had survived the crash. That made me smile. I packed him away in my new bag. I then came across my small Olympic Torch, sitting neatly at the bottom of my bar bag. It too had survived the crash.

'It survived, Little Flying Cow!' I exclaimed.

My excitement however was then overrun by a huge sense of failure. Not only could I not break the world record and win the race but I also wasn't going to complete taking this little torch around the world. I could picture the disappointment on the kids' faces.

Then I thought, what if that was my new goal? My new reason for continuing? My heart started to race as I felt a flame of excitement inside my stomach for the first time since the accident. That would be it, my new thing: to get this torch back to London in time for the Olympics, which was now about three months away. I still had the rest of America, Australia, Asia and Europe to cycle. Distance didn't matter anymore because I no longer needed to do the 18,000 miles that Guinness stated. I obviously would have loved to do more, but I had already booked my flights, so that couldn't be changed. I now just needed to get back to London by the middle of July so that I had time to get settled for the Olympics. Not many people get the chance to experience the Olympics in the town they live in and I didn't want to miss it.

I wasn't even sure my goal was possible, seeing as I had lost three weeks and still had a sore back and neck. But I sat down, did the calculations and realised it was totally doable. I'd need to average around 140 miles per day just to make it even if I took a more direct route. It was far below the 180 miles a day average I was doing but still not an easy task. I rushed back to Maid Marian II and continued to rebuild her with a new vigour, a new excitement for a new adventure and a new challenge.

It was three weeks before I decided I could get back on the road again. I had been for a few slow rides around Searcy with some guys from the local bike club and although my legs felt strong, my cardio was shot and my neck hurt. Martin suggested I take a neck brace just in case.

The last night with Martin, Missy and their kids was a mixture of emotions. I felt excited to be getting back on the road but sad to have to say goodbye. I had spent three weeks living with this wonderful family. I had met their friends, their family and their parents. They had cared for me, bought me clothes, food and a new bike. I'd been told 'southern folk' are very friendly and generous, but Martin and Missy took this concept to a whole new level. I doubt I will ever experience such selfless kindness and generosity again. These two strangers had not only healed me, but also given me hope and a chance to carry on in my dream of cycling around the world. I'd never forget it.

It was 8 April. The following day it was time to get back on the road. I can't ever remember being as nervous as I was then. My gut was turning on itself, I was having dreams of getting run over again, I could hardly sleep. The only comfort I took was the probably completely unrealistic theory that statistically, seeing as I had been run over once already, the chance of it happening a second time was quite low. I knew that it made no sense but it helped my mind to cope with getting on the bike and not falling apart.

The next day Martin had to go to work so I said my goodbyes and a huge thank you while trying to hold back the tears. I felt very emotional to leave. I knew I had made a lifelong friend and I'd definitely come back and visit one day in the future.

# 10

## GETTING BACK ON THE HORSE

'I can't believe you cycled on this road man. There is no shoulder and it's really quite busy.'

After my accident, a guy called Kurt had contacted me on Facebook offering to show me some better roads out of Arkansas for the next two days.

'Really? It seems OK to me. I've been on a lot worse,' I replied as we met and shook hands.

'Man, this is probably the worst road in the area,' Kurt laughed

'Really? How was I to know though!'

'I guess so. If you don't know any better it's just another road on the map.'

I had decided to go back to where the accident had happened and carry on from there. I didn't want to miss any parts of my route. It was really surreal returning to where I'd been knocked off. I thought it might jog my memory but nothing at all came back. Although the road didn't have a big hard shoulder, it was dead straight and coming up to some traffic lights. This made me really annoyed. I couldn't understand how the driver didn't see me. It wasn't as if I was in the middle of an old quiet back road or anything. This was slightly suburban and there was a traffic light 100 m ahead. He should have seen me. Maybe my red tail light got mixed in with the red traffic light?

'Right buddy. Should we get cracking? I know all these roads. Where do you want to go?'

'Anywhere as long as it's quiet.'

Kurt's knowledge of the area made me feel a lot better because I knew I'd have two days of good roads and someone with me in case anything happened to me. Martin obviously wouldn't have let me carry on if he thought I wasn't ready but I knew full well that only three weeks recovery was not nearly long enough time. Things were going to be difficult but I couldn't delay my departure any longer if I wanted to get to London in time for the Olympics.

I got Maid Marian ready and put my neck brace on. My neck still hurt quite a lot, especially on the bike when I was hunched over. The neck brace was fairly light but got in the way of my beard a bit. I didn't quite know whether to tuck the beard under the brace or have it pushed up and forward out the top. Either way it wasn't comfortable.

Not only did Kurt show me some of the great roads heading west but he also was an incredible cyclist. He often enters 250- and 500-mile races and when I asked him how he did in them his reply was:

'Well, I usually win.'

He decided to use the two days with me to train for his 250-miler on the weekend. He normally does 250 miles in twelve hours but his fastest time was just under ten hours, although admittedly he had an incredible tailwind. Even so, he knew his stuff and it was great to cycle with him. We pushed on until around 3 p.m. cutting south of a town called Conway, which I really wanted to go through but Kurt said it was very busy and hilly. We carried on through a town called England, where I obviously took a photo before stopping in Subway for lunch. I ordered a footlong Italian BMT as always.

'When I do my 500-mile self-supported races I buy four footlongs. I eat one and put the other three in each back pocket of my cycle jersey,' Kurt explained as he finished his footlong before I had even started my second half. This man was obviously an adventure racer and used to eating fast.

I gobbled down the second half of my footlong a little quicker and we hit the road again. Our pace was good as we kept a steady 18 mph through the rolling terrain of Arkansas. Kurt apologised for a few roads that he thought were bad. I laughed because after South America these were probably in the top 10% of all the best roads I had been on. It's all relative though, and I guess he was used to ripping it up on some smooth blacktop. I was just happy if I didn't have to watch out for potholes or rabid dogs.

Annoyingly, with the accident my continental GP4000's tyres got wrecked and I was sent some thin race tyres with the new bike. They were by far inferior and I managed to get two punctures in the afternoon. While changing the second one a huge old rusty pick-up truck came to a screeching halt right next to us. A young fellow in a dirty white vest looked out the window and shouted.

'Hey, did y'all flip the finger to my brother just there?'

He looked angry. Kurt and I looked at each other confused.

'Um, no, that wasn't us.'

'Are you sure? He just called me and said there were two cyclists on this road and one gave him the finger.'

'Well, it wasn't us buddy, as you can see we are here fixing a tyre.'

'Oh, OK then. Bastards. I'll find them.'

'Bloody redneck.' Kurt looked a little embarrassed.

'Ah well. What can you do?'

'The problem is he probably had a gun in his car so you don't want to piss him off.'

Imagine getting run over and shot within 50 miles of each other. My mother would have a hernia.

My neck was getting worse and worse all afternoon and by 5 p.m. I realised my brace was doing nothing at all. My neck could still pivot at the base and that's the part that hurt the most. I took another painkiller which I should have taken a few hours earlier. The one good thing about America is they aren't shy about giving you medication and I had enough painkillers to forget my name if I wanted. I have never been a fan of them, but there comes a point when you have to forget your own preconceived ideas and give in because they do work. As Kurt said, 'Your body can do a lot more than you think it can. If your mind isn't telling you to stop, then you can push harder.' In theory that was fine, but I'm not sure the long-term effects would do you good.

It turned out that Kurt lived roughly 100 miles west of where we started, which worked out perfectly. He planned a great route that ended at his home where his wife had a huge bowl of lasagne waiting for us. Kurt was cycling mad and had every sort of bike and bike part lying around his garage. He even opened a beer suggesting that it was good calories.

I hadn't had any alcohol at all since I started but I figured surviving day one was worth celebrating.

The following morning I was up at 4 a.m. and ready to get going. I didn't need to do big mileage but really wanted to, to get my confidence back and prove I could still do it. Although it was tough, I really did enjoy racing and pushing the big miles. Today would be the test.

Kurt was up and we set off at 4.30 a.m. It was great to have him with me as I would never have chosen any of the roads he had taken me along so far. We pushed on to Arkadelphia for breakfast. Kurt had a friend who lived there and we stopped in for a breakfast of bacon, eggs and toast and butter. It was a good combination of carbs, fat and protein, although I probably could have done with a little more toast (carbs) for extra energy.

After breakfast it was time to part ways with Kurt*. He was off to do a route heading round and back home. He gave me some good roads to take heading towards Dallas but after that I'd be on my own again, which was quite a nerve-racking prospect.

I had a new respect for the road and drivers, so decided to keep to all the back roads as I made my way towards Texas. I even passed through New York. If you think of a town as opposite as it is possible to the actual New York then this was it. A tiny farm town, or village even, in the middle of nowhere. I liked that I was passing through so many smaller

---

* *In 2015 Kurt went on to break my hero Tommy Godwin's 'Most miles cycled in a year' record by cycling over 76,000 miles in a calendar year. It was an honour to have cycled with him for two days.*

versions of major places I still hadn't visited. So next time someone asked me whether I have been to New York, I can say yes.

My failed attempt with the neck brace resulted in it going in the bin. I regretted the decision within a mile as my neck started to hurt again. I only had about 40% movement and wouldn't dare to try going into tri-position. I was hoping that after day one it would loosen up and feel better but it was actually stiffer. I was stopping every half an hour to try and stretch it and give it a rest. The relief was always short-lived as it would start hurting again on the next hill. It didn't help that I had a small headwind which made me have to strain my neck even more. The other thing was that my backside was starting to hurt. My lovely Brooks saddle had been trashed in the accident and I was now on a Selle Italia, which although good, wasn't my Brooks. My bum had moulded perfectly to my Brooks and I didn't get any saddle sores whatsoever. I guess it would just take time to get used to a new saddle. I'd certainly need to make some fine adjustments over the next few days in order to get comfortable again.

By 7 p.m. I had done 165 miles, which I felt good about. It was over the 140 I needed to get to London in time but I felt like carrying on and trying for the all-important 200-mile mark by the end of the day. I stopped in a service station, had a protein shake, some beef jerky and some nuts before getting back on the road for the last few hours. I was doing well and just when I started to get a tailwind I landed up in a three-mile section of roadworks. They had closed one lane which was now all dug up and sandy. The other lane had stop-go traffic which was way too thin for me to cycle on and I didn't fancy getting run over again. I had no choice but to try and cycle on the sand. I made it all of ten metres before my front wheel sunk and I stated to wheel spin. It was just too soft and dusty. Annoyed I got off and started to walk, my head hung low trying not hurt my back as I pushed Maid Marian through the sand. It was a slow few miles and put me about 45 minutes behind schedule, which meant I was going to be about ten miles short of 200. Tired and annoyed I stopped in Texarkana for the night. This was my first night alone in almost a month. I thought I'd find it uneasy and lonely but was surprised to find myself falling right back into my previous pattern. It's what I was comfortable doing.

Before the accident I was averaging five to six hours of sleep a night but now I thought I'd push that up to seven or eight. Along with more sleep I could also now afford to sit down and eat a lot more and didn't have to rely on eating on the bike. All this said, I wanted to try and push some big days. Anything above 168 miles a day made me feel really good, and that I was at least achieving something. My legs were strong and my cardio was getting better, and as long as I didn't injure my neck and back any more I wanted to see if I could still push myself. Although my new goal required only 140 miles a day, I did still want to challenge myself rather than just coast through. I guess deep down I was scared of cruising through anything as that's what I did in photography and it hadn't worked out well. Looking back now I think that was very relevant. I wanted to challenge life and justify that my decision to carry on was bigger, bolder and more impressive than just idly pedalling around the world on a jolly.

By sunrise I was already in Texas and greeted with the best road I had ever seen. The hard shoulder was as wide as the main road and it also had the aggressive rumble strips along the yellow line stopping cars using it. It seemed a massive waste of tar and money, but I wasn't complaining. It was great for cycling. Texas, after all, is one of the richest places on the planet, richer than most countries in fact.

My plan was to go around the bottom of Dallas and then head west towards the Rockies. By mid-afternoon the wind had different plans for me as a southerly picked up again. I tried to fight it for a while but then looked at my map and decided I could in fact head north again and pass Dallas on the east and go over the top of it. The road continued to be good but slowly the chip-seal turned to rock-seal. By mid-afternoon I couldn't do much more than 15 mph on the downhills as the vibrations on the big stones were just too much for my neck and back. But another benefit of now heading north again was that I got to go through Athens, another *European* city I had never been too. I managed 195 miles by nightfall and was just on the outskirts of Dallas.

The following morning I had breakfast in the south-eastern outskirts of Dallas: a footlong Italian BMT, a huge Coke (and when I say huge, it must have been well over a litre) and three choc chip cookies. I tend to keep the cookies for the road as it was hard enough for my stomach to fit the footlong and Coke. My stomach seemed to have shrunk since the accident, which meant I was getting full really quickly. It was a real struggle to eat as much as I needed too.

Dallas was a beautiful city: very green with scenic residential areas. I was still a little disappointed I hadn't seen a cow, or a cowboy, or a man with a gun. That's what it's like in Texas, right? Men walking round with cowboy hats and guns. The only thing there seemed to be a lot of were huge moustaches. That's probably law in Texas. You must grow a moustache when you turn thirty. That thought made me smile.

It took forever to get out of the never-ending suburban streets before I eventually hit farmlands north of the city. My plan was to head west but I still had a strong southerly wind so decided to head further north and make the most of it. I had heard of the American grid system roads before. I had seen a few that were kind of wiggly grids at best but nothing in comparison to the section of farmlands above Dallas. I looked at Google, which showed me a sprawl of squares covering an area the size of London.

I figured I'd turn off the main road I had used to get out of Dallas and work my way north and west for the rest of the day. I'd head north for a while and then turn left and head west until I saw a nice looking northerly road again. The exact grid formation allowed me not to have to think about route choices. As long as I was going west and north then I'd land up in the right place by the end.

This was prime tornado-looking country, even more so than Alabama. Texas is the tornado capital of America with over 120 tornadoes touching soil each year. What's more worrying is that most of those happened around this time of year. A huge tornado had caused a lot of damage in Dallas only a week earlier where a few people died. Parts of the city were completely demolished and the cost was well into the tens of millions. Looking around, the countryside looked exactly like you see in movies. A few white barns dotted here and there, straight roads flanked by green fields. It was also slightly overcast, giving it a sense of gloominess and impending disaster. I hadn't really thought about it at all but if a tornado decided to come and I was out alone, I'd have nowhere to hide. Also with no access to news while cycling I'd have no clue if one were sneaking up on me.

Then at 2 p.m. I saw my first tornado casualty: a white wooden house, not completely torn apart but more slightly knocked off-centre on to its side. It had windows broken, doors missing, and large holes in the roof. It couldn't have been more than ten metres off the road and looked like the family just took everything out the house and moved somewhere else. I decided this wasn't a place to hang around so I picked up my pace and passed it quickly – it was eerie.

The problem in doing small farm roads was that every now and then the nice fast blacktop tar roads turned to gravel for about five miles. This annoyed me because Google didn't differentiate between a perfectly good tar road and a slow sandy dirt track: Google knows the colour of the tiles on my roof at home so why not the difference in tar and gravel roads?

When you managed to forget that you might be swallowed up by a tornado anytime soon the landscape was rather peaceful. Green fields contrasting soft, clouded skies let my mind wander and think about being back on the road again. I was getting back into the swing of things finally and my confidence was slowly returning. A small part of me winced every time I heard a truck coming up behind me but these were getting less and less frequent as the hours rolled on by. I kept thinking about the world record and how my mind and legs still wanted to push big miles, but my back and neck weren't so keen.

The southerly winds kept pushing me northwest towards Wichita Falls. By 7 p.m. I had done 150 miles so stopped for some dinner and looked at the map. The plan was to cycle to Nocona for the night. It was only 25 miles away, but a part of me felt like cycling through to midnight. I wanted to do 200 miles as I hadn't quite managed a 200-mile day since the accident yet. I still loved the feeling of seeing the odometer clicking over to 200 miles. No matter how tired I was it always brought a smile to my face. I saw a section on the map that showed a loop into a farming area, which looked like it would add an extra 30 miles to my day. Perfect. I headed north again towards what looked like a winding river on the map. The scenery changed from the square flat lands to rolling green pastures with cattle. Finally! I had spotted a cow. Still no cowboys, though.

It had been flat all day but this section dropped a few hundred metres down towards the river. It got a lot more forested and a little spooky to cycle through, all alone at night. This wasn't a through road, which meant it was very quiet. I must have passed, or rather been passed, five times in two hours. As it was a loop, the downhill to the river resulted in quite a long uphill again. The night was pitch black and for the first time since the Atacama I noticed the array of stars in the sky. It was truly a beautiful night and I was glad I'd done the extra loop.

# 11

# TORNADO ALLEY

My plan now was to carry on towards the Rockies. But the following day, the wind had different ideas as an even bigger southerly picked up. I looked at the map and saw the Route 40 Highway, which was the old Route 66 further north. I had to go check it out. From there I could head west, which seemed the perfect plan.

The power of wind was impressive. I carried on west for a little, leaning quite far into the road as I balanced against the heavy side wind. It was only a ten-mile stretch but took me an hour. I then turned north and immediately sped up to 19 or 20 mph. It was glorious. My neck and back were feeling a lot better and I managed to get into tri position for the first time in a while. This was by far the best tailwind I'd ever experienced and I couldn't help the huge smile on my face as I zoomed up towards Oklahoma City. You can be cycling through the most boring scenery, in the snow, rain, hail or anything, but if you have a 40 mph tailwind, it'll be the best ride you've ever done. I just hoped this wasn't a tornado chasing me.

Famous last words! The wind started to get stronger and stronger and after half an hour it started to rain. Normally you get heavy raindrops in the face, but even cycling along at 20 mph I could hear the raindrops hitting the back of my helmet. Then I noticed some clouds building up to the southwest of me. I didn't think they looked too ominous but they were definitely darker and a little lower than I'd seen before. I was just switching off when a car drove up next to me. The lady wound down her window. She seemed to be in a real panic.

'The tornado is coming, are you OK?'

Really? The weather didn't seem that bad. I looked behind me to see if anything had changed but nothing but those same dark clouds about ten miles away.

'You better get some shelter soon. I'm hauling my ass home right now.'

'Oh, OK then.' I still felt a bit nonplussed. 'I think I'll be fine.'

'There is a town ahead, take shelter there. This is going to be a big one.'

With that the lady sped off leaving me in a cloud of spray. Should I be worried? I'd heard that Americans can be quite dramatic. Maybe she was just being overcautious. I stopped on the side of the road and looked back to where the wind was coming from. It really didn't look that daunting at all. It wasn't anything like the movies. The town she was referring to was about five miles ahead. I decided I'd make my decision when I reached it. It started to rain a little heavier the closer I got to the town but still nothing the good old British winter hadn't thrown at me during training. If someone was going to know all about wind and rain, it was me. I lived in Britain. I knew weather.

I reached the town, which was actually no more than a few farmhouses and a gas station. The weather hadn't changed much and there was nothing around except some heavy clouds. Surely there wasn't going to be a tornado. If I wanted to do 200 miles then I couldn't afford to hang around, for a little drizzle.

'Screw it, Little Flying Cow. Let's carry on. How bad could it be?' I said out loud. Little Flying Cow was now pretty drenched and sad on my handlebars.

I jumped back on Maid Marian and immediately heard the distinctive sound of air bubbling out of my front tyre. Great. A puncture. Thankfully I was right outside a gas station. It was pouring with rain so I nervously left Maid Marian outside and went in. As I opened the door the staff looked up at me. They too looked rather agitated.

'Are you cycling today? Are you mad? There's a tornado coming.'

'Yeah, someone told me but I can't see it.'

'Bring your bike in, quick, it's not far from us now.'

They seemed a little frantic. I needed to change my front inner tube anyway so brought Maid Marian in and started taking off the front wheel.

'Look,' one of the attendants pointed, 'the storm chasers are here already.'

Yeah right, I thought, Storm chasers surely only lived in Hollywood film screens. But I looked out the window and sure enough, there was a huge Hummer with some satellites on the roof. Shit. That's cool.

'So there is really a tornado coming, then?' I asked.

'Sure is.'

'But it doesn't look that bad.'

'It can change suddenly,' I was told. 'It's all happening above us. That tail can strike at any time,' explained the older of the two.

Just then I looked outside. The wind had started to really pick up and then all of a sudden did a 360 and became a northerly. It had completely changed direction. Then the hailstones started. They were golf-ball size. Smash, crash, bang! They came down onto the tin roof. A few cars pulled into the gas station to take shelter under the roof. One had a completely broken windscreen.

How could it have changed so quickly? I was shocked. Signs were blowing over, windscreens cracking, leaves were getting stripped off trees as if being shredded by a huge invisible blender in the sky, and a 100 mph wind was heading in the exact wrong direction. I realised that had I not got a puncture when I did, I wouldn't have stopped in that gas station and I would probably have landed up right in the middle of the storm. I vowed to never complain about getting a puncture ever again. That one saved me, by the looks of things, from almost certain death. One 100 mph golf-ball-sized hailstone to the face would have been the end of me.

Then as quickly as it started, the storm disappeared. The hail stopped, the wind changed back to a southerly and the rain dried up.

'That was close, ' said one of the attendants. 'And it's not over yet. There is another one coming here in two hours.'

'Really?' I asked now with a little more respect for the weather than before.

'Yup, from the southwest and heading in a northeasterly direction.'

'Where is the tornado heading?'

'It's going to be hitting Oklahoma City in three hours' time.'

I looked at my map. That was pretty much the exact time I was planning to arrive there. I didn't know what to do. I couldn't hang around for three hours as it would then be nearly dark and I'd have nowhere to stay, and I certainly wasn't going to outrun a tornado at night. I decided to try and make a dash for it.

I got back on the road and the sun came out delivering a comforting soft orange light over the bright green fields, contrasting with the black clouds to the east. I stopped to take a selfie with the Olympic Torch. It looked nothing like it did ten minutes before. The tornado had passed about a mile ahead of the town. Although it hadn't 'touched down' as they say, it had caused a lot of damage. There were no torn-down houses or anything but loads of hail, grass and water everywhere.

Apart from the advice of the garage attendants, I had no idea where or when the next storm would hit. I was cycling blind. That was not a good idea. I needed to somehow work out when this next storm was coming up behind me. I was going forward with a whole new level of respect for tornadoes. This wasn't Hollywood dramatised drama. This was the real thing.

'Twitter?' I swore Little Flying Cow shouted at me.

'Genius, Little Flying Cow!' I shouted.

I immediately tweeted my exact position and asked if anyone knew where these tornados were. I didn't wait more than a minute before Ian, one of my cycling friends who had joined me on my opening ride to Gatwick, tweeted me back: *Mate, there are a few, what's your number, best to call.*

I gave Ian my number and he called me straight away. It was good to hear a familiar British calm voice, a nice contrast to the frantic way in which some people here had been delivering me tornado information.

'Listen,' he said, 'I'm on the Oklahoma weather website which has live tornado tracking. There is one coming up from the southwest in about an hour. You can either push it fast for an hour and it'll pass underneath you, or you might need to wait around for half an hour or so. There doesn't look like there is much between you and your next town.'

'Right. So I need to do about 21 miles in an hour to miss it?'

'Yeah, you better get going mate!'

It was going to be a huge push but I didn't feel like going back to the gas station and hanging around. I decided to go for it. I ate the last of my choc chip cookies and put my head down. My legs were burning and my heart rate jumping out my chest but with a good tailwind I was averaging 23 mph. I should make it, providing the Oklahoma Weather website was accurate and Ian had interpreted it correctly. I'd never wanted my lightweight fast carbon bike so much as I struggled to push a now waterlogged Maid Marian north and out of the way of potential death.

I used every bit of energy I had to push eighteen of the twenty-one miles before the rain started to come down again. I felt knackered, but knowing how quickly the weather changed, I didn't want to be caught again. I stopped under a row of huge trees to get out the rain. Maybe I should just stay there. At least the trees would shelter me. The rain started to come down hard as puddles started to take over the entire road. I waited for a few minutes and then decided that actually a tree probably wasn't the best pace to wait. It didn't shelter me from the wind at all. I had to risk it and make a dash for the last three miles.

There's nothing quite like playing chicken with a tornado. My heart rate was already high from pushing it and the added nerves certainly didn't help. I jumped back on Maid Marian and made a huge push to the next town, the rain still thumping down. At least the wind was still a southerly. If it turned to a northerly then I knew I'd be in trouble. Head down, I cycled on, only looking up every ten seconds to see if there was anything in the road to avoid. Eventually I reached the outskirts of an another small farm town. The little sprint had taken it all out of me. There was a café just off the road with a few sheltered cars parked next to it. I parked Maid Marian under the awning and went into the café. A few other people had the same idea and there were a few laughs as I sat down, pretty drenched to the bone, a sizable puddle already on the floor below me. The rain carried on for a while but nothing like as hard as before. I asked one of the waitresses and she said that it was due to pass just south not long from now. Yes! I'd outrun a tornado. I'd never have thought I'd ever say that in my life but I had and I felt epic.

I was now just short of Oklahoma City where I was told the tornado hit properly and caused quite a lot of damage. It was time to start heading west again as I had already come a lot further north than I'd expected. The old Route 66 was now Highway 40 but there were parts of the old road you could still cycle on. I followed a few of these heading parallel to the highway, taking in the now peaceful picturesque sunset ahead of me: it was a complete contrast to the earlier storms. By nightfall I had done 182 miles, which slightly annoyed me: I'd most definitely have reached the 200-mile mark without all the tornado lark. Maybe tomorrow I'd make it. But at least the upside of not reaching 200 miles was that a day of playing chicken with tornados and surviving had rekindled the sense of adventure again.

The next day the landscape changed from green farmlands to shrubby grassy rolling hills. The wind was good, the road was smooth, and the sun was shining. I was in a great mood. I had a late start but with such a great tailwind I'd surely do another big day. I pushed on, head down, while listening to Mumford and Sons for the twenty-seventh time on my iPod. I was just switching off a little when something caught my eye. Just off the side of the road was a golden Labrador. It was just sitting there looking lonely and confused. It wasn't another 100 metres before I realised that I hadn't seen a house for miles and there didn't seem to be anything ahead of me either. Maybe the dog was injured. I turned around and started to cycle back up the road. The wind was so strong I could only do 8 mph, which gave me even more appreciation for the tailwind I had. As I was nearing, the dog got up and started to walk along the fence about ten metres off the road. It looked excited to see me but didn't want to come near the road. I got off Maid Marian and walked over. It was clearly a pet and surely very lost. There was nothing around. Not a house or farm barn in sight. I sat there wondering what to do. Hopefully a driver would see it and help it. I had heard of stories where people lost their wallet or bag and tweeted for help and got it back. I decided to do the same so tweeted that there was a lost dog just south of Woodward. Hopefully enough people would retweet it and someone might find it. I knew that the probability of that working was second to none but at least I did what I could. I got back on Maid

Marian. The dog looked so miserable. I felt just as awful as when the kitten followed me up the hill.

The tweet about the missing dog had a few people asking for more details. By now I had mastered the art of tweeting and texting while in tri position. I could happily rest my elbows on the pads while holding my phone as you normally would, and still dodge potholes and take corners. It became such a natural position that I'd often catch myself deep in thought with my hand under my chin while playing with my now slightly unruly beard. As I was tweeting while listening to music, all the things you shouldn't do while cycling, a police truck came alongside of me.

'Pull over please, sir.'

Bollocks, I thought. I was going to get busted for dangerous cycling. Damn it, just what I needed. The police truck stopped up ahead. I discretely put my phone away hoping that they didn't see me. They obviously had though. I watched as the two policemen stepped out and walked towards me. The driver had the biggest grey moustache I had ever seen in real life. It looked exactly like Hulk Hogan's one. He had a sheriff badge on his chest. He looked very scary and didn't smile at all as he walked over to me, almost in slow motion.

'Afternoon, sir.'

'Afternoon, officer.' Hugh Grant accent in full force.

He paused and looked at me and then down at Maid Marian. This was it. Certain jail!

'Sir! There is a tornado due here in about half an hour. Can we give you a lift?' said the other policeman who had a rather tiny moustache in comparison to Sheriff Hogan.

'Oh really?' I tried to sound like they were really helping me out here. Maybe I wasn't going to get arrested after all.

'How far is the next town?' I asked

'About five miles from here. We can lift you.'

'Thanks, but I'm kind of in the middle of this race and not really allowed a lift.' It was easier to say I was in the race rather than say I had this no-lift rule because of, well, pride. They couldn't argue with race rules.

'OK. You be careful out there.' And with that they left.

I pushed on to Woodward and stopped at a restaurant as the rain and hail started to come down. Perfect timing. Restaurants tend not to like it when you come in dripping wet (unless there is an impending tornado), so always try and look desperate and cold to get the sympathy vote. I walked in and it was quite empty except for a few people glued to the TV in the corner. It was showing a live tornado weather tracking. I've seen world cup cricket matches with audiences not as interested as these people were in *Tornado Live Watch*. They barely even looked up at me when I walked in.

The first thing I heard the weather reporter say was:

'We are going to get storms today that make the history books, people.'

Just my luck. I sat down and looked at the menu. They did a wild boar burger. That sounded delicious. I ordered two.

The weather channel showed the storm passing slightly west, heading north through the entire area over the next hour or so. It covered a much larger area than before and I didn't really have any other choice than to wait it out. I was more worried about the Labrador that seemed to be right in the path of another one of the storms. If Americans were as kind to dogs as they had been to me then I was sure someone would find it and look after it.

The TV was showing live storm chasers chasing tornados looking for 'touchdowns', which I've learned is when you get the twister bit hitting the ground, causing chaos. There seemed to be loads of chasers, though they were of a type: all similarly over-dramatic, all in their huge Hummers. I'm not a huge fan of the vehicle – parking must be a bitch – but if I were going to chase a tornado, I'd definitely take one of them. I've heard that some storm chasers have built a tank-looking truck that if in trouble, shoots huge stakes into the ground to stop it from taking off. That I'd love to see.

Despite the fact my plan was to head west, because of the wind (and the fact west was hilly) I decided to carry on north. Although I was going to be doing good miles, they actually didn't count towards the 140 miles a day I needed to do to get back to London in time. I really needed to start heading west again soon. According to the weather channel there were still a few storms heading up to the west of Woodward, which meant I couldn't really go west anyway. I decided to make the most of this southerly tailwind for one more day, which would send me out the top, where I could then cut around and back down out of the risk zone, or Tornado Alley as it's known. I only wish someone had told me such a place existed. I might have skipped it.

The wind pushing me north got stronger and stronger all afternoon and I managed to do fifty miles in two hours. The wind was so strong that stopping became difficult. Also I had to face oncoming traffic when taking a pee in order to go with the wind and avoid peeing on my leg. There weren't many trees to hide behind either, which resulted in a few cars hooting at me. What was I to do though? I was planning on getting to Dodge City for the night and by 6 p.m. I had reached the last town where I could get some food and water before the thirty-mile stretch to Dodge City. I stopped at a gas station and stocked up on some beef jerky, nuts, tinned tuna and some cheap cake. I wasn't normally a fan of cake, especially the 99c ones that only go off in five years, but today I felt like it.

The teller, extremely skinny and gaunt, barely noticed me as she mopped the floor in aisle two. I had to wait a good minute at the register before she decided she wanted to come over and serve me. When I told her where I was going, she had news for me.

'Dodge City? There is a tornado coming through between here and there in the next hour,' she said in a matter of fact kind of way.

Great. 'Is there anywhere I could shelter between here and there?'

'Nothing at all. It's all flat country. I wouldn't take the chance if I were you. Look at the weather here. It's looking bad.' She showed me the weather channel on her small TV behind the counter. Tornado watching really was like a sport here.

I sat down and ate some cake, deciding what to do. I'd had two close shaves with tornados. Was three pushing it a bit much? It had already started to rain again and the wind had picked up.

'Are there any motels here?' I asked.

'There was, a long time ago, but it closed down. Nothing I'm afraid.'

Well, I'd have to make a dash for it then. Just as I was about to go, a kid walked in. He was about eighteen years old and covered in tattoos.

'Hey Jim, are there any motels in town? This fella needs a place to stay.'

'Na Julia, nothing. But, I think they leave the church open. They have a tornado bunker.'

The church was as described: a white wooden building with a brick holding the door closed. It started to hail as soon as I arrived so I went in to check it out. It seemed like a good place to stay. I decided to wait and see if the storm would pass. I sat on the floor at the back of the church to finish my sandwich. I felt sitting on one of the pews to eat dinner was probably not going to make the man upstairs happy.

By 7 p.m. it was still raining, windy and getting dark. I wasn't in the mood to get cold and wet again so decided to settle in for the night. I unpacked everything and lay down on one of the pews. It was surprisingly comfortable. I had only managed 160 miles, and probably could have done way over 200 with that tailwind and no stopping for tornados. I was nervous about the morning because I'd have to head west and then south no matter what the wind was doing. My tornado dodging had pushed me way too far north and I couldn't afford to go any further from LA as my flight, which I had meticulously prearranged for optimising my race, was in just over a week. At this rate I'd need to do 150 miles a day to make it. If there were any headwinds then that would almost be impossible, and missing one flight meant I might miss all the rest going forward, which I couldn't afford.

I was just nodding off to sleep when I heard the church door open. I froze. I lay there quietly as I saw a figure walk in through the door. It was almost pitch black and I couldn't see much. The figure then started to walk down the side aisle right next to where I was sleeping. My heart started to race.

Should I say something or just keep quiet? For some reason I decided to speak out.

'Hello there . . . ?'

A lady let out a huge scream and jumped up against the wall with her hands in the air. 'Oh my. You nearly scared me to death, you did.'

'Sorry, I'm a cyclist and was told I could stay here the night.' I was now trying my very best Hugh Grant accent. I definitely nailed it this time.

'That's fine,' the lady said getting her breath back. 'There's a bunker below. I'm just making sure it's stocked up in case things get worse in the night.'

We said a few more pleasantries before she went off to the bunker and then left again. My heart was still racing. I decided that I might find a more secluded place to sleep. I found a row in the corner and used the kneeling cushions to make a small bed on the floor. There was quite a lot of lightning outside, which made the stained glass windows glow with every strike. It was so memorising I don't remember falling asleep.

The next day I decided to get up at 4 a.m. because of my early night. It was a freezing cold start, which I wasn't prepared for at all. I reached the outskirts of Dodge City before sunrise and desperately needed a coffee to warm me up. The sun did eventually come up and brought with it a heavy headwind. Just the thing I was dreading but it was inevitable: the closer I got to the Rockies the more likely I'd get headwinds as they are predominantly westerly. My pace dropped to a dismal 6 mph as I struggled through the flat windswept Kansas countryside. I found myself stopping every half an hour to look at my map to try and find a better route. I kept asking people if it was normally this windy to which they'd all laugh and say that it was in fact quite a still day! Brilliant: first Tornado alley and now possibly the windiest place in the world. Good planning, Sean!

Every now and then a truck would pass me and give me a brief glimpse of what it would be like without a headwind, before I'd get smacked in the face again, putting me firmly back in my place. It was really tough going. My normal water and food rations would get me at least sixty miles before I needed to restock but on a day like this it'd only get me about twenty-five miles. It took me fourteen hours to do the first 100 miles. By this point, it was 6 p.m. and I was buggered. I sat eating a burger, deflated at my slow progress. I figured I'd try and do at least another twenty miles and then cut my day short. Hopefully the wind would be better in the morning. I got back on Maid Marian and straightaway noticed that something was different. I was doing 15 mph, easily. I realised that I now had a tailwind. How was that possible? For a moment I thought I had got really confused and was heading back the way I'd come, something easily done when many towns look the same. I stopped to try and work it out. Surely that didn't happen. I'm usually quite good with directions.

'The sun rises in the east, and sets in the west.' I started to talk to myself while pointing to my left and right trying to visualise a compass. 'The sun is now off to my right which means north is behind me. South is then in front of me, which means I am in fact going south.' I felt like I was talking to a five-year-old. I turned around in circles while double and triple checking my findings. Every which way I looked at it, I was in fact still going the right direction and now, for some strange reason, had a tailwind. I jumped back on

Maid Marian with a huge smile on my face. Tailwinds all the way north for three days and now tailwinds south again. Bar the last fourteen hours of headwind hell, the tailwind gods were looking after me. I decided to make the most of them. I searched for 'Don't Stop Me Now' by Queen on my iPod and turned the volume to eleven.

I didn't stop at all. By 10 p.m. I had done 175 miles. The next town was still fifty miles away but at the rate I was going I'd make it there in less than three hours. I decided to go for it. At 11.33 p.m. my odometer ticked over the magic 200-mile mark. I could feel myself well up with excitement. I still had it in me. I could still push the miles even though I was injured. A tear ran down my face, more with relief than sadness. I was on a very different journey now but a part of me always wanted to see, just once, whether I could still push the big days. I felt all the weight on my shoulders disappear. I was truly happy.

'We did it, Little Flying Cow. We did it!' Eventually at one in the morning I reached Pampa and had covered 225 miles. I was knackered but still buzzing. I sat in the motel not really sure how what had begun as my slowest day had somehow resulted in my biggest day on the bike. Imagine how far I would have gone if I hadn't had the headwind in the morning. Three hundred miles, surely.

# 12

## PRAYING TO THE WIND GODS

I had just about made up for going too far north but was still cutting it fine to get to LA in time for my flight. I now just had the small issue of The Rocky Mountains to conquer. With climbing higher than the highest ski resort in the Alps, it would be the largest mountain range I'd have to cycle over. This was the hardest part of my American leg: I'd be cycling up to nearly 8000 ft where it would be a lot harder to cycle and a lot colder. I'd most certainly get some heavy headwinds up there, too. Although I was quite excited to have some hills, I was still worried about my knees. The next few days were going to be tough for sure.

After my longest day on the bike, I had battled my way through more headwinds before reaching Roswell, famous for its alien connections. The following day, the terrain changed from arid flat land into the foothills of the Rockies. Up and up I climbed and eventually came to a small summit. I stopped to look at my very first downhill in nearly a week. The hard shoulder was nearly as wide as they were in Texas and also had the heavy-duty rumble strips stopping cars moving into it. I knew I could bomb it down at 30 mph. I stopped to check that my brakes still worked before taking a huge gulp of water. '*Yeee-haaaaa!*' I shouted in an overly American style as I began the descent. It was incredible. Wide shoulder, smooth tar and no wind. I couldn't have been happier.

It wasn't long before I was doing 30 mph but then suddenly I saw something long and thin going right across the entire hard shoulder. It was about 30 m away. It looked like a stick that was about as thick as a tennis racket handle. There was no way I'd be able to stop in time and I couldn't move into the road because of the deathly rumble strips stopping me. Maid Marian, although light for a touring bike, was not exactly a gymnast and I'd never be able to bunny hop over it. I'd just have to hold tight and pray for the best. Hopefully it would break as soon as I hit it.

I sped towards the stick trying to work out the best place to go over it. The end bit nearer the edge of the road looked thinner. I started heading nearer the edge of the road when the stick suddenly moved. I got the fright of my life and nearly went right off the road. It wasn't a stick. It was in fact a huge two-metre long snake, and I rode right over the back of its tail and it recoiled into a circle, its head centimetres away from my leg. I immediately felt awful as I am quite fond of snakes. At least I had only gone over the last 10 cm of its tail. I had no idea what type of snake it was (and never managed to find out) but was pretty sure any bite from a snake of that size would be rather unpleasant. I slowed my pace to 20 mph and started to scope the route ahead just in case I needed to stop quickly, all the while still feeling incredibly guilty.

I had no idea if I was actually in the Rockies but figured because the hills weren't as bad, I still had them to come. Dark tar roads slowly worked their way through drying riverbeds and dead grassy fields. It looked dry but not arid, wild and untouched. This was the first time since I started my American leg where I wasn't cycling through farmland. I pushed on to Carrizozo, New Mexico, where I had a bacon and cheeseburger from a typical American diner. I had another long stretch to Socorro but wasn't nearly as worried because, although there was a slight headwind, it wasn't nearly as bad as it had been. I restocked my five water bottles and carried on west.

By nightfall I could see the lightened sky over Socorro. I saw a few more snakes making the most of the still warm road as I bombed down, but none nearly as big and scary as the first one. The final stretch was fairly urban with quite a few houses dotted on each side of the road. I had my headphones in and wasn't really concentrating until a dog burst out of a driveway nearly knocking me over and giving me the fright of my life, for the second time in one day. I gave out a pretty embarrassing yelp and took out my headphones to shout at the dog. Although small it was pretty determined to bark its lungs out and chase me away. It wasn't just this dog that was going a bit mad either. There seemed to be a few behind me too. Had I inadvertently been playing my Chasing Dogs game without knowing it? I imagined a few dogs running after me and because I had my headphones in I was none the wiser. I could have had a wolf on my tail and wouldn't have known.

I decided not to play Chasing Dogs with this little nipper still giving me grief, so just stepped it up a gear and he soon gave up. I settled back into my rhythm and decided to only put one headphone in just in case a wolf decided to chase me. Good thing I did because it seemed every house I rode past had a dog that barked and a gate that didn't work. Nowhere else have I seen so many aggressive, cycle-hating dogs in my life.

I was excited to be nearing the Rockies and the next day was on the road just before sunrise. The climb out of Socorro was slow but beautiful. The sun came up, sending golden shadows ahead of me. The elongated version of my body on the road made me look very thin. I knew it was all an illusion but I felt skinny and lacking energy.

As soon as the sun rose, so did the wind. There was no getting away from it now. The invisible army was back and they were taking no prisoners. The road did a few switchbacks before the first long straight heading up and around the first big mountain range to my right. By now, the wind was relentless. Not gusty, not aggressive, just one huge steady invisible wall of pain. My pace dropped to just four miles per hour as I stared at my groin again. The worst part of going so slow when in tri position is your face is about five centimetres away from your cycle computer, which is shouting at you because of how slow you are. Eventually I got so annoyed I covered up the speed with my neck scarf. I hoped that if I couldn't see my slow pace I'd somehow feel better. It actually worked a treat. I wish I had tried this trick earlier.

By midday I had reached Magdalena, for which I am sure the expression 'one horse town' was invented. It was a typical Western-looking town with old buildings, one main street and a few side streets – straight out of any Clint Eastwood film. It looked like it hadn't changed in 200 years. The first thing I looked for was some tumbleweed. If there was ever a time and place for the Western stereotype to appear, this would be it.

I didn't find any tumbleweed so looked for breakfast instead. There wasn't much to choose from except a small café opposite the very typical old-sheriff-looking police station. Breakfast was scrambled egg and some oatmeal porridge sprinkled with little tiny raisins. Porridge had been my staple breakfast throughout my training: I wish I had put raisins in mine too; it was delicious. After my feeding and a brief chat with the actual sheriff of the town I carried on west and into the heart of the rocky plateau. I had another climb up and out of Magdalena. The wind didn't change at all and I was still sluggishly pushing along. About ten miles outside of the town I came to a roadside picnic spot and saw another cyclist sitting in the bench, an elderly woman. Brilliant, someone to cycle with. I cycled over with a sudden burst of energy. She waved and smiled when she saw me, revealing a huge gap in the front of her teeth. She looked in her late fifties and didn't look like a cyclist at all. She had what looked like steel-toed builder's boots on and her bike looked more suited to a scrapyard than a Rocky Mountain expedition. She had a pannier rack but no panniers: all her stuff was wrapped in black bin liners and tied to the rack.

'Are you heading into this bloody headwind too?' I asked.

'Sure am.'

'This is the worst wind I have ever cycled in. I can't do more than five miles per hour.'

'At least you can cycle. I've been pushing all morning. It's taken me two days to get from Socorro.'

'So where you heading?' I asked, before she realised I left Socorro six hours ago.

'The plan is to eventually get to San Diego. I've been on the road for a few months this time round.'

'So you've been cycling a while then?'

'Yeah, I've done about 125,000 miles so far.'

I nearly fell off Maid Marian. There I was, with arguably some of the best cycle equipment available for touring, and complaining about a headwind, when this lady, who had builders boots on, no teeth and a bike older than me had done 125,000 miles.

I cycled off up the hill with a new lease of life. What an amazing woman. I only wish I had a photo to remember her by. I didn't even get her name. In some sort of way, though, I liked that. She was this anonymous person, just happy to be on a bike. Such a simple, yet wonderful way of life. I found myself questioning the reasons and motives that made me try to break records. If only I could find happiness in other ways. I was just too scared of just existing again; I needed to push myself to feel alive. This person had somehow found a way of living and being happy without the need to prove anything to herself or anyone else. Maybe that came with age? Maybe when I turned sixty I'd say, 'Fuck it I'm disappearing', and ten years later an insecure young ginger cyclist would come across me in the middle of the Himalayas and ask for a photo.

The more I climbed, the stronger the wind got. It was obviously the day for cyclists because I saw another chap coming towards me down one of the never-ending climbs. Bastard must have the best tailwind known to mankind. I was very envious. I slowed down and was preparing to stop, hoping to chat about what I was in for. Better the devil you know. But he was bombing down the hill with a huge smile on his face, looking straight ahead. His smile made me smile back but he didn't even look my way. He didn't slow down either and before I even realised he had flown past me without a head nod or anything. What a cock. Besides the old lady, this was the first proper touring cyclist I had seen since the start of my ride back in February and he didn't even say hello. I went back into tri position and turned my music up to hide the sound of the headwind going past my ears.

Wind, wind, wind. Nothing in the world is more demoralising. The harder I tried, it seemed, the slower I went and the worse my neck felt. The strain of keeping my head down against the wind was really taking its toll. Eventually I gave up. I got off and started to push Maid Marian for a while. Pushing was actually only one mile an hour slower than cycling – I cheated and took a sneak peek at my speedometer – but at least I could rest my legs a bit, use some different muscles and stretch my neck. I walked for about ten minutes and then decided to lie down and take a break. Rested I carried on walking for another ten minutes before something caught my attention off to my left. About a mile ahead was a field of gigantic satellite dishes. There must have been thirty of them. I jumped back on Maid Marian with a new small ball of excitement. I had seen these in a film with Jodie Foster, I thought.

The road had plateaued a little, which was good because I didn't have a hill to climb, but bad because I had no shelter from the wind. There were some very dry areas occasionally interrupted by some wooded outcrops and ranches off the roads. It must have been incredible exploring this part of the world 200 years ago on horseback. I guess horses had the same problem when battling into a heavy headwind.

By 3 p.m. I had been on the road for nine hours and only done fifty miles and my neck and back were killing me. It's the worst they had been since the first day back on the bike. Not even the painkillers were working. I knew I should probably have rested for longer after the accident. I reached a small town: if Magdalena was a one-horse town, then this was a no-horse town. Just a petrol station, a small restaurant and a few houses here and there. I was pretty low on energy so stopped in the restaurant for a burger. Inside it seemed so calm and peaceful. There was a very Western-looking gentleman sitting on the table next to me. He had cowboy boots and a cowboy hat on. He looked like he came from the area, or at least must know it.

'Is the wind always this bad and from the west?' I asked.

'Yeah, It's pretty heavy today. Hasn't been this windy in days, and yes, it's generally always from the west up here. Where are you heading?'

'I was trying to get over the Rockies today but it's taken me nine hours to get from Socorro, so it looks like I'm staying somewhere up here for the night.'

'If it's that bad, we live about ten miles up the road where there are some nice places to camp. We have a pick-up and can give you a lift if you want.'

I sat there contemplating my options. My back was sore, my neck was killing me, I was tired and in theory, could easily take a lift because I wasn't going for the world record anymore. It seemed sensible. Surely carrying on would injure my neck even more. I then suddenly realised what I was thinking. No way! I would never accept a lift. I was annoyed that the wind had even made me think about it at all. As tempting as the idea was, I would not get a lift.

'Thanks, but I've got this personal goal to cycle all the way, no matter what.'

'Sure. Well in that case Pie Town is about twenty-five miles from here. There is a lady who has a traveller's house. It's called the Toaster House. Go through the town and down the hill. Take the first left 100 metres down and then go about 200 metres up the dirt track until you see a house with loads of mismatched chairs on the porch and a bunch of toasters hanging on the fence. She lets travellers stay there. You might even get a hot shower.'

I reached Pie Town at around 7.30 p.m. and decided that I'd quickly go and see this Toaster House place. The cowboy's directions were spot on. The Toaster House was an old wooden house with the most random collection of objects all over the garden. There were car seats on the porch, sofas with mismatching cushions and various items hanging from the porch roof. It also had a variety of toasters all hanging from the doorway, thus giving it the name the Toaster House. I immediately fell in love with it.

I knocked on the door, slightly nervously as it all seemed quite empty. A few moments later a fairly young woman, in her late twenties I guessed, came to the door.

'*Bonjour!*'

'Ah, *bonjour*. How are you? I take it this isn't your house then?'

'No, no. I am just stopping here for a few days while travelling.'

'You're obviously from France. I live in London.'

'Ah, *oui*! Very cool. Come. Come, I show you everything.'

The woman, Nicolette, showed me everything about the toaster house. There was food in the fridge, I had a bed and there was hot water. It was brilliant. It didn't cost anything except a donation to restock the cupboard with tea, coffee and some supplies. Between the supplies and what other travellers had left there was enough to feed a peloton of hungry cyclists. I hadn't planned on staying the night but considering it was cold, I was tired and in pain, and there was nothing else for another thirty miles, I decided to give up. I had only done seventy-six miles, my first sub 100 day since I started. I wasn't sure why I felt so bad. I wasn't racing anymore and could legitimately take a day off or do a shorter day. Then Nicolette came bouncing into the room I had found for myself. She was very bubbly and funny. We chatted all about our adventures. She was walking through the Rockies and had decided to take a few days off to rest and write. She also had an interest in stars and was just about to head off for the night to look at them with an actual astronomer who knew 200 stars by name. I knew one, Orion's Belt, and that wasn't even a star. It was a shame she had to leave. I was feeling pretty lonely and bored of all the wind and it would have been nice to chat more about our respective adventures. But I was so tired I probably wouldn't have been much fun in the chat department.

At 9 p.m. I said goodbye to Nicolette as I would probably be gone by the time she got up and decided to look at my route to LA. I had six days till my flight and after my few very short days I'd now have to do 180 miles a day to get there in time. With this headwind, and my neck and back that seemed to be getting worse, that wasn't possible. I lay there trying to work out a plan. Maybe the wind would be better in the morning.

It was still quite cold as I made my way out of Pie Town the following morning. At least there was a slight downhill which lifted my spirits slightly. The wind wasn't nearly as bad as it had been but there was still some climbing to do. It was a beautiful morning cycling through ranch territory as I dreamt up scenarios of face-painted Native Americans running down the valley trying to cut me off before I reached the next river crossing. Every now and then I'd see someone on horseback wandering along a riverbank, the horse's hooves kicking up water which glistened in the morning light. My iPod had randomly chosen some Native American chanting music, which fitted perfectly.

By early afternoon I was starving so stopped into a gas station to fill up on supplies and have a banana. I kept forgetting to have electrolytes in my food and bananas are full of potassium, which helps carbohydrates bond to your muscles for energy, or something of that nature. As I sat on the pavement deep in thought hoping a typical Western gun battle would happen in front of me a lady came out the station.

'Where are you heading?' she asked. 'Into the wind or with it?'

'Into it, unfortunately.'

'Yeah, it can be bad around here. Are you heading to Show Low? You should take the inland route instead of the desert.' She pointed to the mountain range off to my left. 'It's a long fifteen-mile climb at first but then pretty much all downhill from there.'

'Oh, OK!' I wasn't convinced. I couldn't bear any more climbing.

'The problem with carrying on through the desert is it's much hotter and there are loads of ups and down. It probably works out the same. Also the route through the trees shelters you from the wind.'

I hadn't thought of that. She might have a point.

'That's sounds tempting. I don't have a map though. Is it easy to find my way?'

"I have one in my office. If you wait here I can go get it for you.'

I thought she was going to walk literally around the corner but she jumped in her car and sped off down the road and out of sight. I carried on eating my banana trying to weigh up the options. Big climb for three hours and then downhill in the shelter of the trees, or slightly flatter but a bit hotter and possibly a lot more windy. The lady eventually came back and proceeded to show me the route through to Show Low via the Pinetop ski resort which was 3000 m above sea level. The map she showed me showed her proposed route in a nice green colour: my original route through the desert looked very dry and brown.

After more persuading I decided to go with the inland route. I had just eaten, which meant I could use all my energy getting up the big climb and then coast down to Show Low. I immediately appreciated my decision as the wind was pretty much non-existent as I made my way up the Alpine-looking hill. My pace was slow but I knew I'd have a long downhill. In all the faffing with deciding on a new route I had forgotten to go to the toilet. I then suddenly realised I had also run out of toilet paper and hadn't replaced it. I tried to hold it in but only lasted another ten minutes before I really had to go. Luckily I was in a forest this time so ran a hundred metres off the road and out of sight of passing cars. Grass was slightly better than a rib bone for toilet paper but still rather prickly. I'd work out this cycle touring logistics thing soon, I hoped.

I carried on climbing to 3000 m and even passed some patches of snow. I didn't really need to fill up my water bottles with snow but did it anyway to feel like a proper adventurer. The route got more and more scenic and at times I thought I was in Switzerland. The alpine forests and crystal-blue lakes were a nice change from the hot, windy flatlands in New Mexico. The route down to Show Low was pretty much all downhill, the idea of battling through the arid desert now a long lost memory. It's amazing how easily you forget the bad times. All in all, getting help from the lovely map lady was the best thing that had happened to me in days.

The forests continued as did the never-ending downhill. Then about five miles from Show Low my back tyre gave in. Normally I'd be really annoyed but I was in a much better mood because the wind had died down. Also, I could finally get rid of the old tyre and save another 220 g which I'd been carrying around for nearly a week. I knew in the grand scheme of things it didn't make a difference, but if in your mind you are as light as possible, you cycle better. The back tyre is always a lot more of a faff to change, especially when you have a Rohloff. First you have to put it in 14th gear, then unscrew the gear-changing mechanism and slide the wheel off. I unpacked my new Specialised tyre and started to put it on. I was sitting on the floor with the wheel in between my legs. I got most of it on except the last bit, which was a lot tighter than normal. I didn't want to use the tyre levers to get the tyre on in case I caused a pinch flat, which had happened a few times before. But no matter what I tried I just couldn't get it on. It didn't help that I had broken both my thumbs skiing a year before, so couldn't really use them to push the tyre onto the rim as normal, as they were still weak. I decided the best way was to try standing on the bottom of the rim as I pulled the tyre up. I put my shoe between two of the spokes and with both my hands on the tyre gave a hard pull upwards. As I did that a sharp pain shot up my back. I dropped the wheel and slowly sat back down. The pain had been brief but very sharp. I tried to bend over forwards to stretch it, but that hurt even more. I had to keep my back as straight as possible for the pain to go away. I decided to lie down for a bit.

'Shit! Not now!' I said under my breath.

I lay there for a while and tried to get up. I felt the sharp pain again. It was as bad as it had been the day after the accident when I couldn't get out of bed. The only way to get up was to roll onto my side all the while trying to keep my back as straight as possible. I hobbled over to Maid Marian, took another painkiller and sat back down. Time seemed to go into slow motion as I sat on the side of the road, my kit sprawled all over the place and a bike with no tyre. I waited for the painkillers to kick in. I really had to get the tyre fixed. I decided to use the tyre levers and hope for the best. If I punctured the next inner tube I'm not sure I'd have enough strength to change the tyre again. I managed to get the tyre back on the rim and after another ten-minute rest got back on Maid Marian. At least Show Low was only five miles away and it was all downhill. If I kept my back as straight as possible and didn't push it then it didn't hurt as much. The plan was to try and go slightly past Show Low but I decided to cut my day short and rest up. Hopefully I had just tweaked a nerve or something and it would all be fixed in the morning.

That night, I managed to sleep on my back, which seemed to help. Although very stiff, I could still just about get up and walk around. I just hoped that like my knee in South America, it would get better as soon as I warmed up. At least my route down to Phoenix was mainly downhill. It soon became clear, however, that I had in fact reinjured my back. I struggled on and stopped again to have a burger before the first major decent into the Arizona desert. It got hotter and hotter the further down I went and eventually by the time I reached the bottom it was nearly 40 degrees.

I had been told the route from here would have three very big climbs before the long descent to the city. I reached the bottom of the first climb and looked up. It must have been about five miles long and would take me an hour. With the sun beating down I started the climb, my back hurting with every pedal. My pace was slow and it was extremely hot, so hot that I even came across a car that had to stop because it was overheating on the climb. I pushed on at a frightfully slow pace, stopping every few miles to try and stretch my back. Nothing helped though. Up the first climb and then down the other side, up the second climb and then down again. I passed another truck that had overheated just before the final climb and rested for ten minutes under a tiny bush trying to get some shade. As I sat there I knew that the odds of getting to LA in time for my flight were pretty impossible. Not in the state I was in. If I missed that flight, then all my other flights would be affected, and considering my pace was so slow, even getting those flights would be tight. I decided to get to Phoenix and then check my options from there.

I got back on Maid Marian whose black metal frame was so hot it nearly burned me. I started up the final climb and hadn't gone more than 100 m before my nose started bleeding uncontrollably. I tried putting my head back but the feeling of warm blood running down my throat made me nearly throw up. I cocked my head over again, hurting my neck in the process, while letting out a waterfall of blood from my mouth and nose. Half of it landed up on my shirt too. I stood there for another five minutes as warm crimson blood came streaming out my nose and into my beard. It was so ridiculous that I eventually even videoed it. I had never experienced a nose bleed like that in my life. It was unreal. Eventually after about fifteen minutes trying every which way possible to try and make it stop it slowly dried up, forming a crusty layer of blood on my nose and in my moustache.

The final descent to Phoenix was sluggish and hot. I also got a slow puncture about four miles from the centre, so carried my pump in my back pocket and gave it a few bursts every 500 m or so. There was no way I'd be able to do another tyre change. I reached Phoenix by nightfall and had only done 130 miles, even though most of it was downhill. My back and neck still hurt like hell and I really needed to rest them both. I looked at the map to decide what to do. My flight was in four days, which meant I really needed to get to LA in about three so that I could arrange a bike box and sort things out. Even if I left tomorrow, which at this rate wasn't going to happen, I'd still possibly not make it. And that was providing I didn't get a headwind.

As I sat there deflated I realised that I was possibly at the end of my American leg. I started to cry. I'd always dreamt of cycling coast to coast in America but knew that if I pushed my flight back again at a cost of around £100 a go I'd then have to push back all the rest of my flight too. There was no way I'd be able to afford that. I knew it was over. I'd have to end my American leg here in Phoenix, rest my back up and then continue my journey from Australia. It didn't seem right that I was skipping a 300-mile section. Would it completely undermine the whole 'Around the World' concept? I thought for a while and then remembered that all the other riders going east around the world probably got halfway across

Turkey before flying to India. In theory I was doing the same; only the fact that there was an ocean at the end of America made it seem like cheating. I hated giving up but I knew I really had no other choice.

I had tried to not think about what Mike and the other riders were up to as it made me a bit depressed that I wasn't part of the race anymore, but at the end of my American leg I decided to see what was happening. Mike was still way ahead and putting in some big miles across Australia. Martin was a close second with Richard in third place. I couldn't find much on the others as they weren't sharing online, except it looked like Paul and Steven had both pulled out of the race. So three had stopped, four were still racing, and five, myself being one of them, weren't racing anymore. Although not racing I was still keeping up similar mileage and more at times than the others. It was hard to avoid the inevitable depression every time I thought about it. I quickly got my Olympic Torch out to keep focused on the new goal.

America had been one of the most incredible places I have ever cycled in. Americans are without a doubt the friendliest people I have ever met. I had battled through some of my darkest days and although my record attempt had been taken from me, the kindness of two random strangers had allowed me to carry on my adventure with a new goal and a new focus. I was gutted to not have completed my US leg as intended, but I really needed to rest up and think about my long-term health. Australia would be a whole new chapter with hopefully a revived excitement.

Bye bye, USA. You were really, really hard, physically and mentally.

# 13
## G'DAY MATE

'Good morning ladies and gentleman. Welcome to Sydney. The weather is slightly overcast and 16 degrees Celsius with a slight southerly wind. Thank you for flying with Air Canada. Enjoy your stay.'

Sydney is a very, very long way from LA. Just look at a map – it's literally across the world. I appreciate we probably flew around the other side of the world but still, it's a long time to be in a small seat at 33,000 ft. The whole transfer took twenty-four hours, and because of the time change I lost an entire extra day. For me, 28 April did not exist: I left on 27 April, flew for a day and arrived on 29 April. My brain, although rested, was still too tired from a restless flight to work it all out. Also, 16 degrees and cloudy? I thought Australia was meant to be sunny and warm?

My flight had been pretty awful but at least I was feeling fresh and excited about starting my new leg. Although carrying on from the accident was a new beginning, America still seemed a bit tainted in my mind as I struggled to come to terms with the whole ordeal. At least now I was in a new continent, a new country and feeling revived and fresh again for a new adventure. Also on the map it now looked like I was cycling back home rather than away from it.

The first task on my list was to get to Brisbane, which was 620 miles away. One of my closest cousins Chris lived there and it would be great to see him and his new fiancé Sian. It was extra important to see them because I had planned on getting back to the UK in time for their wedding but due to the accident I was now going to miss it. This made me sad. I had originally wanted to get to Brisbane in four and a half days (today being the half day as I'd only leave the airport by midday), which meant averaging 140 miles per day in line with my new goal of getting back to London for the Olympics. I was feeling quite fresh and strong after my four-day rest so decided to try and make Brisbane in three and a half days, and therefore earn a day's rest and catch up with family. The research I had done on this part of the journey suggested it would be flat and I'd have a tailwind all the way up the coast, which would make the 620-mile stretch just about doable. It was going to be tight, but I was excited about getting back on the road again.

I had by now mastered the art of putting Maid Marian back together and was on the road again by 11.30 a.m. I left the airport and started bombing down the road, excited to be on a new continent. I came around the first corner and a taxi driver was completely cutting it, so much so that he was literally all the way on my side of the road. I ducked onto the pavement and he swerved at the last minute, hooting as he shot past. How dare he hoot? Cheeky bugger! I got back on Maid Marian and yet another taxi came hurtling down the road in my lane. I jumped onto the pavement again. What side of the road did Australia drive on? Two more cars came in both directions answering my question for me. Australia drove on the same side of the road as Britain! I hadn't even thought about it. Since Spain, where, ironically, I made the same mistake, I had been cycling on the right. Slightly embarrassed for being annoyed at the taxi driver I crossed the road and decided to get away as quickly as possible.

I must have gone no more than another 50 metres when I heard a massive explosion. Naturally, hearing a bang in an airport made me think of terrorism, but straight away I felt my front tyre was flat. What a great start to Australia. The tube blowout was so big it tore the tyre right off the rim. I realised straight away my mistake. I had changed back to Continental Tyres in LA and, because my back was still sore, I'd used tyre levers, which must have put a small pinch in the tube. I'd also then forgotten to let some air out my tyres for the flight, which meant they probably expanded due to the low pressure in the cargo bit. Lesson learned!

After a hasty inner tube fix, all the while expecting the Australian bomb squad to appear, or an angry taxi driver telling me off, I was finally on my way, heading north. Annoyingly, Sydney Airport was quite far south, which meant about 30 miles of busy city traffic to contend with. The one good thing was that I could at least go via the Sydney Opera House and take a photo with my Olympic Torch. It took a good hour to do the ten-mile stretch to the harbour bridge where I took a quick photo before heading over the bridge and on through the northern suburbs. I was planning to get near Newcastle for the night, which I thought was about 100 miles away, but was shocked to see a sign saying it was 180. How had

I got that so wrong? If Newcastle was 180 miles away then I'd seriously messed up my planning, again, and would never make Brisbane in three and a half days. I spent the next hour contemplating whether to take the slightly shorter inland route when a second sign came up: Newcastle 155. What? There was no way I had just done 25 miles. Then it hit me: Australia must be in kilometres. Duh! Somehow my brain decided that because I was cycling on the 'correct' side of the road, like the UK, it was in miles. I felt like such an idiot, but at least my planning was in fact right.

The going was slow as I made my way through the leafy northern suburbs. I was right about my tailwind, but very, very wrong about Australia being flat. The northern parts of Sydney were extremely hilly, and I spent all afternoon climbing up a few hundred metres and then heading back to sea level. I managed to find a small back road next to the main highway that was at least very quiet. I reached Gosford by mid-afternoon and decided to head towards the coast so that I could avoid the busy Pacific Highway. It became a lot flatter and I was now making good progress. I was out of the city and all the stress they bring and onto the open road again. The excitement for my adventure was slowly starting to come back.

By nightfall I was in Swansea and decided to call it a day. I had done just over 100 miles and felt good. I hadn't slept well on the flight, so decided to stay in a cheap motel for the night. There weren't too many to choose from but I found the one that looked the cheapest. I was shocked when they told me it would be $80 for the night and they were the cheapest in town. $80? Although fairly clean it looked pretty rundown: a similar motel in America would have cost $29 and the US and Australian dollars were pretty much like for like in terms of value. I was incredibly tired and decided to treat myself to one night of good rest. I actually enjoyed camping out but was still without a tent or usable bivi (I hadn't used my useless one since I got drenched that night in Chile), which would make the whole process a lot more exciting and adventurous. However, that would be tomorrow's challenge.

I slept like a baby and was ready to get going by 5 a.m. I headed out of Swansea and carried on up towards Newcastle for breakfast. My phone had died in the night and for some reason wouldn't charge from my dynamo. I tried everything but nothing seemed to work. I'd have to buy a wall charger to get it going, and buy a map in the meantime to direct me. I stopped for some breakfast and nearly fell off my chair when I saw that a simple English Breakfast cost $15. Has Australia heard about this credit crunch or were they just so far away it didn't affect them? I thought $15 for breakfast was ridiculous. To avoid embarrassment I stayed, hoping it would be a breakfast that would change my life. It wasn't and I left annoyed at the sheer boldness that they could charge that much for a breakfast I could get in London for £6 ($9).

The next stop was to get a phone charger so that I could use Google to try and find some cheaper supermarkets for food. I stopped by a petrol station and saw an array of various wall chargers. I didn't really know if my phone was a thin or thick USB so went back to Maid Marian to get it. Just then I saw another touring cyclist go past the way I was heading. The first proper touring cyclist I had seen going in my direction. A flame of excitement started in my stomach: maybe we could cycle together for a bit? It would be great to actually cycle with someone for a while, compare stories and learn a thing or two from each other. Overly excited I ran back into the shop and hastily worked out the right charger before jumping back on Maid Marian to try and catch my potential new cycling partner.

I zoomed out of the station with new vigour and pushed my pace up to 18 mph to catch him, hoping he hadn't turned off. I thought I'd catch him within a minute or so but after a good three or four minutes there was still no sign of him. I was just about to give up when I came around a corner and saw him 100 m ahead. I couldn't believe he had gone so far ahead in such a short period considering he had five huge panniers of gear. A strong cyclist obviously. I stepped it up a gear, like a predator after its prey, until I came right up beside him. He was Japanese and nearly fell off his bike when he saw me.

'Hey dude. How's it going? Where are you heading?' I asked still overly excited.

'I do seven month. Perth to Sydney. Now up to Darwin for five month.'

'Wow, really. That's awesome.'

We chatted for a little longer but his English wasn't that good, which made it quite hard to find out the kind of adventure he was having. With slight disappointment I realised we probably wouldn't be good touring partners, mainly because I needed to average 175 miles a day to get to Brisbane in time. I gathered he was doing about 50 miles per day. We were on completely different missions with different goals. I'm sure he thought my challenge was completely daft: I said *sayonara* and carried on.

It was another 30 miles before I decided to look for a cheaper place to eat. I opened my top bar bag to get my phone.

It wasn't there. Strange. I always put it there. I searched all my pockets, my other bar bag and even my food bag. I had the charger I bought but no phone. I racked my brain and then realised what had happened. In my excitement to get the charger and catch the cyclist I must have left my phone on the counter at the service station. I could even picture it on the counter.

*Shit. OK. Make a plan, Sean.*

If I could phone the service station, somehow, then I could get them to give my phone to a driver heading my way and ask them to give it to the ginger bearded cyclist. Perfect. The only problem was where to find a phone. This part of the road was pretty quiet. Eventually, after an agonising ten miles I came across a small tavern on the side of the road. I rushed in to the glares of quite a few locals drinking XXXX and VBs. I guess this was the Aussie version of Ye Olde English pub. The lovely bar lady knew of the service station I was talking about and called directory enquiries to get the number. She called them but they didn't know anything of it.

'Sorry kiddo. They don't have it.'

'No worries. Thanks for trying anyway.'

I was annoyed. I had left it right on the counter and unless another customer saw it and took it then one of the staff must have picked it up. Luckily I had backed up all my voice recordings in America, but I lost all the photos I'd taken that I hadn't uploaded to Facebook or Twitter. It also had all my maps on it for Australia. I'd have to buy a paper map to get me to Brisbane and then hope for the best. Dejected I walked back to Maid Marian and then realised that I didn't have cousin Chris's number either, so he'd have no idea when I would arrive. I only hoped he was following my tracker and would then somehow meet me along the route. Brisbane is the biggest city in the world when it came to land area and I had no idea which part he lived in.

'Cross that bridge when we get there, Little Flying Cow. Let's try and get there first,' I said to myself. I'd been talking to myself a lot. I used to feel embarrassed but now didn't care. It's just one of the side effects of solo touring. I still wouldn't have it any other way though. Even though I wasn't racing and had done my first 200-mile day since the accident, I still wasn't missing company and was enjoying being on my own.

The rest of the afternoon was pretty uneventful as the frustration at losing my phone with all my photos outweighed my excitement for exploring. The terrain was pretty boring and just before nightfall, it started to rain. I wasn't sure how much I trusted truck drivers to see me at night, so when it finally got dark and hadn't stopped raining I decided to try and find a place to camp. I went another few miles without seeing anything suitable when finally, just off the main road, was a small bus shelter. It wasn't ideal but at least I'd be out of the rain. It was a tin shelter on small stilts, which meant the water was coming in through the bottom. I'd have to try and sleep on the one-foot wide bench to avoid getting wet. Although not the most comfortable looking place to sleep it was still a lot more adventurous than a motel and that excited me. I had done 170 miles, which was about 20 miles short of where I wanted to be but just about on target to get to Brisbane in time for a rest day with family.

If it wasn't the deafening sound of rain against a tin roof, it was the sound of trucks bombing along the main road that kept me awake. I must have had three hours at the most. Bleary eyed and still half asleep I made my way to Kempsey for breakfast and then carried on further along the coast. The map I bought wasn't nearly detailed enough to show any back roads so I kept to the main road all morning. Drivers weren't nearly as good as they had been in America and even with no oncoming traffic, wouldn't move over, even a foot. This resulted in a few curses as a gust of wind nearly took me off the road. Bastards!

I saw my first dead kangaroo at around midday. I felt quite bad for the poor guy. He didn't look more than a few months old. It was only after I passed it that I smelled it. The stench was almost unbearable: the Australian heat and humidity really made these carcases rot. At least smelling it after I saw it meant I had a tailwind, so that was one positive thing I could take from the situation. By 10 p.m. my restless sleep from the night before decided to catch up with me. I had done 165 miles, which left 190 more miles to Brisbane. A long push but doable, as long as I managed to get a good night's sleep. It was slightly drizzling again but I managed to find a small café that was just on the edge of a roadside caravan camping spot. I ducked behind the café when no cars were looking and made camp on one of the porches down one side that was shielded by bushes. My head hadn't even hit the floor before I fell fast asleep. A long, slow, and wet day but at least getting to Brisbane, and having a rest day, was looking likely. I set my alarm for 3 a.m. to give me two more hours to do the 25 extra miles.

'Sir, sir. Sorry, you can't sleep here.'

A very bright light was shining in my face. I was confused. For a moment I had no idea where I was.

'Sir. This is private property. I am going to have to ask you to move please.'

'Really? I'm not homeless or anything. Just a cyclist and I'll be gone in the morning.' My half-asleep voice made me sound like Johnny Cash. Nice!

'I can appreciate that but it's an insurance thing. Sorry mate. I'd let you stay but it's not my call.'

'OK, cool. Can I sleep round back?'

'Yes mate, as long as it's not in the café section.'

I slowly packed everything up and wheeled Maid Marian round the back. It was still raining a little and there was nowhere to sleep with shelter. I walked down a few stairs and saw the café was about two foot off the ground on stilts. I went under to inspect it. It was dry but a little stony. I heard a rustle off to my left. I looked up to see three geese all sitting up looking at me. If they thought it was a safe place to sleep then I guess it would do. I dragged Maid Marian on her side and made a patch to sleep on. Apparently geese are the best guard dogs so I felt quite safe having them around. That's as long as they didn't see me as a threat. I hadn't thought about that.

Getting up at 3 a.m. was really tough, the jet lag, hills and pretty awful sleep taking their toll. My body wasn't used to it but after an orange juice and some nuts I said goodbye to my geese flatmates and pushed Maid Marian round to the front of the café. As I started to pedal my right leg slipped and the pedal spun round and hit me slap bang in the middle of my shin. I tried to avoid shouting as there were a few caravans around and I didn't want to wake them. Instead I mimed a loud scream while rubbing my now bleeding shin.

I became even more worried about the day ahead when I passed a sign for Bald Knob Road. Shivers ran through my spine. Bald Knob was the place I'd got run over. I'm not superstitious at all but there can't be too many places in the world called Bald Knob and I managed to pass them both. I decided to be a little more aware and check my mirrors a little more often.

The rain and the hills continued all the way to Byron Bay where I finally dropped down and left the Pacific Highway to follow a quieter coastal route. I saw a huge sign saying: Sunshine Coast. They couldn't be serious? It had rained more on me in the last four days than it had my entire trip, excluding the tornado-chasing malarkey in America. How could this be the Sunshine Coast? I pushed on north stopping for some food and at a bike shop to get a few more inner tubes to replace the burst one and have a spare one. According to the map there was no way of getting to Brisbane without doing a huge loop inland. My initial plan was to follow the Pacific Highway, which I had been on all along, but from Byron Bay they didn't allow cyclists. I really needed a better map, so stopped in a service station to get one. It too looked like I'd have to go inland. I sat down deflated. This inland loop would add another 40 miles to my day, which meant I'd never get to Brisbane by nightfall. I looked at the map again and then noticed, right next to the main highway, a very thin white line. Was that possibly a road? It was worth checking out.

I was in luck. The thin white line was a service road running parallel to the highway. It was quiet, smooth and had one of the best cycle-friendly hard shoulders I had seen since I landed in Australia. I pushed on north extremely chuffed that for the second time in nearly as many days my planning, although partially accidental, had worked in my favour. Even with the faffing trying to find a map I was still looking to get to Brisbane by nightfall. I still had no idea how I was going to get hold of Chris but figured I'd make a plan when I got there.

The route into Brisbane got even hillier with some long climbs and tons and tons of traffic lights. The aim was to head for the centre of town and then wait there and hope Chris would be following my tracker, realise I had stopped, and come and find me. Option two was to call the only number I knew by heart, my old business partner. Get him to call my mother, who might have my aunt's number who would have Chris's number. I figured option one was more likely as half the people involved in option two were asleep on the other side of the world.

It was around 8 p.m. when I eventually reached what I thought looked like the centre of Brisbane – or at least, the part of the map where 'BRISBANE' was written. I was just about to settle in for what was bound to be a long wait when I suddenly remembered something. I was sure Chris had once given me his number on Facebook, way back when he moved to Brisbane. Right! All I needed was to find an Internet café, get the number, find a phone box and call him. Or . . . I could just ask someone to use their phone. It was a long shot but I figured I'd try. I started pushing Maid Marian down the fairly empty street looking for someone to ask. A girl on her own would never say yes. It would have to be two people or a couple. I waited a good ten minutes before I saw my first target – a young couple waking towards me.

'Hey guys, sorry to bother . . .' I explained my situation, expecting them to say no.

'Yeah sure, no worries,' said the girl who seemed really excited to help. I was quite taken aback at how quickly she said yes. There wasn't that awkward moment when she had to think about it at all. What legends. That would never have happened in London. Her boyfriend, who looked like he owned a gym, or was a lifeguard, or something else that required having lots of muscles, was also on the case. They were like a well-oiled machine. Facebook. Login. Messages. Chris. Scroll, scroll, scroll. Write number in notebook. Dial number. Ring, ring, ring!!! Before I knew it I had their phone in my hand. Wow! I was almost speechless, literally, which isn't ideal when making a phone call.

'Hello, Chris speaking.' Chris answered in the slightly professional way we all do when we see a number we don't recognise.

'Hey, mate. It's me. I lost my phone and am borrowing someone's.'

'Ah, right. Cool. You're not far. I've been following your tracker. Epic effort mate. Driving to Byron is a long day in the car even. That's incredible.'

'Ha-ha. Not going to lie, I'm pretty knackered. I would have been here earlier but struggled with the route and hills.'

'Cool. Right. Keep heading north towards the bridge. I'll meet you there.'

'Cool. See you in a bit.'

I gave the phone back to the girl and asked her how I got to the bridge. Again, as if she had done this a million times before, she opened her notebook, drew me a map, tore it out and gave it to me. We said goodbye and I carried on towards the bridge still not really understanding what just happened. It's not often that people go out of their way like that.

I met Chris on the other side of the bridge. He had cycled from his flat, which was about a mile down the road. There was that awkward moment when we tried to have a conversation across four lanes of traffic but soon realised it wasn't going to happen so signed to each other to meet on the north side. Brisbane at night was a spectacular sight, especially from the bridge with the river reflecting the city lights. I stopped and took another photo of me and my Olympic Torch.

'Mate, welcome to Oz.'

'Thanks. Good to be here. Although no one told me it rained so much. I thought it was meant to be flat and sunny here.'

'Just you wait till you go inland. You'll be happy for the rain.'

# 14

## MIND GAMES

Chris's boss let him take the morning off, which meant he was able to cycle the first 20 miles out of the city with me. As it turned out we did his exact cycle route to work, which meant a precise route of various back roads ensuring the quickest and least stressful route out of the city. I do love how commuting cyclists operate: sprinting between traffic lights; dodging cars and jumping the odd pavement here and there. I could barely keep up with Chris at times.

Northern Brisbane was very beautiful with some incredibly big houses and one very steep hill. It was just what I needed to get the legs going again, although I didn't think so at the time. Armed with a better map, and having my very own tour guide, we made good progress before cutting across towards the quieter coast route. It wasn't much further before Chris had to turn around and head back to work. It was great to catch up with him and Sian, which made me feel a little better for missing their wedding.

By early afternoon it started raining. Again.

'Come on Australia,' I shouted. 'It's meant to be hot and sunny.'

My coastal quiet route had come to an end and I was back on the Pacific Highway. The going was pretty slow and became extremely bumpy. I had been warned that the roads, although generally good, were made up of quite large chip seal, which was not only pretty bumpy to cycle on, but also kills the tread on your tyres. I battled on north along the A1, which at times had no hard shoulder at all. This wasn't the place to listen to any music as I had to keep pretty aware of what was going on around me. Once or twice I even had to go off the road onto the grass when I saw a huge truck coming towards me and another one coming up behind me. This road wasn't big enough for the three of us and to avoid another Bald Knob incident I dashed off into the grass coming to a quick halt as various gusts of wind slapped me around the face for a few seconds. Then it was back on Maid Marian and onto the road again. It was very tiring.

My final stop for the night was going to be in a town called Gympie. Just when I though the road wasn't going to get any worse, it did. There was a stretch where Australia had finally realised the A1 wasn't wide enough and were building a new lane. This would be great when complete, but what it meant now was that on each side of the already thin road was a huge two-metre high concrete wall. The roads were busy, it was raining and I couldn't turn back. I looked behind me to see a long line of cars flying by. There was no other option, I had to go for it. I waited to find a decent gap in the traffic before putting my head down and making the dash of death. I pushed my pace up to 24 mph which, at a push, I could hold for about fifteen minutes, at the most. I had no idea how long this stretch was but I dug deep and pushed hard, all the while repeating in my mind, 'You've been run over already. It won't happen again.' The gap in the cars ended and after a few hairy moments and some angry hoots I popped out the other side and ducked off the road onto the grass to catch my breath. That was it. I was done. I needed to rest. Time to find a place to camp for the night.

It was still raining and I still didn't have a tent, so kept a look out for some shelter. It wasn't long before I cycled past a house with an open garage just off the side. It was perfect. The garage was unused and even had some soft grass to sleep on. The lights were on in the house and I figured it would probably be better if I asked first so that I wouldn't get woken in the night by security again.

Knock, knock, knock. I figured three knocks was the appropriate amount. Two was not personal enough and four was too aggressive. I waited a good few minutes before I heard a stir inside and the door flew open.

'G'day mate. Yes?'

A very small fellow with nothing but a tracksuit bottom on stood in the doorway swaying a little from side to side. He was covered in tattoos, which looked like they were made with a spoon in 1957. He had a cigarette hanging from his lip.

'I'm cycling up to Darwin and need a place to crash for the night. Any chance I can stay in your garage.'

'Darwin? Mate, that's miles away.'

'Yeah I know. It's going to take me a while.'

'You're mad, but yeah, sure. Go ahead.'

'Thanks mate. I'm Sean by the way.'

'Roland. Nice to meet you.' We shook hands, but it was a bit awkward. With that he closed the door and I went back to

Maid Marian. After my little sprint, and now a firm believer that food was more important than sleep, I decided to get something to eat first before bed. I saw some lights a few hundred metres up the road so headed to see what I could find. It turned out to be a service station, so I stocked up on some peanuts, fruit juice, a banana and some milk. As I was heading back to my 'motel' I saw Roland coming out of the garage with a torch and a blanket in his hands.

'I thought you'd changed your mind ay! I was going to bring you a blanket. It gets quite cold at night.'

'Ah thanks, mate. Very kind of you.'

'Listen Sean, you seem a nice guy. Why don't you stay in the house? It's warm, I have beer and my flatmate is away so you can have her room.'

I wasn't sure. He looked pretty rough and a little drunk too.

'Where you from mate?' Roland asked. 'I detect an accent.'

'I live in London at the moment.'

'No way. I'm originally from Liverpool. I even have a dog called Scouse. Come and meet him."

A bed would be nice, I guess. Better than a damp garage. Also Rowland seemed a little too drunk to be a real threat anyway.

'Are you sure, mate? As long as it's no problem. Also I have to leave at around 5 a.m. if that's cool.'

Roland led me around the back where I left Maid Marian and we went inside. Scouse, the little white Jack Russell terrier, started to bark at me. Roland was having none of it and banished him to the kitchen.

'Beer mate?'

'OK thanks. That would be great.'

We chatted for about an hour as he told me all about his life in Liverpool as a kid, which mainly revolved around smoking and drinking in the park. He was a funny chap.

Roland took me through to his flatmate's bedroom. I opened the door to see a huge poster of tigers on the wall. She did like cats. It didn't stop there. She had cat ornaments, cat toys, cat stickers on her mirrors, photos with her and cats. Pretty much everything in the room was cat oriented, except her duvet, which was a dog. Maybe they ran out of cat ones and that was the next best thing?

'How old is your flatmate, Roland?' I asked, worried that she was twelve.

'She is twenty-eight mate. Yeah, it's weird.'

The following morning, the mist rolled in as the sun was coming up. Although quite scenic I couldn't really make the most of it because there still wasn't much of a hard shoulder. It was a lot colder than I had planned because I should have been in Australia at the beginning of April instead of the end, which would have been a bit warmer. Once I got going it was OK: it's just those first few minutes that bite deep. If it was going to be this cold I'd definitely need to get some winter gloves. My fingerless ones were just not cutting it.

The rest of the afternoon was pretty uneventful except that the forested areas I cycled through smelled like my shower gel. At least it masked the actual smell coming from my clothes. Eventually, at around 4 p.m., I managed to find a slightly quieter route off the main side road. I pulled off and hadn't gone more than 100 m when a car came up beside me and a man shouted out the window.

'Are you a crazy Conway?'

I looked through the window hoping to recognise who it was, but he didn't look familiar at all. He pulled over and I came up alongside wracking my brain as to where I may have met him before.

'Hey, Sean. My name is George. You don't know me but I know your father from Rhodesia days. Your cousins in Brisbane mentioned you might be coming up this way so I've been tracking you. I was waiting on the main road. Luckily I saw you duck down this road or I'd have missed you.'

It was nice to know one person at least was following my tracker.

'Listen, where are you staying tonight?' George asked. 'I live about 30 miles further along and you're more than welcome to stay and have a shower and a real bed.'

I had only done 105 miles and if I stayed with George I'd land up doing only 135 miles. But it did mean I'd get a real bed and possibly some local knowledge about the route heading north that wasn't the busy A1. It was worth it.

'That would be great.'

'Can I give you a lift?'

No thanks. I'm not allowed lifts really.' It was so tempting though because technically the 30 miles was off-route. I had set myself a goal though, and wanted to stick to it.

'No problem. It's easy. Ten miles ahead there is a T-junction. Turn right then look out for some cane fields on the right. I'm in there somewhere. Follow your nose. I'm sure you'll work it out.'

I managed all the way to the cane fields with no problems but then didn't really know where to go. I came across a small farm road that had some recent tyre tracks so decided that's where my nose would take me. I cut through the cane fields and out the other side to a larger field. About a mile further along was a water tower and what looked like a large aerial within a clump of trees. I headed that way completely off the road and through the muddy field. It wasn't the easiest cycling I've done, especially on race tyres, but I still felt excited because, even if it was for only a mile, I was on an off-road adventure trying to find a house with my nose.

I came up to the house and knocked on the door. An old man, who wasn't George, answered.

'Sorry to bother you. Does George live anywhere around here?'

'Over at that next clump of trees.' He pointed slightly back to where I had cycled past.

George had moved from Zimbabwe a while back and taken up farming. He was now a retired farmer who had a few fruit trees to pay the bills. I liked the idea of that. It seemed like quite a good retirement fund. Instead of paying into a pension, buy a small plot of land, plant some fruit trees and sell them. It also gave you something to do in your old age. What a great idea.

I nearly froze my fingers off leaving George's farm at 5 a.m. It was by far the coldest I had been since I started. Because of my shorter day I decided to push on to Gladstone, which was 150 miles away. I had a good tailwind and put my head down all day. I was pushing it a little fast and by the time I reached Gladstone was a little dehydrated. I wasn't in the mood to camp under a bush, so splashed out on a hotel that was attached to the pub.

I really needed to do something about the cold and also finally decided that some sort of shelter was in order to cope with the dewy nights. The next morning my first port of call was Rockhampton. I arrived at 10 a.m. and nothing seemed open at all. I had no idea what day it was but I was almost certain it wasn't the weekend. Eventually, after wandering the empty streets looking for food, I was told it was a bank holiday. If anything were to be open it would only be at 11 a.m. Rockhampton was a fairly large town so I decided to head all the way through it and try and find some food and a camping shop.

Finding food was simple but getting some sort of tent shelter wasn't. There was nothing suitable less than a kilo. After trying various outdoor shops I decided to buy a large waterproof tarp sheet and then cut it down to a usable size. Worst case, I could just put it over me at night to stop the dew settling on me. By 9 p.m. that evening, I had done 140 miles. A little short but it was to be expected after all my faffing around trying to find a tent. I saw a sign for a campsite so decided to see if I could get some free accommodation. Not only did I get a free night's stay, the lovely campsite owner gave me three eggs, some potatoes, tinned soup, half a loaf of bread and some milk. There was a communal kitchen that I could use and a fridge to leave anything I didn't eat. How kind of her. Just as she was walking away she warned me that her father was a little senile and might come and wake me up in the night asking me whether I had paid or not. I laughed at the idea of an old man knocking on people's doors demanding payment. I love old people. I'm going to be a nightmare pensioner.

I settled in for the night. Not only was I now sheltered, it was also a little bit warmer. Just as I was nodding off I heard a huge splash from the pool near me. It was midnight. Why on earth was someone swimming at this time? I couldn't see them but heard them splash around a little. They couldn't have been in there for more than a minute before I saw a guy, around my age, walking across the field pushing a bike. He was in full cycling gear, and dripping wet. He pushed his bike back to the road before jumping back on it and disappearing back into the darkness. For the first time since getting back on the bike I properly thought about how I wasn't racing anymore. It made me sad. I missed racing. I missed having to find ways to get sweat off your clothes at midnight. I so had it in me to break the record before the accident but was now busting my back for no real reason at all. It wasn't fair.

The following morning was slow and boring. I didn't care to explore. I wasn't in the mood at all. I kept my head low and music loud as I pushed the miles along. The scenery wasn't changing much, which just added to my foul mood. The only positive thing that happened all morning was a recommendation I got from a gas station attendant to do a quiet route that went off the main road. He was right. It was a lot better but only because there was less chance of getting run over, and the scenery was still the same.

I was just about coming to the end of the side road when I saw a guy pushing a trolley ahead of me. I pulled up beside him. He had a child's pram with a solar panel on the top. On the front it said, *OzOnFoot.com – Walking for Cancer.* He looked about my age and wore a very tattered hat with a flap that covered his neck. It had started out life very pink but was nearly white with the amount of sun it had received. He really could have done with a new one but I know what it's like when you have something for so long it becomes part of you.

'Wow, around the world?' The guy, who was called Andrew, looked impressed when I told him what I was doing. 'That's cool. I'm just walking around Australia. It's for my friend Simmo, who died from complications related to myelodysplasia.'

'Sorry to hear that. That's incredible.'

My little self-centred ride fell into insignificance when compared to his incredible journey. I felt like an idiot for being in a foul mood all day. This chap was pushing a huge pram all the way around Australia for his friend who died. I needed to get things into perspective a little.

'I'm actually on day 499 today,' Andrew told me. 'I've got another two months I think. I finish in Sydney.'

'That's nearly two years on the road. Wow! How much food and water do you carry? Where do you sleep? How far do you walk a day?'

I had so many questions.

'I sleep wherever I can, carry just about enough food for a week and generally walk about 70 km a day, but if there is a headwind then a lot less.'

I hadn't thought about headwinds for walking but I guess if you are pushing such a wide load it would be a lot harder. Also 70 km per day was nearly two marathons, while pushing that cart. Amazing. Andrew showed me more of his setup. He had a solar panel charging a little motorbike battery, which powered everything from his phone to a small fan, which he used to keep flies off his face in the outback. Genius. But I guess after 499 days you've ironed out all the problems. I also loved the little rear-view mirror he had installed. It was a very cool setup. He told me that he had been through nineteen pairs of trainers, and judging by the ones he was wearing he could have done with a few more in that time. They were pretty tattered.

'So is there anything I need to worry about?' I asked. 'Any headwinds?'

'Mate. I went the wrong way round and have had headwinds for the last six months pretty much. Probably more. I've given up counting. You'll have a tailwind all the way to Darwin.'

A six-month headwind? Shit! And there I was complaining about three days of headwind in America. I needed to man up.

I jumped back on Maid Marian with a new sense of reality and purpose. It's strange how things work. The gas station attendant could easily have not bothered to recommend the quieter back road. I would have not met Andrew and I'd still be grumpy. Sometimes things just happened and today was one of those days. What an inspiration.

*It saddened me to hear that soon after Andrew completed his incredible walk, he was tragically killed in a motorcycle accident. He was a true adventurer and a real inspiration.*

*Rest in peace Andrew 'Cad' Cadigan.*

# 15

# THE EXCITEMENT RETURNS

The days were definitely getting warmer the further north I rode. That suited me just fine. As I said earlier, I preferred the heat. Not much happened for a few days as I averaged around 170 miles per day. My final stop along the busy Pacific Highway coastal route was Townsville. From there I'd head west along the Overlanders Way highway and right into the heart of the great Australian outback.

I had no idea what lay before me but I definitely needed to get a few more supplies. First on the list was a set of new tyres as I was certain I couldn't get any in the outback, and secondly, a couple of extra water bottles, which I tied to the front forks. I could now happily carry four and a half litres of water, which should hopefully see me through the long stretches of nothingness. It was a fine line deciding how much water to carry. Water is one of the heaviest things on your bike. The more water you carry, the slower you go, so you therefore need more water. It's a catch 22. I still haven't worked out the exact system but I figured four and a half litres should do me 80 miles in the heat with no headwind. It was all total guesswork because I had no idea how long my longest stretch would be.

I felt extremely excited and a little nervous about heading right into the middle of Australia. Right up till now I hadn't really had too many long gaps between towns. Even in the Atacama there were truck stops spaced every 60 miles or so. This Outback stretch was surely going to test me.

The first bit out of Townsville was a small climb passing a huge sign saying OVERLANDERS WAY. Seeing the sign made me nervous. It felt real now. The roads remained fairly good and were a lot quieter than the Pacific Highway. There also seemed to be a lot more dead kangaroos around. One every few miles. I felt sorry for the little buggers. I still hadn't seen a live one yet. But if there were that many dead ones it surely wouldn't be long.

It was great to be able to switch off a little. The concentration needed for busy roads really took the energy out of me. I pushed on towards Charters Towers where I would probably need to sleep for the night. It was the last major town before a few long stretches and I wanted to get a good sleep and a decent breakfast in the morning. I managed to find a small campsite and the owners offered me a free patch of grass. Although I had only done 125 miles I was starving, so after setting up my shelter I went off for some food. The nearest place open happened to be a pretty posh restaurant. I looked at my clothes. They were pretty tattered and dirty. I thought they'd never let me in but they did. Most of the menu was pretty standard until I came across Crocodile Pasta. Done! I'd only ever had crocodile once and it could very well have been chicken anyway. I was really excited. The outback awaited and I was having crocodile for dinner. Life couldn't be better.

I'd been warned of the big hills to come as I approached the Australian dividing range the following morning. Looking ahead it didn't seem possible but maybe they were hidden beyond the curve of the earth. I'd climbed ever so slightly to around 700 m when I came across a sign saying I was at the top of the dividing range. I burst out laughing. They could not be serious. That wasn't a hill. But I guess when you live in a place that is pretty flat, 700 m is huge. At least I had a small downhill to get excited about. I started down the other side in tri position with my hand under my chin in thinking mode. As I was switching off, something caught my eye in the bushes about 100 m ahead of me. It was moving quite quickly. Was it a kangaroo, my first live kangaroo? I was excited. Yes it was. It was bouncing gracefully at about 45 degrees to the road. It was quite a small one. I was in a trance as I bombed down the hill and my new friend bounced through the grass. We were finally almost right next to each other when the kangaroo decided to change direction and head straight for the road where I was just about to pass. I was still in tri position with my hand under my chin and before I knew it, it jumped right across the road only a few feet from my front wheel. I didn't have any time to react but swerved into the road while trying to balance and get out of tri position. I was already a full 20 metres past when I had recovered and managed to look back to see it but it was gone. I slowed down a bit. Stupid bloody animals. No wonder they all get run over.

There are towns almost every 30 miles or so through this section, which made it pretty easy cycling. My first stop included a brief stop for a pie and to refill my water bottles.

The truck-stop owner was a real character. He wore very short shorts straight out of 1973 and an open shirt revealing a much-sunburned belly. He also said he had the cure for cancer but the 'corporates' kept it very quiet. The truck-stop owner said he had cancer but was passed down an old recipe, which was a mixture of bicarbonate soda and authentic Canadian maple syrup. Apparently, if you had it three times a day you'd be cured in six months. He was deadly serious too.

There wasn't much between stops, which meant I switched off a lot as I kept my head down. The quiet was however disturbed every 20 minutes or so by one of Australia's famous road trains. I had heard of them but still didn't really know what to expect. Luckily, they didn't really sneak up on you because they were HUGE! The first one I saw came up from behind me. I had no idea it was a road train at first because from the front it just looked like a huge truck. It was only when it bombed past me that I realised how immense it was: a massive American-style truck with four long trailers winding from left to right as it snaked along the middle of the road. I got such a fright the first time, I ended up going off the road. The wall of wind the road trains brought with them was incredible. I had to hold on tight as the gust smacked me on the back of the head, and then lean a little away from the road so that the draft of it going past didn't suck me in. The one good thing was that the road-train drivers were extremely cautious and gave a lot of space. This was only possible when there was no oncoming traffic. I'd most certainly have to move off the road if there was oncoming traffic.

By 6 p.m. I'd only managed 125 miles. It was the third day in a row that I was under mileage. Even with the tailwind I just didn't feel like I was getting into the swing of things.

I was about 30 miles from Hughenden and stopped in a café, which was just about to close. The very friendly owner decided to stay open and make me a huge bowl of spaghetti carbonara. It was incredible. Halfway through my dinner her son came in and offered me a few beers. I landed up staying there for nearly two hours as I chatted and found out more about life in the Outback.

I very nearly decided to quit for the night and stay in the family's garden but fuelled by two beers decided to push on to Hughenden to make up the mileage. I left the café and hadn't gone more than five miles when I saw the lights of Hughenden ahead of me. It looked no more than a few miles away. I stopped and looked at my map to double check I was going the right way again. I was but Hughenden was most definitely still twenty-five miles away. Maybe there was another town in between. I carried on but this town never got any closer. For two hours the lights stayed on the horizon until I eventually came into Hughenden. The air was so crisp and the road so flat that you could see for miles.

The following morning I made good progress. The wind picked up nicely and I managed to push out 75 miles in five hours. The roads were flat and very quiet: I could listen to music and not have to keep my wits about me every few seconds. The temperature reached 42 degrees by midday and I was drinking about a litre every hour. Although I was running out of water fast, I knew I'd make it to Richmond in time so didn't worry too much about it. It was slightly more humid than the Atacama but not too bad. At least it wasn't raining. I was going to push through and not stop again when a young guy in his late twenties wearing skinny jeans, thongs (an Australian word for flip-flops) and a T-shirt, came walking into the road waving me down. He had been parked at a roadside stop. I slowed down.

'Hey, man. My name is Frederik. My girlfriend and I have seen you for two days now. We keep overtaking you. How are you doing so much kilometres?' He spoke with a slight European accent.

'Yeah, I'm trying to get back to London by July for the Olympics, so I'm pushing it a bit.'

'Wow. When we saw you this time my girlfriend and I made you a plate of food. Come and join us.'

I walked over to the bench where his girlfriend, who introduced herself as Natalie, had literally made me a feast. Some cheese, ham, nice bread (it had been a while since I'd had some good old wholegrain bread) and fruit. What a treat. Frederik and Natalie were from Switzerland and had hired a car to travel around Australia for a few months. Such a lovely couple. Although younger than me, Natalie was forcing food down me like my mother would.

'Come on, eat. You need it,' she kept saying with a huge grin on her face.

After a feast and stocking up with some water I said goodbye and carried on. They overtook me about ten miles later with huge cheers and a loud hoot. This Outback leg was turning out to be a really friendly experience and a lot less harsh and barren than I expected. I also now had more than enough water to get me to Richmond, which meant I could pour some on my baking head to cool me down. What a luxury!

Richmond was the last town before a 100-mile stretch of nothingness. This was going to be the longest section I had done with no food or water since I began. There was a huge fountain just before the town, which was far too inviting to miss out on. My clothes were starting to get brittle again with the amount of salt build-up and I really needed to wash them out. The fountain was no ordinary one. There was a mushroom-shaped sculpture with water coming out the top and falling all around. I stood there surprised at how cold it was for a good ten minutes. It was the most refreshing thing I'd done since that cold shower at the edge of the Atacama.

For some reason the supermarket in Richmond was closed, so I could only stock up on supplies from a small service station. It wasn't ideal but I wasn't worried about food. It was water that I was concerned about. Four and a half litres to do 100 miles was pushing it a little. Before doing a long stretch it's best to eat and drink as much as you can so that you can do at least the first hour without food or water. You can probably hold a litre and a half of water in your stomach, which makes a lot of difference towards the end of the day.

I managed the first 20 miles without touching my water supplies, but once my stomach was empty the water started to deplete quite quickly. It was about 33 degrees, which was a little cooler than it had been. The problem was that there was a tailwind that was exactly the same speed as I was cycling. I found myself in this bubble of warm air. I tried to push it a bit to get a cool breeze on my face but became too tired. I then slowed down to try and get a slight tailwind on the back of my neck, but that was too slow and would add an hour to my ride, meaning I'd definitely run out of water. I had no choice but to plod along in a heat bubble. The other problem with going the same speed as the wind is that the flies keep up and you also suddenly realise how smelly you are. And this was *after* my fountain shower. I tried to drink only one litre every 20 miles but soon started to get a headache and knew I was getting dehydrated. I decided to drink an entire litre just in case, which then left me two litres for the last 50 miles to Julia Creek. It was 4 p.m. and I knew at least it would start getting cooler. Could I make it through?

I rode on into the evening getting slower and slower. I was tired and getting quite hungry. I was still 20 miles from Julia Creek when I eventually ran out of water. I stopped on the side of the road and rested for a bit. I needed to make it to Julia Creek. I pretty much had no food or water left and I needed something before bed otherwise I'd crash massively in the morning.

It took me over two hours to do that last 20 miles and was dark by the time I sluggishly I made my way into the town. I stopped at the first sign of life, the Julia Creek Hotel, a white wooden double-storey building with a blue balcony all around. The warm glow streaming out the windows took my mind away from the fact I was on the verge of serious dehydration. I stumbled through the door and fell onto the stool at the bar. There were about ten people also sitting at the bar. Conversation stopped as I sat there staring into nothingness. It had been a long hard 170 miles and I really needed some food and water.

'Jeez mate, you've come far, ain't ya?'

'Hey, yeah. Long day on the bike. I've come from Hughenden.'

'No way, mate. That's over 250 km.'

I ordered a glass of water and asked the bar lady if she had any food. She didn't but said she had crisps. That would have to do.

'What you drinking water for, mate. Come one, I'll get you a beer. Oi, sexy!' he shouted to the bar lady. 'Give this dude a schooner, will you?'

'Shut your mouth you old hag!' laughed the bar lady. Everyone seemed to know each other. It was pretty jovial.

'So where you from, mate?' asked a younger chap who didn't have nearly as harsh an accent as the others.

'I live in London at the moment.'

'No way, I'm from Croydon, south London.'

The guy, Jason, was a little drunk but incredibly friendly: he had a caravan in his garden that I could stay in. After another schooner (a glass slightly smaller than a pint of beer) Jason and I wandered off down the back streets of Julia Creek. Most of the houses were bungalows with a corrugated iron roof, a large garden and a fence with a 'Beware of the dog' sign on it. I'd figured Jason's caravan was disused and rusty, so was taken aback to find a brand new, incredibly clean caravan in the open garage next to the house. Jason went and got me a towel and said I could have a shower. The evening was turning out pretty well for me considering at one point a few hours outside of Julia Creek I very nearly decided to give up for the day and sleep under a bush.

The next morning I had another big day ahead: 170 miles to Mount Isa with another 90-mile stretch in the middle with nothing. This time, however, I was told by a builder at breakfast I would be able to fill my water bottle at a roadside stop after around 45 miles. This was a great relief because I wasn't in the mood for another long, dehydrated session. I put my head down, pretty keen to get the first 45 miles out the way. With more water available I knew I could push it a bit and not worry. By the time I had reached the water stop I had drunk three and a half litres, which only left me a litre. I felt good though, and it hit home how dehydrated I must have been the day before.

As the builder had mentioned, at the road stop was a huge tank of water. I got all my bottles out in a row and turned on the tap. Nothing came out. I waited for a while but there was nothing at all. I hit the side of the tank. I'm not tank expert but it sounded decidedly empty. I tried to feel if the bottom half of the tank was colder than the top half, which happens where there is water in it, but again, nothing. I sat down. There was no way I'd make the 45 miles with only one litre of water. I'd have to ask a driver when they came past. I figured it would be harder to stop a car, so waited patiently at the roadside stop for someone to come by. After about 20 minutes a car and caravan stopped. I was just walking over to explain my situation when the driver saw me and said.

'Hey, didn't we see you yesterday just outside Julia Creek? You've done well today!'

'Not that well, actually. I thought I could get water here, but it's empty.'

'Well, we have loads. Come inside. Can we make you a cup of tea?'

Although it was 32 degrees a cup of tea sounded like a great idea. We chatted for a while, and I discovered all about Silver Nomads. They are all the older generation who when retired sell their house, buy a caravan and travel around Australia for years and years. I hadn't really noticed it but when looking back it was true. At least eighty per cent of the campers I had seen looked older than sixty. I liked the idea of that.

After my cup of tea and filling my bottles I hit the road again. The route towards Mount Isa was getting a little hillier, which was a welcome break from the monotony of the flat roads I'd been on for days. I stopped again for lunch at another roadside café where I met a few more Silver Nomads before the start of one of the big climbs of the day. I must have climbed for about half an hour before realising my food bag wasn't on Maid Marian anymore. I stopped and realised I had left it at the roadside café. I looked at the map to see if I could make Mount Isa without food, but it was still a good six hours away. I had to turn back. It only took me ten minutes to get all the way back down to where I had left it on the bench next to where I was sitting. I put it back on and started the long climb back up the hill again. That little detour along with the time I'd to wait for water had put me over an hour behind schedule. I decided that I should treat myself to a motel after two long days.

The hills kept coming as I cycled into the night. If it wasn't for the fact I was going to stay in a motel I would have given up earlier, but eventually, at 11.30 p.m., I made it to Mount Isa. I stopped at the first motel I could find. They had a few rooms but the cheapest was $150. That was too much so I carried on to the next one. It had a sign on the door saying full, as did the next two. Eventually I found one that didn't and went in and asked. They too were full but forgot to put the sign up. The receptionist was very friendly and phoned around for me. Turned out there was only one with a room available. It was $80 and still another five miles out of town. I was too tired to carry on, plus I also needed to be near the centre of town for breakfast and to refill my almost empty supplies. I carried on towards town looking for another place to stay. I was almost near the city centre, right by the Tourist Office, when I saw a small park on the right, with a row of bushes surrounding a picnic table. I figured if I went behind the bush it would put me out of sight. I waited for the roads to be empty before ducking down to inspect my camp spot. It was perfect: out of the wind, out of sight and on soft green grass. I was glad I hadn't wasted $80 when this place did the job.

I wrapped up warm under the bush tying my sleeping bag really tight so that the hole was the size of a tennis ball. The nights were getting quite cold after all. I was asleep even before my head hit the pillow I'd made out of my cycle jackets. But not for long.

*Crash, crash, thunder.* In the middle of the night I woke to feel water pouring in through the small hole. I woke up with the biggest fright I've ever had. I thought the world was coming to an end. Why was it raining? Nothing in the forecast suggested rain. I sat up and struggled out of the small tennis ball-sized hole. I sat there for a moment still a bit confused and sleepy trying to work out where I was. I looked up to the clouds to see the rain but it wasn't coming from above. It was coming from below. That didn't make sense. I was even more confused. I looked down and then realised what had happened: I had cleverly decided to sleep about one foot from a pop-out-the-ground sprinkler that was designed to water the bush I was under. I jumped up and tried to use my tarp which I had used as a mattress to cover the water. I eventually managed to stop it and get everything out the way. Still a bit perplexed I stood there completely wet. Everything was drenched: Maid Marian, my clothes, my bags, my sleeping bag, the works. It was quite cold and I started to shiver, not really knowing what to do. It was 4 a.m. and too early to get up and go. I tried to put my sleeping bag back in the stuff sack but it was too wet and just wouldn't fit. Also I didn't really want to have a wet sleeping bag for the next night. I decided that the only option was to get back into my cold wet sleeping bag and hope that my body heat would dry it. It was a long shot, but I figured if I moved to the picnic bench where it was a bit windier it might work. I moved everything onto the picnic table and squeezed back into the bag and fell asleep again still thinking that maybe it had all been a dream.

I managed to sleep until 7 a.m. under the picnic table, waking to find a few homeless people on another bench staring at me. I looked around to see if anything had been stolen but all seemed to be intact. My theory had worked. The wind and my body heat had dried my sleeping bag. At least something had worked out in my favour after a pretty disastrous night.

# 16

# NOTHINGNESS

The next leg was 130 miles of nothing. I figured that because I had done two fairly big days I wouldn't go further than the next major town, which was Camooweal. That way I'd be able to get a good dinner and breakfast there before the next very long stretch of nothing. With a short day of 130 miles ahead I took my time in Mount Isa getting breakfast, water and stocking up on supplies for the day. I bought two footlong Italian BMT sandwiches from Subway and also decided to get another one-and-a-half-litre bottle of water, bringing my total to six litres. If I left Mount Isa with a full belly I wouldn't need to drink for at least the first 20 miles. I'd then have six litres for the remaining 110 miles. That was just about doable. After a breakfast of pancakes and chocolate cake I drank nearly two litres of water before struggling to get on Maid Marian. I thought I was going to explode, my stomach was so full.

The route out of Mount Isa started off northerly before turning slightly northwest again. It got a lot hotter as the morning sun rose higher. This route followed an old World War Two road. Why was there a World War Two road in the middle of Australia? I wished I had taken history at school. The day continued to get hotter and by 2 p.m. it was 38 degrees and I had only managed 40 miles. I still had another 90 miles to go. It's a daunting idea in this heat to try and carry eight kilos of food and water: that's basically the same weight as a Tour de France race bike. I chuckled slightly to myself at the idea of Bradley Wiggins cycling along with another bike strapped to his back. Considering I drank and ate around three kilos of food and water for breakfast, and I'd eat and drink another seven during the day, I was consuming my entire body weight every six days. That was a scary thought. I had managed to put on some weight after the accident but most of it had gone again and I was back at around 64 kg. My stomach just wasn't big enough to eat as much as I needed to.

The flies also started to get quite bad the further into the outback I went. They seemed really aggressive too, trying to burrow between where my sunglasses met my cheek. My salty skin must have been some sort of catnip for flies because they seemed to be going a bit crazy. They loved the vacuum of air that was in front of my face caused by the fairly strong tailwind I was getting. I've never complained about a tailwind but there were a few times that afternoon where I had a slight sense of humour failure. How did these bloody flies survive out here? Why were there so many? I'm pretty sure I even ate one that landed on my sandwich at lunch.

I pushed on through the afternoon and into the evening, my two long hot days taking their toll, but I didn't feel too bad knowing I only had 130 miles to do. I was managing my food and water quite well and would drink one litre every hour and eat a footlong every two hours. I finally felt in control of my adventure and knew how to cope in the outback.

I was about three miles from Camooweal when I got a puncture on my front tyre. Luckily it was a slow puncture, meaning I was able to pump it up every 500 m instead of changing the tyre in the dark. It was on the fourth time I had to pump the tyre when I saw the light from a truck coming up behind me. I knew straight away it was a road train. It was bombing along as I was still half straddling Maid Marian while leaning over to pump her front tyre. I then noticed the truck moving ever so slightly towards the side of the road. I stopped pumping and lifted my head. Maybe the driver hadn't seen me. Surely he could. His lights were still on full beam. After another 20 m he was still heading dangerously close to where I was standing. Surely he'd seen me? I stood up and waved my hand in the air. At that moment the truck swerved right into the middle of the road with the long tail of trailers weaving back and forth while the tyres screeched along the tarmac. In the same moment I kind of fell backwards with Maid Marian as I tried to get us out of the way, only just managing to keep upright. By the time I got everything out of the way the truck was a good 100 m past snaking along the middle of the road. That was a close one.

'Bonjour Sean.'

In Camooweal, I'd found a small pub that had a campsite out back. When I arrived, there were two French lads, Mikael and Alain, washing up from the meal they had just cooked. They were off to do strawberry picking on a farm for a while to fund the rest of their gap year around Australia. It turned out we were both leaving at around 6 a.m. and they offered to make me some breakfast, which I gladly accepted.

'Morning chaps,' I said still blurry eyed as I crawled out of my sleeping bag. It was still dark.

'You want some juice? I have orange and apple.'

When the French do travelling food they do it properly. When the pair had offered me breakfast the night before, I was thinking cornflakes and maybe some bread. Mikael and Alain went the whole hog with eggs, fruit, juice, yogurt and even a proper tablecloth which they put over the bench. It was brilliant.

My next leg was 200 miles with no food or water stops. I only just about made the previous 130 miles with six litres and I still had no idea what I was going to do. We were just finishing up when Mikael finished the last of his water from a 1.5 litre bottle and threw it in the bin. I suddenly had an idea. What if I got them to leave this bottle about 70 miles ahead and then another one 150 miles ahead? Mikael and Alain were happy to oblige and after looking at the map we decided to leave the water below the signpost signalling the next picnic spot. If there was no signpost then right next to the road at the entrance to the picnic spot would be fine too. The only problem was that they didn't have another water bottle to leave at 150 miles. We searched every bin, the back of their camper, everywhere, but nothing. I'd just have to make do with one water refill. I now had 7.5 litres for 200 miles but hoped that I'd be able to find someone at the next picnic spot and ask them to do the same.

This part of the outback was pretty barren. There had been trees for most of my route but now there were patches of nothing but grass. It was still pretty quiet on the roads, which was good for cycling but not so good for trying to find someone to take more water ahead for me. If the French guys pulled through I'd have enough for the rest of today but still needed a few litres for tomorrow. I really needed to find someone to ask. I figured the best thing was to get the bottle the French guys left and then give another driver the empty bottle and hope they had some spare water for me. I felt pretty organised for the first time even if my organisation relied completely on someone else.

I was still about 20 miles from where the French chaps had hopefully left my water when a car drove up next to me.

'Wow, you've done well mate,' the lady shouted across from the driver's seat. Her husband in the passenger seat barely looked up and kept reading the paper. He wasn't interested at all. I recognised them though. They were a couple I had met a few days before at the picnic spot where I forgot my food before Mount Isa. She stopped and jumped out the car with a bag of nuts and two apples.

'I thought you might need some food. It's quite desolate out here.'

What a lovely lady and the perfect person to ask to leave me more water. She didn't have a big bottle but managed to find two small ones and filled them from the five-litre bottle she had. We looked at the map and I asked her to leave them another 100 miles ahead, which would be about two hours before the end of my day. Perfect. If the French guys forgot then I'd have a back-up plan. If I managed to get both drop-offs then I'd almost have too much water, which was never a bad thing.

The plan worked. I was happy to find the first bottle exactly under the sign we had guessed would be there. Even though it was practically boiling from sitting in the sun all day at least I could fill up my stock.

The couple didn't forget and just as before I had another litre of boiling hot water to keep me going. I felt a lot better now that I definitely had enough food and water. I worked my way towards a rest stop where I stopped for the night. I wrapped myself up in a little cocoon and fell asleep on the stony ground.

My next stop was Three Ways where I met the north-south road heading through the heart of Australia. A few hundred miles south was Ayers Rock. I was initially a bit gutted that I hadn't planned my route past it but was told that the flies were sometimes so bad you'd easily have 100 on you at any one time. That sounded like hell. I got another puncture near Three Ways and after faffing around I decided to stay there the night. I was feeling a lot more tired than I should have felt. I think the last few days had taken it out of me a little. I had only done 130 miles but I was still on target to hit Darwin on time. After a nice bowl of spaghetti Bolognese and a few beers that a very drunk and overfriendly motorbike tourer bought me, I decided to treat myself to a motel for the night. I really needed to wash my clothes, with soap this time!

A short day plus a proper bed completely revived me. I left Three Ways heading north towards Darwin in great spirits. I hadn't gone more than a few hundred metres when I hit a huge stone in the road and got a pinch flat. As I've said before they are the worst because they are a lot harder to fix. I patched the inner tube and put the tyre back on the rim, which always hurt my back. After using tyre levers I got the tyre back on and continued. I couldn't have gone more than 100 metres when I got another pinch flat. I stopped again, cursing the road. I inspected the tyre and discovered my patch hadn't quite stuck and it had leaked some air. The self-stick patches are convenient but not as adhesive. I decided to get rid of that tube and put a new one in. That was my last inner tube. I always like to keep two spare but had somehow lost one. The problem with having Continental GP4000s tyres is because they don't get punctures very much, you get a bit negligent at keeping spares. Another lesson learned. Keep more than two spare inners.

Fitted with a new inner I carried on towards Elliott, which was 140 miles away. I went another 20 miles and got yet another puncture. I fixed it and carried on but a few miles later got another one. It didn't make sense: my tyre wasn't worn and the road didn't seem that bad. Four punctures in four hours: damn the Puncture Gods! My back was starting to feel it every time I tried pulling the rubber over the rim. Just before I arrived in Pamayu, I got my fifth puncture for the day. I flopped down on the side of the road. How was this possible? Fitting that fifth tyre really put my back under strain. It wasn't nearly as bad as that time in Arizona but still enough to need to rest it. I limped into Pamayu roadhouse and sat down under a tree. I had only done 88 miles, my second sub-100-mile day. I hated it. I felt bad for stopping so early but knew I need to rest up.

I was umming and ahhing as to whether getting back on the bike would warm me up and help a bit. I was just going to give it a go when two girls came over from the campsite next to the roadhouse.

'Hey, how's it going?'

They were English.

'I'm good thanks, just taking a break from the heat.'

'Yeah, it's proper hot. We're hot in the car. I can't imagine cycling. Where you are heading?'

'Elliott for the night.'

'Elliott? Don't go there,' they said looking worried. 'We don't know why but we've been told on three separate occasions that whatever happens we are NOT to stop in Elliott. It's very dodgy apparently. Full of homeless people.'

'Really? It can't be that bad.'

'That's what we thought, but after the third person literally made us swear not to go there we thought we'd stay here instead.'

I was now even more intrigued. I hadn't seen anything even remotely 'dodgy' at all in Australia. Everywhere seemed pretty pleasant and safe. What was this place?

'You are more than welcome to stay with us. We are in the van but have a tent for you if you want.'

I didn't know what to do. I was in two minds. My back was sore and I could really do with the rest, but then I had also only done 88 miles and hated doing a short day. I also had survived many parts of the world that were surely a lot more dangerous. I'd hate to find out that Elliott was in fact not that bad. In the end, I convinced myself I needed to rest my back anyway. I'd find out what Elliott had to offer in the morning.

Kate and Jessica were nineteen years old, lived in Surrey and were on a gap year. They were on their way to Darwin to look for bar work for a few months before carrying on their adventure. They had bought a van from another traveller, who had bought it from another traveller, and, well, you get the idea. It was a 1990s VW Camper and judging by the number of coats of paint it had, it seemed it had had its fair share of adventures.

The two girls invited me for dinner, which was nice of them. They were cooking, or heating rather, a can of spaghetti and meatballs while sitting in the doorway of the van. They only had one set of cutlery too, which we shared. I laughed at the difference in food choice between the French chaps and these two English girls. What a contrast. I pictured an Outback Traveller style *Come Dine With Me.* Although the tinned spaghetti meatballs were surprisingly good the French chaps definitely would have won hands down. I mean, they even had a tablecloth!

The next morning, it was about 40 miles to Elliott and I was really interested to see what all the fuss was about. On approaching I noticed that it looked a little rundown, with broken road signs, uncut grass and disused plots of land full of rubbish. There was a roadhouse in the centre of the town where I had to stop and get some food. Opposite the station on the grass were about six people lying on the grass. They kind of looked homeless I guess. I went and got some food and as I sat outside on the park bench to eat, a stray dog came over and started foraging around the bins. This was different to the last few towns I had come through. The town seemed forgotten in history and a little neglected, but I didn't feel threated at all. I would have probably been all right finding a bush to crawl under but under the cover of darkness it probably looked like any old town. In my experience it's often the poorer people in the world who are the friendliest. Another reason not to listen to the naysayers.

There were a lot more stops in this part of the outback heading north, so I didn't need to carry the extra water bottles. I kept the two fork bottles though just in case. About 15 minutes after leaving Elliott Kate and Jessica drove past and stopped. They offered me some water and for the first time I actually didn't need any. It felt good to say that. They were hoping to get to Darwin by the afternoon and we promised to catch up when I finally arrived.

There seemed to be a lot more dead kangaroos on the road here for some reason. It was sad to sometimes see a mother and baby lying dead on the road. I also cycled past a herd of about ten cattle that had also been wiped out by a road train. It was carnage: carcasses lying everywhere. I felt ill. It was such a terrible sight. Road trains can't stop for anything and are equipped with huge bull bars to deal with these sorts of accidents. Apparently the average truck hits about twenty kangaroos each night. I could well believe it.

By 7 p.m. I had made it to Daly Waters and found the only place that looked open, the Daly Waters Pub. It was heaving, the busiest place I had seen outside of Mount Isa. There must have been 100 people in the pub and spilling out into the beer garden. Where did they all come from? Hanging from the ceiling were hundreds of caps and scarves and you couldn't see the walls because they were covered in thousands of beer mats, and various notes of money from all over the world. It was an OCD nightmare but I loved it. I ordered a schooner and heard an eruption of laughter from outside. I went through to the beer garden area where they had a rustic, corrugated stage set up and a guy in his late fifties, wearing a Stetson cowboy hat, was playing the guitar and singing what must have been a politically humorous Australian parody or something because everyone one laughed at something that didn't make any sense to me.

'This is the Daly Waters Pub and listen, you can have a good time tonight, you can roll around, you can drink yourself stupid, you can brawl, you can fight, whatever, because this is the only pub in the world that the bouncers throw you back in.' Everyone cheered. What an amazing pub and what an amazing character. The guy was called Chilli and he has been performing at the pub for quite some time. He carried on his set for over an hour, playing guitar, telling jokes, singing songs and reciting poetry. It was a great evening.

The following morning, I got some good news when looking at the map. I somehow only had another 400 miles to do in four days, which was 100 miles shorter than I thought. This meant I didn't have to push it and could take it easier. Considering how expensive Australia was I didn't want to have to hang around Darwin in what would surely be a very expensive hotel. The other bit of good news was that the flies seemed to have gone, which was a huge relief. I no longer had to check whether they were caught up in my beard anymore.

The days were getting hotter and at one point I even cycled through some fires. They weren't that bad and probably set on purpose as a fire break, but they still packed a bit of heat as I went past. The smoke reminded me of camping wild, which brought back some good memories as I plodded along. I was quite enjoying this new, less stressful way of cycling, finally. I was glad I had pushed it a bit at the beginning to give me these few easy days. I seemed to be getting a lot more attention on this section too. Loads of friendly hoots and waves as people drove past. I felt part of a little community like I had when cycling on the Pan-American through the Atacama. After about the tenth wave and smile a young chap in a van drove past, waved and stopped a few hundred metres ahead. He jumped out of his van and asked me if I needed some water.

'So where have you cycled?' he asked.

'Just come up from Sydney over the last three weeks.'

'Three weeks. What? Really? I'm just about to cycle around Australia and it's going to take me six months. I'd love to hear your stories. A few of us are heading to Mataranka to the hot springs at around five. Come join us for dinner.'

Mataranka was now about 100 miles away, bringing my daily total to 130 miles. A bit further than I needed to do but the offer of hot springs and food was too good to miss. The springs were located a few miles off the main road down a small road and then along a path into a very pretty, almost mystical forest. The hot springs weren't just ponds as I had expected: it was a full-on river that you could float down. Markus, the young chap in the van, was there already and came running over.

'How awesome is this place?' I said. 'Have you been in? Is it warm?'

'Very.'

I kept all my clothes on except my shoes. I learned my lesson after my fountain swim. My shoes weren't as breathable as before and didn't drain the water or dry as quickly. I walked over and jumped in.

'Woooahhhhh! This is amazing!' I shouted out.

I swam around in circles, trying to get as much water through my salt ridden clothes as possible. I hadn't washed my clothes in at least a week and certainly not in warm water.

With every dive I felt the salt draining out my clothes. It felt glorious.

After the swim Markus and I joined a few of his traveller buddies for dinner in the car park for the springs and invited me to join. I was very impressed at the facilities. There was a gas-powered stove that anyone could use – free of charge. We all stood around, making pasta and tuna, showing each other photos and videos and generally talking nonsense. It was strange being in and amongst this group of young guys. I was definitely what you'd call a mature traveller. Part of me really enjoyed the conversation and banter between lads around the fire, but I was surprised that another part of me wanted to go off on my own, make my own fire and read a book. All this time alone you'd have thought I'd be craving company but strangely, I wasn't at all.

Although I didn't need to get up early the next day, I did anyway as I always feel better getting a good chunk of the day's mileage done before midday, when it was at least a little cooler. As I was leaving the campsite, heading back to the main road, I saw my second kangaroo bouncing a few hundred feet from the road. It looked so graceful. Then another one appeared just behind it: then a third, fourth and fifth! Within a minute there must have been about twenty all heading in the same direction bouncing through the recently burned landscape. It was a very surreal sight. It almost felt like the end of the world was coming and all the animals were running away through the charred and smouldering landscape. Listening to 'Angel' by Massive Attack on shuffle just added to the mysterious feel of it all. Then as soon it started, the burned section ended, the kangaroos all disappeared into the bush and Massive Attack made way for: 'It's Raining Men.' What an anti-climax. Also, how did The Weather Girls land up on my iPod?

I carried on heading towards Pine Creek. I hadn't gone more than five miles when Markus drove past and shouted out the window.

'Where you staying tonight man?'

'Pine Creek, I think.'

'OK. I will wait for you there and you can sleep in my van if you want. I only have to be in Darwin tomorrow anyway.'

'Really? That would be very cool.'

I decided to put my head down and push it to Pine Creek. I went into tri position, looked ahead at a clear road and then put my face down, using only the white line to direct me. I hadn't played white line chicken for a while. It's amazing what you see on the road when you're concentrating on it so much. I was spotting shapes and patterns all over the place. Darker patches that looked like countries or cracks that looked like an army of stick men without heads. It certainly kept my mind busy. There was even a filled-in crack that looked exactly like a pair of breasts. I thought I was seeing things, so stopped and went back to have a look. I was right. There, on the tar were two boobs. Obviously an Aussie road worker with a sense of humour. I wonder how long it had been there and how many other people had seen it?

I reached Pine Creek at around six, where Markus was waiting for me in the bar. We chatted for ages as I found out more about his adventures. He too had been run over in South America while cycling. He was going to walk the length of Africa but decided to cycle around Australia first with a few other people. There were four of them leaving

Darwin in a few weeks. Although envious, I had done a good stretch in Australia and was excited to carry on to Asia.

Pine Creek was about 150 miles from Darwin and instead of pushing it in one day, I decided to divide it up over two days and do a few scenic back roads. It was the first time I'd made a conscious decision to do a shorter day. I felt strangely guilty. What I loved was hitting the 200-mile mark on the bike and what I absolutely hated was a day under 100 miles. I was going to be doing two of them now. I even looked at the map to see if there was a way of adding more mileage so that I could do two bigger days, but there was nothing that didn't involve me cycling somewhere and then coming back again on the same road. I resigned to the fact I'd just take it slow.

I decided to do some back roads so stopped for some supplies and a beer. I had never taken a beer out cycling before but figured it would be nice to find a quiet spot under a tree and have a cold beer in the afternoon sun.

'These three pies and those two cans of VB, please,' I said to the shopkeeper, feeling quite smug.

'Sure buddy. Do you have your ID?' he asked. I was honoured he thought I was under eighteen. I had my UK driver's licence and produced it. He tried to scan it.

'Sorry, mate. This is not valid.'

'I'm over eighteen, I promise.'

'It's not that mate. I just can't prove that you are not on the banned list. Unless you can prove you aren't on the list by giving me a valid form of ID then there is nothing I can do. You can buy a beer in the pub, just not take-out.'

What? You can get banned from buying alcohol? I guess that was a good thing but surely the fact that I wasn't

Australian meant I couldn't get on the list anyway? Or could I? If they had this rule in Faliraki every visiting Brit would probably end up on the list. Maybe this was the Faliraki of Australia. It seemed highly unlikely though, as the only other people in the store were Silver Nomads stocking up on tinned tuna for their campervans.

'OK, just the pies then,' I said without hiding my annoyance. I hate it when rules don't involve a little thing called common sense.

The final stretch to Darwin was quite busy, so heading off-route was exactly what I needed. I wandered along slowly, swam in some creeks, and looked around a bit more. I didn't see anything more exciting than usual. Same trees, same grass, just moving past at a slower pace.

Australia had thrown everything at me: hills, rain, heat, hunger, dehydration and a lot of nothingness. I had conquered the outback, nearly ran over a kangaroo and got the world's dodgiest fingertip tan. Although I had really enjoyed the journey I was ready to carry on and explore a new continent. My average pace had dropped down to around 140 miles a day, which although a lot less than before, was still on target for getting back to London in time.

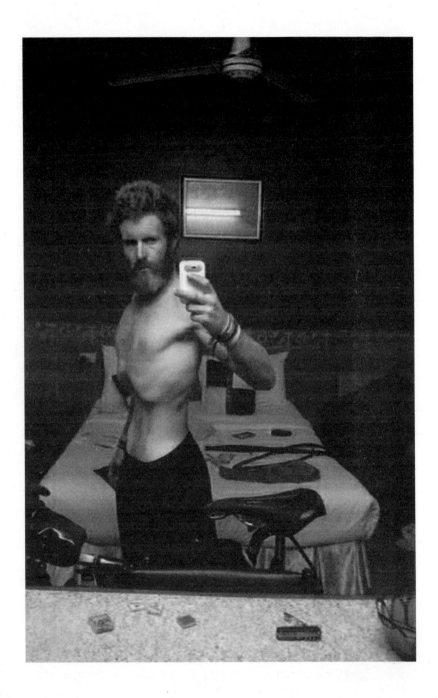

# 17

## NOODLES AND SOUP

Sweat was pouring down my face and into my eyes, and I hadn't even started cycling yet. It was so humid. I'd landed in Singapore soon after ten in the morning and it was already 32 degrees. I didn't have a map but had figured it couldn't be that difficult to get off the island and into Malaysia. As it turned out I was very wrong and spent a good few hours breaking various laws as I cycled on the main highway and down one-way streets. I was getting really hungry and thirsty but hadn't bothered to get any Singapore money as I knew I'd only be there for a few hours. I didn't even know what currency they used in Singapore. To make matters worse, I got an early puncture too. I tried to patch it but the humidity stopped the patch from sticking. Everything was wet. Luckily I had the sense to buy three new tubes in Darwin so could use a fresh one. It took me three hours to work my way to the northern tip of Singapore and cross the bridge into Malaysia.

I had originally planned on doing a slightly longer and flatter route towards Bangkok that would take me about eight days, giving me two days' rest before India. Although flat it was along the fairly busy main roads. But I decided instead do a more scenic and slightly shorter route. My flight out of Bangkok was in eleven days and I had 1300 miles to do. This meant I only needed to average 130 miles per day with half a day to sort a box for Maid Marian. I figured I might as well spread it out instead of busting my ass and then having to wait around in Bangkok. It was now the end of May, which gave me just over a month and a half to get to Bangkok, across India and then from Turkey back to London. That seemed an impossible task when looking at the map, but I knew distances were actually shorter than they looked in Europe because of the curvature of the earth. I had no idea on the distance but I guessed it was around 5–6000 miles.

I decided to try and head for the coast as soon as possible. There was no point in coming all the way to this part of the world and not experiencing the beautiful coastline it has to offer. There seemed to be many more towns along the coast too, which would make it easier to find a place to stay. From the outset I had budgeted for cheap hotels in Asia instead of camping. There's always that feeling that you are a walking wallet in developing countries: I didn't want to take any chances and with most hotels being under £10 for the night I could afford it. Food was also dirt cheap in Malaysia. My first meal, which was obviously noodle soup, was all of £1.50. It seemed a bargain, although after my first spoonfull, I was convinced that £1 of it was the amount of chillies they used. It nearly blew my head off. I tried to carry on eating it but had to give up halfway through. I was still starving though, so I got up, took a chilli in my spoon and walked back to the counter and asked for another bowl but signalled for 'no chilli' as I pointed to the spoon. They all laughed at me and I can only imagine what they were saying: 'Stupid white man can't eat spicy food.'

The temperature soared to 38 degrees and was so humid that I was completely wet, my clothes sticking to my skin. I think if I had jumped in a pool I would have come out drier. It was so bad that the touch screen on my phone didn't even work. I worked my way towards the coast and finally started to head north. Once again, it was great to be on a new continent with new people, new challenges and new adventures. Everyone seemed really friendly and it was nice to be back in a country where a lot of the population used bicycles as a means of transport. The roads were designed perfectly for this too, as I was presented with a decent hard shoulder, then a one-metre wide bike lane and then the main lane. The bike lane was mostly designed for scooters but still made for easy cycling as most cars expected traffic on their inside lane so gave a wide gap when overtaking.

I originally started with three full bottles of water but would barely finish half of one before I came to the next place where I could get water. I decided then to cut down to only one bottle to save some weight. I didn't have to carry any food either. Whenever I felt hungry, within ten minutes there would be a roadside stall for me to get food. The third time I stopped to get more food, some of the roadside stalls looked as if they had closed for lunch and were just opening up again. I walked in and used what I thought was the international sign for food (putting the tips of your fingers together and bringing them to your mouth) to see if they were serving yet. They didn't seem to understand and just looked confused and shook their heads. I carried on for a few stalls and the same thing happened. Eventually on the fourth stall the lady obviously knew what I was on about and re-signalled a 'spoon to mouth' sign as if to say that's how I was meant to do it. *Aha!* They did eat a lot of noodle soup so I guess that made sense. I naturally sat down and had just that – without chilli.

The first day in a new country is always exciting. There are so many things to take in. It was getting dark at around 5.30 p.m. in Australia, which made the evenings very dull and seem to last forever. It was therefore a pleasant surprise to find out it was still light at 8 p.m. in Malaysia. Because I didn't have to push it to get to Bangkok in time, I decided against any night cycling. Although the roads had been good, the cars and trucks weren't so. There were a few occasions when I saw big trucks with a completely smashed window still driving, along with the driver practically looking out the side window. I didn't want to take any risks. Just before nightfall I had reached the town of Batu Pahat. I had only managed 106 miles but that was to be expected after trying to get out of Singapore.

Dinner was another bowl of noodles from the only café in town that had Wi-Fi. I didn't have a SIM card for Malaysia and it didn't seem worth it for the three or four days I was there. I used Wi-Fi to update my blog, Twitter and Facebook but also, and more importantly, to download the next few days' worth of maps on Google. The new phone I'd bought in Australia was brilliant. Whenever I viewed a map on Google, it saved it to the phone's memory. This was great for zooming into towns to find a good route through because my paper map wasn't detailed enough.

After dinner I found a cheap hotel which cost £8 and, as always, made sure they would let me take Maid Marian into the room.

It was a pretty dirty and rundown hotel and the receptionist was fast asleep on the wooden bench near the door. He nearly jumped out of his skin when I rang the overly loud doorbell. The receptionist was still asleep on the bench when I woke up at 5 a.m. I had been locked in and felt extremely guilty waking him up to let me out. I was surprised to find that many roadside food stalls were open at this early hour. I stopped for a breakfast of rice and some sort of curry. I hadn't had curry for breakfast in a long time but I was starving so didn't care. I tried to get a cup of tea but they didn't have any. I was certain Malaysia was British once. Why hadn't they left their tea-drinking mark here too?

I'm not sure what Delhi belly is called in Malaysia but I had rumblings in my stomach all morning. That'd teach me for eating curry for breakfast. It wasn't nearly as bad as it could have been but I was worried because I didn't have the luxury of just going to the loo anywhere as in the desert. Flanking both sides of the road were people's homes or stalls and it had been like that since I reached the coast. It was nice that I didn't have to plan much for food and water but I found it hard to switch off. I dared not listen to music either, as there was just too much happening on the roads. Going to the loo in a restaurant also meant leaving Maid Marian unattended for a few minutes. This was a slight concern and I managed to control my rumblings for another hour. Eventually, I had no choice and found a petrol station with a toilet. I'm always surprised by the seeming lack of regard for ablution cleanliness in many developing countries. Even the very well-looked-after petrol station had pretty awful toilets around the back.

Feeling a lot better, I carried on along the coast slowly getting into the swing of things. I cycled past, on two separate occasions, two guys fishing while still wearing their motorcycle helmets. Apart from looking hilarious it must have been boiling hot. My mind was also kept busy by trying to work out how many things people were carrying on their motorbikes. When fully loaded was able to cycle faster than them. I'd see them 100 m ahead and then put the bets on with Little Flying Cow.

'One, no, two goats, three passengers, a chicken and a bag of maize.' I was confident I had nailed it. I was, however, very wrong. On reaching the motorbike it had five passengers: Mum, Dad and three kids, a goat strapped across the back, a cage with two chickens, the weekly shop and one of the kids holding a puppy. Anything seemed possible in this chaotic yet amazingly accident-free society. It was more of a case of how far could your imagination take you.

I was getting a mixture of attention from people as I cycled past. Some weren't bothered at all and didn't even look twice, while others smiled and waved. Many kids even tried to race me on their bikes too, which was fun. After the third time I suddenly had a brainwave. I hadn't played Chasing Dogs in a while. Maybe I could play Chasing Kids instead? I burst out laughing at the concept. Was that bad? Probably!

Nevertheless I spent the rest of the entire afternoon playing Chasing Kids and had the most fun I'd had in a while.

Although my mind was strong and happy, my body felt weak. I seemed to be starving within an hour of eating and just couldn't push much more than ten miles every hour because of all the times I had to stop and eat. There just wasn't nearly enough calories in the food. I needed more fat but Malaysian food seemed very healthy. I would need to start stretching my stomach by force-feeding myself. Anything to be able to get more noodles in me.

By nightfall I had only done 116 miles to Port Dixon, a scenic holiday seaside town with palm trees and perfect sandy beaches. It was a nice change from the busy roads I had been on all day. I worked my way through the town and found a hotel along the beachfront. As I was wheeling in I saw a massage parlour next door. Although my legs felt OK I really could do with loosening my quads up a bit. I checked in and went back to the parlour. It seemed very clean and was only £5 for an hour's massage. They were very friendly and spoke a little English. I was still wearing my Lycra and managed to get across the idea that my legs were tight. I was asked to wait a few minutes and then a tiny Malay women in her mid-forties asked me to follow her through the door to the back. She took me down a dark corridor that was lined with curtains covering about ten doorways. She took me into her little cubical, which was simply a mattress on the floor.

'Take off please.' She pointed to my clothes. I took off my shirt.

'Also off.' She pointed to my tights. I blushed immediately and my heart jumped. There was no way I was going to get naked as that would surely result in a situation I didn't want to land up in towards the end of my massage. Instead I rolled up my tights into speedo shape. She seemed annoyed but told me to lie down anyway. The next hour involved her jumping all over me while digging elbows, knees and feet into various parts my body. It was painful but good and I think once she realised that all I really wanted was a proper massage, she focused on that, rather than trying to seduce any 'extras' out of me.

After a good beating I wobbled out to pay. I felt like a new man. Just as I was leaving the receptionist said that she could send someone up to my room anytime until 2 a.m. I laughed and said I was fine. I knew that Thailand was known for its casual views on prostitution, but not Malaysia.

Breakfast in Port Dixon included a curry-flavoured sauce with a sweet fried pancake-style bread made with dough, eggs and sugar. The contrast between sweet and spicy was surprisingly good and I knew I was getting some good protein for the first time in a while. Noodles and soup really wasn't able to give me the nutrition I needed to recover.

At 11 a.m. the humidity finally decided to turn to actual rain. This was no ordinary rain either. It bucketed down. The roads soon became rivers and my pace dropped as I prayed there wasn't a pothole in every puddle I went through. The other problem was that I now had three days' worth of salt build up in my shirt, which ran down into my groin. The mixture of salt and water started to cause a painful chafing rash on the inside of my thighs. Eventually I stopped, bought a bottle of water and immediately poured it down my pants to the very confused look of the stall attendants. My shoes too had become completely waterlogged, which made the skin on my feet very fragile. I decided to stop and try to dry myself out and get more food in me. It didn't really work though because the humidity was so high.

The biggest challenge for the day was to get past Kuala Lumpur. The city with a population of 1.5 million was certainly going to take time to get beyond. Luckily, the main part of the city was slightly inland and I was able to keep along the coast a little as I worked my way up the maze of roads through Klang and onto Kuala Selangor. The going was slow but at least it had stopped raining and the sun had come out. I even bumped into a young couple, Bill and Julie, who were cycling along with their twins, who couldn't have been more than a year old, in a buggy behind them. They called themselves Biking with Babies. Bill was pulling the heavy trailer as well as carrying all the panniers because Julie was ill and had no energy. It was nice to have a proper conversation in English that didn't involve charades and pointing at things. Their biggest concern was finding roads with a good hard shoulder. The buggy was pretty wide and they couldn't just duck off the road like I could. Fair play to them for touring in this environment with very young children. Maximum adventure points.

By nightfall I had managed to claw back some of the miles I had lost on the first two days, and stopped at Sungai Besar, having completed 141 miles and successfully navigating my way past the never-ending maze of roads through Kuala Lumpur. My legs were definitely feeling a lot better after my massage. I'd clearly need to get a few more done while I could.

I hadn't been listening to any music at all since I reached Asia, but the following morning I decided I fancied something to keep my mind busy. Annoyingly, my iPod had run flat and somehow my battery pack wasn't working again. The dynamo itself was working but for some reason the battery pack wasn't charging. It had been on and off throughout Australia even after I tried to fix it in Brisbane. This time, though, it seemed broken for good. With all the rain from yesterday I wasn't surprised.

It's weird how your brain works. I'd been happily cycling for a few days without music but the moment I wanted it, and couldn't have it, I became annoyed with little things like a small click from my right pedal and the grating sound my brakes made because of the wet roads. There was nothing I could do. Once you are aware of the noise, you can't get rid of it. It stays in your mind all the time. Click, click, click! I was going mad.

The heavens opened again at around midday. I thought the day before had been bad but that seemed a light mist in comparison. It rained all afternoon. Everything was getting soaking wet. I even had to buy some plastic bags to cover one of my bar bags because it even gave up trying to be waterproof. At least the sound of the rain drowned out the clicking in my pedal and it was warm. After a few hours I even started to get granny fingers as if I had been in a bath for too long. It was at that point that I decided I should probably stop and have some food and dry out a bit.

After lunch number three I decided to put my head down and try to get as close to Penang as possible. After a good 155 miles I decided to call it a day. I managed to find a whole new level of dodgy hotel: no lights, unidentified stains on the sheets and a shower that was pretty much above the toilet. After a 'shower' I wandered into town, bought a wall charger to charge my phone and iPod, ate some spicy noodles because I forgot to ask for no chillies, and then headed back to the hotel. Just as I was getting near I saw a huge truck driving down the street spraying smoke into the air. I asked the hotel owner what it was and he said it was for mosquitos. Shit! I had totally forgotten to take my malaria tablets. I was told to take them for Malaysia, Thailand and India and should have started them in Australia. I ran to my room and started my dose. I didn't have any bites on me so figured it wasn't too late.

The next day, the plan was to get to the Thai border by nightfall, which was only 110 miles away. After passing Penang, I decided to stay on the main road towards the border so that I could get there early in case there were problems. For some reason, or lack of preparation as usual, I hadn't got a Thai visa beforehand. I knew this probably meant going to a different queue first, which might add some time to my crossing. I was also slightly worried about my passport. It had got completely wet in my bag and the plastic that covered my photo page had started to split on the edge, making it look as if I had tried to put a different photo in there. Irish passports still laminate the actual photo you send to them as opposed to scanning and printing it onto the page. Most of my visas had smudged and I looked nothing like my photo either, now that I had quite dodgy looking facial hair.

At the border crossing were several queues I had to join, and the police didn't know if I should go through the pedestrian lane or the car lane. Eventually I made it through to the other side and into Samnak Kham. It was too late for me to push on to the next town, so I decided to end my day early and try and get a few things for my next leg.

At first impressions Thailand seemed to be a lot more First World than Malaysia. There seemed to be quite a few Western shops like 7/11 and KFC dotted around. I used the evening to get some food, a map of Thailand and a SIM card for my phone before heading back to my hotel. It was a big building and I was on the sixth floor. The seventh had 'Massage Spa' written next to it. Perfect. I really needed another beating. I worked my way up and went through the door to the reception. I was lead through the door to the side of reception to a large room where around seventy girls all sat on a mini grandstand that took up three sides of the room. As soon as they saw me there was an eruption of gasps and giggles as they pointed at me.

'You can choose your girl, sir.'

My pulse shot up and I immediately felt my cheeks blush. I didn't know where to look. How could I choose? If I said yes to one, I'd be rejecting all the others. It was very intimidating. I couldn't do it. Also if there was ever going to be a situation that I didn't want to land up in, this 'massage parlour' was probably where it would happen. 'Sorry, I don't want it now. I'll come back later.' I turned around, red-faced to the giggles of seventy girls and went back to my room still a bit embarrassed for some unknown reason, had a warm bath and went to bed.

Good morning Thailand! The weather was warm and the roads were even better than Malaysia: very smooth tar with a large hard shoulder. I was slightly behind schedule so decided to put my head down and head straight up to the east coast of Thailand. The going was fast even though I had a slight headwind. I made the coast and turned north. Lunch was more noodles and chicken, which was almost too spicy to eat: I had to wash it down with warm water. I'd often be given a glass of ice with every meal but decided against using it. Sometimes they use tap water for ice and that's how you get ill. It was so hard to see ice-cold refreshment right in front of me as I drank my warm water from my bottle.

The route north along the coast was incredible. The only annoying bit was, like most places in Asia so far, that the road was lined with houses and stalls which meant I couldn't actually see the beach at all. I could hear it, smell it and even taste it, but only now and then did I get a glimpse of it through the gaps in houses or trees. What I did see looked idyllic though.

Even with a slight headwind I was making a lot more progress north along the coast. Many of the roads on the west coast of Malaysia were fairly winding and doing a 100 miles would probably only take me 60 miles closer to Bangkok. It felt good to be taking up a huge chunk of the map each hour I pushed north. By nightfall I had made it into Nakhon Si Thammarat. As I was bombing along I went past an Irish bar. I stopped immediately. An Irish bar in Thailand: now that I had to try. I stopped outside and went in. It was pretty authentic looking and also did food. Perfect. I sat myself down and ordered a Heineken and spaghetti Bolognese. I hadn't noticed when I first walked in, but there happened to be a European-looking chap, around my age, sitting with a Thai woman at one of the tables. We both caught each other's eye and did the classic thing of nodding at each other. I guess it's a familiarity thing. For all I knew he was from Russia and spoke less English than the average Thai person.

My first beer went down a treat, as did the second and my spaghetti. It was nice to eat something that didn't blow my head off for a change. An hour went by in the bar as I blankly stared out the window. I wasn't tired but had become so used to my own company that I found myself switching off quite a lot. It was 9 p.m. by the time I decided to head off to find a hotel. I was just heading out when the European chap walked to the bar and ordered a beer. He had a Yorkshire accent. The sense of familiarity was great to hear and without even thinking I shouted out:

'From up north right? What brings you here?' I could feel the effects of two beers making me speak a little fast. I had become such a lightweight.

'Yorkshire born and bred but I live here now. That's my wife over there and our fifteen-month-old daughter.'

I hadn't noticed but there was a baby at their table. His wife waved at me.

'I met Kate in England where she was an au pair and then we moved over.' By now he had two beers in his hands and was looking like he wanted to head back to his wife. 'We're expecting a few friends in a bit. Come and join us for a beer if you want.'

The Yorkshireman was called Mark and he introduced me to his wife Kate, whose real Thai name I couldn't pronounce even after trying four times. Kate and Mark had moved back to Thailand to take over Kate's family noodle shop in the market around the corner. I thought that was brilliant. An English chap from Yorkshire running a noodle restaurant in Thailand. We were joined by a few more of Kate's friends. The beers kept rolling and stories kept flowing. It must have been about 11 p.m. when I eventually decided to say my goodbyes and asked Kate for a hotel recommendation. She looked me in the eye and in a very drunk state said:

'As long as you don't murder us in the night you can stay in our spare room.'

I laughed and realised she was actually quite serious.

'Don't worry. I'm a good guy. You can google me. I'm part of this race thing.'

She got out her phone as I told her what to search. Luckily, if you add *'cycling'* to my name on Google I am the first on the list. It happened to be an article about the accident too. Kate immediately felt bad and laughed as if to suggest she was joking all along. To be fair, I thought it pretty brave to let a dirty smelly stranger who she'd only known for a few hours into her home. I was massively appreciative and once again blown away by the generosity of strangers on this trip.

I had now been in Asia for a week and was right in the flow of things. Seeing goats on scooters was now a regular occurrence and didn't even get a second glance. The miles would slowly go by as my mind wandered. I tried to play Chasing Dogs a few times but most dogs weren't bothered by cyclists in this part of the world, so that didn't last long. I then resorted to racing scooters at traffic lights to keep me entertained. In my mind we were having a Formula One style start. The only problem was that most scooters jump the red lights at least one second before they turn green, which meant I usually lost, embarrassing considering they didn't even know it was a race.

I decided on some back roads nearer the coast, which were a lot more scenic. I switched off and plodded along the cement farm roads through green fields and palm trees. A nice change from the busy roads I had been on. I reached Surat Thani by 4 p.m. after having done 95 miles. I was feeling good after my slightly more adventurous route through the farms. I found a small café that had a Wi-Fi sign and decided to check up on Twitter and Facebook, and update people on where I was. I was excited to show everyone some of the scenic coastal roads I had done. I opened Twitter and was about to compose a tweet when I saw one from Mike Hall that caught my eye.

'Thanks for all the messages guys. 18,000 miles in 92 days was tough.'

I sank into my chair. I knew all along that Mike was going to break the record but somehow I felt really deflated. I know I was a month behind schedule from the accident but somehow being on the other side of the world with 6000 more miles to do, and him having finished already, made me feel like a failure. Getting my mini Olympic Torch back to London in time for the games seemed a weak hand-me-down challenge all of a sudden. I had tried so hard to put the accident behind me and move on with a new focus, but now felt back at square one again. I felt like curling up in a ball and hiding from everyone. I hadn't really thought about the other riders at all up till now. How many were still racing? No one was anywhere near Mike, that much I knew. I guess I had tried to push the race out of my mind.

I turned off my phone and left the café without eating even though I was starving. I found a hotel, checked in and lay down and tried to sleep. For the first time since the accident I felt like quitting and taking the first flight home. I had no energy to carry on. Physically and emotionally.

I woke up the next day still feeling depressed. I looked in the mirror. I was the thinnest I had ever been: every time I breathed in my ribcage showed. I had no body fat and my muscles were thinning out. I sucked in my stomach a little to see what I looked like. It wasn't pretty.

I really wanted to relax for a day and get my life back in order but with only having done 95 miles the day before I really had to get going again. I left the hotel and went back to the café for breakfast. I then jumped back on Maid Marian and as I clipped into my right pedal and tried to power into the flow of fairly fast-moving traffic, my foot slipped. I swerved right into traffic and a car hooted. For a brief moment I wished I had been run over again: not seriously, just enough to have an excuse to go home, and for it all to be over. I wasn't in the mood to carry on at all. I managed to pull Maid Marian back and veered off the road again. I tried to take my right foot off the pedal but I was still clipped in. I looked down to see what had happened. The pedal had come detached from the shaft and was hanging off the end. It would have completely come off altogether if it weren't for some of the bearings, which had stopped it. Eventually, after nearly spraining my ankle, I managed to unclip. I put Maid Marian up against a tree and sat on the pavement wondering what to do. I hadn't seen one bike with clip-in pedals at all and knew it would be an impossible task. I sank my head in my arms. For the first time I felt lonely, incredibly lonely. I just wanted to quit it all. I couldn't think of any reason to carry on.

It felt like I sat there for an hour, but in reality it was only a few minutes before I decided to get up. I didn't know what I was doing or where I was going but figured anything was better than sitting on the pavement. I started to push Maid Marian up the road hoping that someone would magically appear with a new pedal. I couldn't have gone more than 50 metres when something caught my eye. On the other side of the road was the biggest bike shop I think I have ever seen in my entire life. There were at least 100 bikes all over the pavement and hanging from the roof. I couldn't believe my luck. I hadn't seen a bike shop at all since Singapore and the time I needed one the most I find a huge one. Maybe someone was looking out for me after all.

I walked over and showed them my problem. The owner tried to get the mechanic to fix it, involving just hammering the pedal back onto the shaft. That didn't work at all. She then looked at the pedal and asked the mechanic to get another pair. He looked confused but was pointed to a box on the top shelf. He took the box down and with it came years of dust. He then opened it and just like in the movies there was a cloud of dust and a brand spanking new pair of SPDs emerged from the smoke. They were silver Shimano knock-offs that only had clips on one side, but I didn't care. They looked beautiful. They were £10, which wasn't too bad either. Within ten minutes I was back on Maid Marian heading north. I couldn't believe my luck. I worked out that there had only been three places to get new pedals in the last 3000 miles, and it happened outside one of them. If this had happened in the outback I'd have definitely taken a lift, which was against my rule.

I carried on north along the coast, taking in more of the back roads. I still wasn't in the mood to explore and just wanted to get to Bangkok and rest. It also rained a lot more and I had to stop twice under some shelter just to avoid the bombardment of splashes from trucks as they overtook me. I was completely in autopilot mode. At lunchtime I stopped at a roadside café and noticed a group of Thai road cyclists all in proper gear. We nodded at each other as I walked in and sat down. I ordered some fried rice, four boiled eggs and a coffee. I was just finishing up when the cycling crowd all got up to leave. One of them walked over to me and very casually said.

'We have paid your food, OK!'

"Oh really?" I wasn't quite sure I understood.

'No problem. Enjoy Thailand' and with that he smiled and walked off. I barely had time to reply. He didn't seem to want any thanks either. I just sat there still a little confused. Surely he hadn't just paid for my meal? Why would he have done that? They all got on their bikes and they rode off. I walked up to the counter to pay just in case I had misheard. The waiter looked confused and said, 'He pay', and pointed to where they had been sitting. I couldn't believe it. What an incredible gesture from a stranger who I didn't even know. I walked back to Maid Marian feeling a lot better than I had when I'd arrived. Yes, I may have failed in my attempt at the world record but I was still in an amazing country with amazingly kind people having the adventure of a lifetime.

'You only get one bloody chance to cycle around the world Sean, so snap out of it,' Little Flying Cow shouted at me.

He was right. I got back on Maid Marian and promised myself I'd not let the accident ruin my adventure again. I had lost focus three times since getting back on the bike: once near Phoenix, once in the outback and once here. I wasn't going to let it happen again. I carried on into the afternoon rain all of a sudden wanting to race little kids on bikes and take more photos. I realised that I needed to make the adventure happen. It wasn't just going to come to me. I was feeling a lot better and even a series of punctures didn't damped my new revitalised spirit. The last puncture was a slow one that I got about five miles before Chumphon, my stop for the night. I had run out of fresh inner tubes so stopped every 500 metres to pump it a bit. It had practically rained on me all day and everything was wet. I had only managed 116 miles. My flight was a 3 p.m. flight in a few days and the plan was to get to Bangkok the night before and then spend the morning before the flight getting a box ready and sorting things out for India. With two slow days, I worked out I'd probably only get to Bangkok at night, so decided to get to the outskirts and then go straight to the airport and fly. A bit risky if anything went wrong but better than navigating the notoriously bad city traffic at night.

The final push to Bangkok was long and boring. Although the roads were good, the traffic was bad. I stopped for the night about 40 miles from the city and then got up early to get into the city. I managed to check Facebook and had a message from Vin Cox (a previous round the world record holder I mentioned earlier) who gave me the name and rough location of a good bike shop where I'd be able to get a box to pack Maid Marian for the flight. As it turned out he had been in Bangkok only a few days earlier. If I had known I'd have cycled a bit harder. What a legend for helping me. I hadn't really thought about it at all and could easily have wasted a few hours trying to find something.

I managed to pack everything up in a box, put a new chain on Maid Marian and get to the airport with about four hours to spare before my flight. Perfect timing. In the rush I had packed my flight details inside the bike box so had no idea what flight I was on, or which airline for that matter. All I remembered was that my flight was at 3 p.m. to Kolkata. Eventually it came up on the board, on an airline I'd never even heard of. I checked in, still dressed in my Lycra and looking quite dirty. I even saw a German-looking tourist take a sneaky picture of me as he walked past. I wonder where that photo ever landed up and what the caption underneath it was?

# 18

## CURRY AND MOUSTACHES

The last time I was in India was a last-minute holiday I took with my mate Maritz. We had £800 each and took a return flight to Delhi. That's all we planned. Over those six weeks we landed up taking a train and bus to Kathmandu; we nearly got arrested for buying beer where we weren't allowed to, climbed up to Annapurna Base Camp, went to Tibet, bought a monk's robe, ate fried yak, drank salt-butter tea, got altitude sickness, built the world's best snowman and generally had one hell of an adventure. India had a lot to live up to this time round.

The first thing I saw when getting into the terminal building at Kolkata was a sign next to a chair that said, 'DO NOT SIT HERE'. I thought that was a bit daft considering the conveniently placed empty chair. I then read the sign again and it said, 'DO NOT SPIT HERE'. Ah! Brilliant. I'd missed India.

My flight landed in the evening so I decided to find a hotel for the night. Luckily I had got a lot of practice the last time so was prepared for the constant attention and seemingly standard practice of 'ripping off the tourist'. The last time I was in Delhi I caught a chap with his hand in my pocket right in front of a bunch of other people. When I told the guy to bugger off and get some practice, everyone just laughed as if I was fair game. I was prepared for this so before I even left the terminal building I found an information desk to find out rough taxi prices. Taking a taxi from the airport to the hotel half a mile away was kind of breaking my rules, but I didn't know where I was going and cycling in India at night was the last thing I felt like doing. Also it was late and spending an hour trying to put Maid Marian together didn't seem fun.

Getting directions, I was told to ask the driver to take me to Gate 4 – there would be many hotels and it shouldn't cost more than 200 rupees (£2). I went outside and was immediately swamped by about twenty taxi drivers, all dressed in white linen shirts and donning matching moustaches. I love that Indians still have the old moustache. I told the first chap where I was going and he quoted me 500 rupees. I just laughed and kept repeating '200 rupees'. Eventually, after a long over-theatrical debate, which probably would have gone on for another hour, and for the sake of 50p, I eventually settled on 250 rupees. The driver tried to make out he was losing money on the ride, which I knew all too well was not true. We managed to fit Maid Marian into the back of the standard Indian taxi, which was a 1960s Peugeot, and he took me to a hotel at Gate 4. I saw the taxi man talking to the hotel owner and then got given some money. I guess he was claiming commission for bringing me there. If the hotel owner said no, he'd just tell me it was full and take me somewhere else. It seemed a decent enough hotel though and came with warm(ish) water and air-conditioning, which was a bonus as it was 28 degrees at night. I definitely needed a shower. The chap who sat next to me on the flight had a look of distaste every time I moved, releasing more fumes from my stinky body.

My Indian leg was to be slightly different to all my other legs because I was going to be filmed the entire way across by an independent film-maker who heard about my story a few weeks before I left. Rachel filmed me a bit at the beginning, and had decided she wanted to come and find me in India. She was going to hire a car and driver and follow me all the way to Mumbai. If you had asked me a week before, when I was feeling depressed, whether I was excited to have some company for this section I'd definitely have said no. I'd become quite used to my own space and a solo way of living on the road. Having to work around a filming schedule and wait for camera angles and carry a clip-on microphone all the time was the last thing I wanted to do. That was a week ago but now I actually felt a little excited to have someone from home soil here. Someone I could chat to and tell my story. I was craving a sense of familiarity I think. I also loved India and was pretty excited to cycle across it. All in all, my mood was high and ready for the next chapter. Rachel was due in Kolkata the following day so I knew I had at least a day off to relax. I needed it after my hectic last day in Bangkok.

I didn't sleep well at all that first night. The driving culture in India has become so hooting heavy that drivers seem to use their horns as a replacement for every other form of car signal available. Hoot when you're overtaking. Hoot when you don't want to be overtaken. Hoot when turning. Hoot when someone else is turning. Hoot at the other cars for hooting. It was ridiculous. Not a minute went by when there wasn't a hooting shootout. Does India still communicate in Morse code? They'd be awesome at it. I had planned on getting up early to sort out some admin in town but after only going to bed at around two I slept until nearly ten. In my sleepiness I nearly drank some of the tap water, which would have ended in a lengthy session on the loo. Must remember to have bottled water only. I then I headed out to sort a SIM card, some money, food and to work out a rough route across to Mumbai.

I couldn't have been outside for more than ten seconds before I started sweating. I'd coped with some pretty warm places up to now – the Atacama, and the outback – but that was nothing compared to the heat in India. The humidity, the smells, the busy streets, the tuk-tuks, all added to the claustrophobic atmosphere, as sweat constantly ran down my forehead and gathered in my eyebrows. Maybe that's why some Indians have moustaches? To stop the sweat going into their mouths. They were like lip-brows. I found myself smiling at that thought and realised loads of onlooking Indians were smiling back, their lip-brows stretching wide. I laughed out loud and so did they. If they only knew why!

First on the list was to get a SIM card, which proved to be a lot harder than I thought: I had to give a passport photo, copy of passport, proof of address in India (unknown) and visa details. After running around for about an hour, which included a full-on photo shoot in a mini studio for a passport photo, I was eventually given a SIM card. But the understanding was that the Vodafone agent still had to send my details to the main head office before they approved it.

The other thing I love about India is the food. I had lost a lot of weight in Malaysia and Thailand and it was time to put it back on. My one concern was Delhi-belly which results in spending at least two full days on the toilet as the universe comes out your arse. I had been to India twice before and no matter how careful I was with hand gels, not having ice in my drink, no salad (they wash the salad in dirty water), no street food, and staying vegetarian, I still got a dodgy stomach. It was hell both trying to remember all the things I needed to avoid and the inevitable two days spent doubled over.

This time I decided that seeing as I was probably going to get it anyway, I might as well enjoy myself. I would still take precautions like bottled water only and no ice, but was excited about eating amazing street food. First on the menu was some potato looking curry served on a banana leaf. Although it blew my head off it was more of a spicy hot, which was a nice change from the chilli hot that seemed more common in Thailand. Dessert was the juice from a coconut that I got from a guy who just had a pile on the side of the road. No stall, no shop, just a pile of coconuts on the dirty pavement. It was glorious.

By midday I had done most things and even managed to find an Internet café, which again involved some sort of security check and copying of my passport. I found out Rachel was due in at five. She had never been to India before, so I decided to go and meet her at the airport. I had no idea how much kit she might have and making her deal with all those taxi drivers wouldn't be a good start for her Indian adventure.

That afternoon I reassembled Maid Marian again in record time and tried to work out how much mileage I'd need to do to get to Mumbai for my flight, with two possible Delhi-belly days in the middle. My original route was to head quite far south so that I could do 2000 miles in the twelve days. If I went directly across to Mumbai I only had to do 1200 miles, which was a great relief. That meant only an average of 100–120 miles per day: I could easily do more so would still head a little south to try and add a few days to the route. I set to work getting everything ready so that I could leave first thing in the morning.

Rachel had a huge smile on her face when I met her, and was all dressed up in scarves, bangles and bracelets. If she wasn't a hippy, she at least decided she was going to be one in India. I, on the other hand, was still in Lycra. We left the terminal building to the bombardment of all the taxi drivers, and again had to play the same game of getting the price from 500 rupees down to 250. Rachel didn't seem to be at all flustered by the whole process and even threw in a few cheeky comments to get them to put the price down like, 'But look, your taxi is dirty, that's cheaper then.' I knew from that moment she'd be fine on her own.

That evening we went out for dinner and somehow landed up in a restaurant that could have come right out of Chelsea. Ordinarily I like to go to the dingy places on the back streets, but it was actually interesting mingling with India's elite. Very eloquent, all speaking English to each other and very well dressed. The difference in classes in India is always something that takes a while to get used to. I'd most likely be on the very other side of the tracks for the rest of my ride through middle India.

I had a surprisingly good sleep and was ready to go by 5.30 a.m. Rachel's driver arrived in a beaten-up Toyota Corolla. He was in his early forties, wore a grey linen suit with sandals and didn't have a moustache. That was quite rare. He introduced himself with a name so long and unpronounceable that he just said to call him A.K. His English was OK but I still found myself simplifying my sentences again, which I hate, but that seemed to be the only way we could communicate efficiently. We chatted about my route and how I wanted to go along the coast for a while. I showed him on the map. He didn't really know and actually was more interested in the map itself. He said he hadn't seen one of the whole of India properly before, which surprised me. Although, in fact, I then remembered I'd had to get this map from Germany as I couldn't find one map of the whole of India. He wasn't too sure about the exact route either, but after lots of hand gestures, shouting and seemingly angry, although probably very civil, fast talking with a few of the hotel staff he seemed happy with where to go. At least that's what I made out. He was probably just chatting about the latest Bollywood film.

Although first thing in the morning, the temperature was already 25 degrees and really sticky. The streets were busy but I was getting a surprising amount of room from drivers and motor bikers. It was a little disconcerting when they spent a good ten seconds looking sideways at me instead of the road ahead, though.

'Watch the road people, not the ginger!' I kept laughing, although I knew all too well they couldn't understand me. It was all smiles though, and I was in a good mood.

The road soon turned west and I got onto the highway. It was a great road. A lot better than I had expected. Good tar with a huge hard shoulder. I decided to try and get a little further out of the city before trying to find some food. By 7 a.m. I had done about 12 miles and saw a roadside stall selling what looked like samosas. Rachel and A.K. caught up with me and we all stopped right on the hard shoulder. Only in India can you sell food on a busy highway. I liked that. I went down to get some food and heard Rachel shout.

'Hold on! I need to film this. Let me mic you up.'

I had already forgotten about the filming side of things. All of a sudden I got nervous about what to say. Rachel hadn't really told me her plans for the film, and probably didn't know herself, but I guessed we were just going to shoot everything. I ordered what looked like samosas and some sweet-looking dough balls. The samosas were very spicy and the dough balls very sweet. The combination was quite nice though. I also needed to get bottled water: this is something that is generally quite readily available and costs about 15 rupees (15p). If you are lucky it's cold, but then normally costs a few rupees more. This stall had Fosters Water – like the beer? I asked A.K. and he said it's because beer companies aren't allowed to advertise so they create a water brand to indirectly promote the beer. Clever!

We carried on west for another 30 miles or so, taking in the Indian countryside. Although the roads were good, there didn't seem to be any rules at all. On a few occasions my hard shoulder turned into an unofficial oncoming lane for trucks deciding that they preferred to drive on the wrong side of the highway. This meant I needed to concentrate a lot and keep my wits about me. It kind of kept my mind busy though and before I knew it I was at the junction where I needed to turn south towards the coast. Leaving the motorway was great and meant I didn't have as many huge trucks to deal with: I did, however, have motorbikes that were so overloaded it appeared all but impossible to ride them.

The road became a little more potholed and soon narrowed down to an almost single track, which barely left enough room for two trucks to pass. I had luckily bought a second mirror for Maid Marian in Australia so that I had one on each side to see what was coming up all around me. I'd often have to duck off the road and onto the dirt when two trucks passed me from both directions.

It was just getting dark when I saw an oddly shaped bicycle in the distance. Well, the bike seemed normal, but the rider was leaning all the way off the side of the bike, so low that he was level with the saddle, like when motorbike racers lean to take corners. I sped up to investigate. It was only when I was about 30 metres away that I realised it was a kid who couldn't have been much more than four years old cycling a full adult-sized bike. He was too small for his legs to reach the pedals so he had to cycle to the side of the bike with his one leg on the pedal as normal and the other going through the frame to reach the other pedal. His one arm went out in front of him to the handlebar and the other then stretched all the way over to the other side to reach the other handle. It was incredible. I followed him for a bit but he soon realised there was someone behind him due to everyone else staring. He turned around and the biggest smile in the world erupted from his little face and in his excitement he nearly lost control. He slowed down and I went up next to him, waved, gave him the thumbs – up and carried on. What a legend. Hopefully India's future Bradley Wiggins.

It was dark by the time I reached the coastal town of Digha, which brought my daily total to 112 miles. It was nice not to have to worry about mileage on this leg, especially as

I also felt as if my body was starting to become quite weak. Except for airport stops and my day in Kolkata waiting for Rachel, I hadn't had a day off since Brisbane, which was nearly six weeks ago. I felt tired, so short days of around 100 miles were exactly what I needed.

Rachel was in Digha already filming bits and bobs and my arrival. I felt a bit dehydrated as I hadn't drunk nearly enough. It had been 40 degrees most of the day. After five attempts at a hotel that wouldn't let me take Maid Marian into the room we eventually settled in. To save money, otherwise Rachel would have had to pay for her own room, we had to pretend we were married. They wouldn't allow non-married girls and boys to share a room. This became good banter as we over-theatrically shouted 'honey' and 'darling' to each other as we filled out the hotel forms and gave them our passports.

How could it be 30 degrees at 6 a.m.? It was so humid it was like trying to breathe in syrup. Most businesses already seemed to be up and running and I stopped for an early omelette breakfast. Within minutes I was surrounded by thirty people just blankly staring at me and Maid Marian. There seemed a lot of conversation around the clip-in pedals and small hard tyres. Cycling in India is seen as a pretty lower-class activity, for poor people who can't afford a motorbike. One of the men asked me how expensive my bike was. I replied with a ridiculously low figure equivalent to £100. I didn't want to be promoting the fact I had an expensive bike. I've never felt threatened in India but you never know. Although I thought maybe if the word got round that my bike was as expensive as a motorbike I'd get priority on the roads. I knew this would never happen but chuckled at the idea anyway.

I left the roadside café to the waves of my new fans. I couldn't have gone 20 metres down the road and looked back to see a completely empty café again. As fast as they had appeared they all vanished again. Just then Rachel and A.K. came alongside me. They had slept in a bit.

'Oi Ginge. How's it going? Can I film you getting breakfast?'

'Ah, sorry dude. Just had it.'

The miles kept rolling that morning, complete with cars hooting and people staring. With every hour the temperature kept rising and by midday it was a staggering 43 degrees. My pace was slow and I really needed to stop in some shade and cool off. I could feel my head thumping a bit; I think I still hadn't recovered from mild heatstroke from the day before. I decided to give Rachel a call to say I was stopping: they surely wouldn't be too far ahead. I tried to call but my phone said 'Sim Card Not Recognised'. I knew straight away that Vodafone had rejected my application. I sat down deflated and tired, as I knew I'd have to go on until I found Rachel. I drank the last of the warm water in my bottle and slowly carried on. This was by far the second dumbest thing I'd done after carrying on cycling with a fractured back.

I limped on slowly and started to feel a little ill. Eventually after half an hour I saw them on the side of the road.

'You OK, mate?' Rachel immediately sensed I was in a bad way.

I just shook my head, I didn't have the energy to speak.

'Have some water.'

I drank it but felt really sick. I needed to cool my head down. There was a stall to my right so I got off Maid Marian and went over and bought a cool bottle of water. I opened it and poured it on my head to the gasps of a gathering of Indians around me. Bottled water, although readily available, is still a bit of a luxury and to buy a cold one and then pour it on your head was just crazy. It seemed to help a little but what I really needed was to cool down properly. I looked on the map to see if there was a town nearby that might have an air-conditioned restaurant. The closest town was Balasore, which was two miles off the main road. I told A.K my plan and he asked the shopkeeper something and they pointed towards the town. I think A.K. was speaking Hindi but I wasn't sure. I could easily have just put my bike in the car and driven there, but I still had to stick to my rule of cycling everywhere so stumbled back onto Maid Marian and went in search of air-conditioning.

The next two hours were spent in an air-conditioned restaurant, eating and trying to recover. It was by far the longest lunch break I had had on this ride and I almost felt guilty. I couldn't afford to get heatstroke again. I was annoyed with myself for not taking more care in keeping cool and hydrated. I was also surprised at how the humidity affects your ability to cool down. The air was so moist that your sweat doesn't evaporate and you therefore don't cool down. I knew this, in theory, but hadn't realised just how bad it would be. Leaving that cool restaurant and getting back onto Maid Marian was the hardest I'd found it all ride. Even worse than those bad knee days in South America. As long as I drank more water and poured some on my head I should survive, but at 45 degrees it was going to be tough.

I don't really remember much of the rest of the afternoon. I just kept my head down and eventually reached Bhadrak just before sunset. It had been a tough day but I had somehow hit the 110-mile mark. My clothes were pretty dirty so I jumped in the shower fully clothed and sat there for what seemed a lifetime trying to recover. In two days my excitement to be in India had turned to a fiery hellhole of heat. At least I didn't have Delhi-belly. Although as I thought it, I knew I had jinxed it. I knew my time would come. It was just a matter of when.

I had been heading southwest along the coast and wanted to head even further but considering I was struggling with the extreme temperatures, I decided to start heading directly west again. I'd also been informed that monsoon season had started in the south and was heading up, pushing the warm winds with it.

I also decided that I'd probably need to spend a good few hours in the middle of the day cooling down in the shade. A bit like lions on the plains of Africa (with my big ginger beard I looked like a lion anyway). With a longer planned lunch break now planned, I left the hotel earlier at 4.30 a.m. It was still boiling hot but I felt a little better than yesterday. Again I left Rachel and A.K. to sleep in and told them I'd find a place for breakfast at around six, about 10–15 miles ahead.

I got my first Indian puncture at around breakfast time and luckily was right near a café so stopped for some chai and omelette. Again, within seconds I was surrounded by about thirty people, now especially interested as I had Maid Marian sprawled out upside down with her wheel off. There seemed to be a lot of interest in how thin and hard my tyres were, with each and every one of them taking a turn to feel them and then comment and gesture how hard it was. Just then Rachel and A.K. rocked up.

'It's not hard to miss you; we just look for the crowds.'

'I know. There was no one here a few minute ago.'

A.K. started to get bombarded with questions once they realised he was with us. I could see he kind of liked it and started to get more cups of chai for us. He was like the boss and Rachel and I were happy to go with whatever he said. Also, he checked the price to make sure we weren't being ripped off. I liked the fact he was getting involved in the adventure. His English was getting better too and he and Rachel had obviously bonded as there was some good banter between them.

After breakfast the first signs of the oncoming monsoon started to appear. The wind picked up and it became a little overcast. Although cooler it was still 37 degrees and the headwind made it worse. By nightfall I had reached Angul and after having to really step up the 'but we are married' façade we eventually got a room. The hotel had Wi-Fi so I managed to catch up on social media and write a blog. I also decided to write a post that said if I raised another £250 for charity by the following evening I'd get my legs shaved by an Indian barber. I wasn't even sure they'd let me, but I liked the idea and it's always a nice boost when I get money in for the charity. It makes it worthwhile when the going is tough.

The following day, I decided to head back up towards the main highway that I started on in Kolkata. I had wanted to go further south to add miles but it was just too hot. I'd make the highway by nightfall and then be on the main road to Mumbai, which should make up for lost time. I struggled to find breakfast but discovered Parle-G biscuits, which have an incredibly high calorie count. They are in fact the biggest selling biscuits in the world and a small pack costs only five rupees (5p) and has about 500 kcal, which is the same as a Big Mac. To date I have never found that many calories for the price anywhere in the world, and probably never will.

At midday Rachel and A.K. drove past me again. Rachel hung out the window.

'A.K. says this is a bad area for terrorism and we can't stop. Apparently two Italians were murdered here a few months ago.'

I hadn't at all felt threatened in India. I never have in fact: they seemed a gentle bunch. But I guess with over a billion people in your country even a very small percentage of 'rotten eggs' is quite a high number of people.

'We no stop and follow OK?' said A.K., looking uncharacteristically serious.

I stepped it up a gear and straightaway heard the distinct sounds of a puncture. Great, of all the places to get a puncture I get mine where they murder Europeans. I fixed the puncture in record pace and went all of 100 m before getting another one. Annoyed, I changed it again only this time realised it wasn't a puncture: it was one of my old patches melting off. I decided to change for a fresh inner tube. I did that but again a mile down the road got another puncture. My patches obviously weren't sticking. I was near a small row of workshop-type stalls and eventually, after asking about five, I found a chap who fixed motorbike wheels. He said he could help and set to work filling, shaving and cutting bits of rubber to fix my tube. He then used some pretty heavy adhesive to fix the tube. It took a good half an hour but the result looked good. I said thank you, paid my 100 rupees (£1) and carried on. The tyre he fixed was good but another few miles down the road another of my old patches started to melt off the tube. The road was just too hot. Four punctures in one day. I don't think I got four in the entirety of my South American leg.

By early evening we arrived in Sambalpur, which was the biggest city we had been in since Kolkata. I found a hotel with Wi-Fi. My Twitter and Facebook pages were overloaded with 'Ha-ha, mate, get those legs out' messages. It looks like I had reached the target and needed to get an Indian barber to shave my legs. Rachel thought this was brilliant, so we went off into the city to find a barber. Eventually we found one and offered him double his normal rate, which was still only £2. For the next hour I had a wave of people stopping to take photos of me and laugh as an Indian chap with a cutthroat gave me the smoothest legs in the world while I tried to decipher the score in the cricket from a Hindi newspaper. England were playing West Indies. Looked like it was a draw.

There followed another hot day on the bike as the monsoon raced north, pushing the warm air with it. I was a bit behind schedule so when I got another early puncture I was a little annoyed. It was the same problems as before: the road was too hot for the self-stick patches. The punctures happened another five times before I eventually ran out of inner tubes. I sat under a tree not knowing what to do. I had no idea how far it was to the next town. Now that I was back on the main highway Rachel and A.K. were ahead somewhere at the next truck stop, but I had no idea how far that was and couldn't call them because no matter how often I told Vodafone, I'm not an Indian resident, I'm a tourist, they still wanted an Indian address for me.

I looked back through all five of my inners, which were now under a bungee on the back of my saddle bag, and debated which was the best one. I decided to put five patches all over the one hole and see how far that got me. It worked for a mile but soon started to go flat, luckily quite slowly. It was my front wheel, so again, much like before, I cycled 500 m, gave it ten pumps and then did another 500 m and so on. It was slow but a lot faster than pushing Maid Marian. Eventually, after an hour and too many 'mini pit stops' to count I arrived at a small truck stop where Rachel and A.K. were, to find them both passed out in the car. I knocked on the window and they both jumped.

'Sorry, are you guys tired? All this driving and being a passenger must be hard work.'

'OK, smart arse. What took you so long?'

'Punctures. I've got no more inner tubes. I need a guy to fix them.'

Luckily most truck stops have some sort of garage and it wasn't long before some kid was working his magic on my inner tubes. I counted that I had eight old patches that had, or were just about to, melt off so asked him to fix them all. This took nearly two hours but I was pleased to have it sorted.

While sitting having lunch I noticed another problem. A mosquito buzzing around my ear.

'Shit!'

I'd totally forgotten about my malaria tablets, again. In fact, I hadn't been taking them since somewhere in Thailand I think. Well, if I was going to get malaria, it was surely going to happen anyway, so I figured starting now was pointless seeing as I only had a week left in India. I had a sudden thought about the headaches from a few days earlier being malaria and not sunstroke. I certainly hoped not.

My aim had been to make it to Raipur but with the worsening road conditions and increasing headwinds, this was looking less likely. My pace barely went into double figures all day. With the decision made to not push it, I decided to take a proper break next to a wide river. I sat on the bank eating some Parle-G biscuits, a spicy samosa and a very small banana. For some reason bananas in India are only about 10 cm long. I also learned that all this time I've been peeling a banana the wrong way. Normally you take the bit sticking out that's normally attached to the tree, and rip it sideways. Sometimes this works, but if the banana is a bit green it bends the banana instead. The correct way, and apparently this is what happens when you give a monkey a banana, is to take the other end of the banana, the bit you usually hold, and pinch it together. This splits the peel and you can then peel it much more easily. At first I didn't believe it when A.K. showed me but it is actually way easier. I'll never peel a banana the other way ever again.

With every mouthful of banana that glistening water looked more and more inviting. Within ten minutes my brain had successfully managed to somehow turn this dirty infested river into a tropical lagoon. I knew there was no turning back. I had to give it a go. I convinced myself that as long as I didn't open my mouth at all, and didn't pee so one of those bugs couldn't crawl up my willy, I'd be fine. I took my shoes and socks off but kept my clothes on as they needed a wash, and waded in slowly. It wasn't as refreshing as I'd thought but still relaxing. Kind of like a warm bath after a long gym session. My watch said the water temperature was 32 degrees. I can believe it considering it was 43 degrees outside. I lay on my back and floated slowly down the river, completely forgetting that a million people probably took a shit in the river upstream. What doesn't kill you makes you stronger, right? Although this was possibly pushing it a bit far. Can E. coli make you stronger?

I ended the day in Pithora, which involved a candlelit dinner because of a power cut due to a huge lightning storm. I love the smell of fresh rain on hard sandy ground mixed with the smell of curry and coconuts. My senses were going crazy, but I wasn't managing to appreciate it as I had one thought on my mind: was the monsoon here to stay now? Was that the end of my dry days in India? When the monsoons starts that's it. It rains for months. I was nervous. Cycling on the same road as cars with no windscreens would surely result in the death of me. Also wet roads covered up potholes, so the chances of getting punctures, or worse, a broken rim, were a lot higher. I fell asleep worried.

I prayed for no rain to every God, but mainly Shiva, promising not to eat beef ever again. He/she obviously heard me as it was fairly dry when I woke up. Another early start got me on the road by five after a pile of Parle-G biscuits and five cups of chai tea. I even tried to make a chai-tea-Parle-G kind of shake so that I could drink it (the biscuits were quite dry), but it didn't work at all and instead I fed it to one of the stray dogs lurking near me.

Heading into Raipur, it was quite busy and exhausting trying to keep my wits about me. There were a lot of festivities and I even passed a wedding ceremony which involved a truck driving down the street with huge speakers, followed by a procession of drummers and then about 300 men dancing along. Kind of like the hippy version of Notting Hill Carnival.

I was nearly pulled off Maid Marian to join in, and probably would have if I'd trusted someone with my bike. They seemed a jolly lot.

Watching all those people dancing made me hungry, so I stopped for lunch at a typical roadside café. I ordered food by pointing to someone else's plate and the cook said something to me in Hindi. I presumed he was confirming what I pointed at so just said yes and mimicked the typical Indian head nod-roll-shake, which is a mixture of yes and no all rolled up into one pretty confusing, yet incredibly comforting gesture. If over-elaborated it acts as a great way to stretch your neck too. Five minutes later I got what I asked for but on the side was a bowl of fresh tomato and onion salad, sprinkled with heavenly coriander. It looked so good. Up to now I'd only stuck to rice and curry mainly, with the occasional samosa. I hadn't had any fresh veg at all. I looked in the bowl. There was some juice at the bottom. Was it water or tomato liquid? I stared at it for ages and then, much like the river swim, convinced myself I'd be OK if I only ate the top layer and didn't touch the water bit at the bottom.

Later in the hotel, however, oh my god, the world was falling out my ass. Even the smallest bit of water used to wash the tomatoes and onions was enough to start World War Three in my guts. I spent about an hour sitting on the loo. Luckily it was a proper loo and not one of the squat ones that India mostly used. I don't even want to know how things would have played out. Who can squat for an hour? Someone told me to have a Coke with every meal in India as that kills some of the bugs that give you Delhi-belly. I thought, I might start doing that.

*

The next day, I wanted to reach Nagpur by nightfall. It was a good 135 miles away, which would be my longest day in India. Of all the days to try and race me, today probably wasn't it seeing as I had my head down for most of it. But for whatever reason this was the day when I had loads of people trying to challenge me on their bikes. Pretty much every bike in India is a solid heavy single-speed bike that looks not that dissimilar to a vintage Dutch bike. These bikes are indestructible and on some occasions have two top tubes to add strength so that they can carry heavy loads. It's quite common to see their owners pushing their bikes, not because they were too heavy, which they probably were, but because there was nowhere left for the rider to sit because of the 300 bags of curry powder strapped all over them. They were incredible machines that never broke and if they did anyone could fix them with a hammer and some wire. I had fallen in love with them and had already decided to try and find one on eBay when I got home.

These bikes, although strong and tough, certainly weren't made for racing, but nevertheless the kids riding them would put on a good fight. They'd come up alongside me, overtake for as long as they could and then give up, graciously of course, with huge smiles on their faces. A cheeky side of me thought about turning Chasing Dogs into Chasing Cyclists. If I went slow enough, how far could I get a chap to cycle away from where he was going? I had to slap myself at the thought because that would just be mean, but it's not like I'd be forcing them or anything.

The road was a bit better than before and I managed to get to double figures on the speedometer. Even though the roads had been widened in recent years, the bridges were still thin and barely fitted two trucks. This made crossing the sometimes 300 m long bridges a bit of a nightmare. At around 9 a.m., when the sun was quite low in the sky and shining right into the faces of oncoming traffic, I approached one of these bridges. It was one of the longer ones at probably 500 m long, so I was relieved to look in my mirror and see an empty road behind me. This was good and meant I wasn't going to get pushed into the barrier as a truck tried to overtake me with oncoming traffic.

There was a steady line of trucks coming the other way and they all waved at me with smiles. Then as I was halfway across the bridge one of the trucks near the back of the line of about ten trucks decided he was going to try and overtake all of them. He swerved into my lane about 100 m away and started to overtake. He hadn't seen me at all. The gap between his truck and my side of the road where the railings were was about half a metre. Five trucks into his ridiculous overtaking manoeuvre and already committed, there was no way all three of us were going to fit on this bridge. My heart started to race as I thought of all the options. Would I have time to get off Maid Marian, lean her flat against the railings and jump into the river which was only a few metres below, or at least hang on the edge. No, that wouldn't work. Just then I saw a slight indent in the railing about 30 m ahead, the truck still bombing along towards me, a cloud of dust behind it. I could just about get there in time. The driver still hadn't seen me, so as I stepped it up a gear I waved both hands in the air. He saw me and kind of gave me the look of, 'Sorry buddy, but what am I meant to do?' Brake! That's what you need to do. Brake! He was already going too fast and I saw he started to brake. The sound of screeching metal suggested his brakes weren't that good. We both raced towards each other in a weird game of chicken. Five metres, four metres, three metres . . . I could see the huge wing mirror heading straight for my head. I closed my eyes and ducked onto the small indent at the last second and felt something hit my helmet with a deafening sound as a gust or air and dust engulfed and disorientated me.

For a moment I didn't know what had happened. I opened my eyes and looked behind me. Off the bottom of the wing mirror was a 30 cm long black rope tassel with a golf-ball-sized knot on the end. That's what must have hit my helmet. I stood there for what seemed an eternity until the bridge was empty again. Still shook up I made the last dash to the end of the bridge and stopped on the side of the road under a tree. I took my helmet off to see if there was any damage but there was none at all. My heart was still pounding. I certainly put the theory that you only get run over once in life to the test. That was without a doubt the closest you could get to being run over without actually participating in the event.

I'm not sure if my near head-on collision had anything to do with it, or maybe I was just bored of cycling all day every day in the heat, trying to deal with getting ripped off every five seconds, and being mobbed all the time, but I was starting to get depressed again. There seemed to be a running theme. I was fine for the first few weeks in a new country but the novelty soon wore off and I'd think about the accident again and get depressed. I genuinely was excited to try and get back to London in time for the Olympics and deliver my Olympic Torch, but it was hard to keep focused when things weren't going well. India was meant to be an easy 110-odd miles per day but it seemed a lot harder than it should have been. Maybe my body was just tired. My total mileage was around

13,000 miles or so. I had stopped counting because it didn't matter, but nevertheless 13,000 miles in four months on the road including one month's rest due to the accident was a lot. I really needed to take some time out again to recharge my mind if anything. Unfortunately, I couldn't because I needed to be in Mumbai in time for my flight in a week. Nagpur is pretty much slap bang in the middle of India but I was over halfway because of my detour, which was a slight comfort.

'Sean, aren't you meant to be on the bike already?'

After Nagpur, I'd done another sub-100 mile day to get to Amravati. It was 7 a.m. the following day and I was still in bed.

'Come one buddy, only another week to go and there's a surprise for you in Mumbai.'

'Really? What is it?'

'I'm not telling, you're just going to have to hurry up and get there.'

Rachel had noticed that I was quite confident cycling in tri position on the bike. The downside is you have no access to brakes, so if something jumps in the roads you have to push yourself up and then find your brakes. I hadn't found many roads in Asia where I could safely do this, so it hadn't been since Australia that I last managed it. I was a bit rusty at first, but like riding a bicycle it soon comes back.

'What else can you do while in tri position Sean?' asked Rachel as she and A.K. came alongside me a mile down the road that morning.

'Anything!' I said.

'Great. Peel and eat this.' Rachel passed me a banana.

'Too easy!'

I needed a banana anyway, so with both elbows on the pads I peeled the banana, and yes, the way monkeys do, and ate it.

'Do it again. Do it again. That's awesome.' Rachel pointed the camera at me while passing me another banana. She was like an excitable child, which made me smile. I didn't think of it as being hard but guess it looked good on film.

'What else? Can you text?'

I got my phone out and pretended to text. A little harder to see what you are writing in the glare of the midday sun but doable.

'How about this?' Rachel passed me a book. 'Can you read and cycle?"

Sudden thoughts of me crashing and trying to explain that I crashed because I was reading a book made me laugh. I could just about read a sentence at a time but then had to look at the road again. It was a lot easier than I thought though, to jump back and forth. I could have easily done it in Australia. I later learned that one of the other riders in the race read a total of six books on his ride. He also crashed into a parked car in Australia and although promised he wasn't reading his book at the time, I have my doubts.

The afternoon's activities got even more exciting when I got to a section of road that for whatever reason had loads of tractors bombing along it at a steady 24 mph. Much like in a Tour de France peloton, if I stayed within half a metre of the back of the tractor I was caught in its back draft and would fly along. Most of their tractors had about five people sitting on the wheel arches laughing and staring at me. It became a fun game even though I really had to concentrate to stay within the optimal distance. If I dropped back too far I was spat out the back, and any closer might result in me rear-ending the tractor. There was a lot of trust here that the driver didn't brake suddenly, but I must say the passengers were quite good at warning me when they were slowing or turning off.

By late afternoon I had done my 100 miles nearly two hours quicker than previously. I'd reached a town called Malkapur and there wasn't much point in carrying on as it might be harder to find accommodation. It was a nice change to be able to settle into a hotel in the daylight and have time to chill out a little before bed.

I could feel the monsoon getting closer and closer. The daunting clouds to the south and the headwinds, mixed in with the occasional drops of rain and humidity, all made for pretty adventurous tropical cycling. I had planned to be in Mumbai by the end of the following day but with these winds, even if I did push it, I'd then have to navigate Mumbai at night. I decided to get as near to Mumbai as I could the next day and then do the final leg in the morning. I knew that there was at least a two- to three-hour cycle through the city. A city of 13 million people. I didn't have a map and had no idea how I was going to find the airport.

'Don't worry mate, we'll find it. A.K. says he knows,' Rachel said with a smile on her face while A.K. did the head nod-roll-shake. He didn't look confident at all. Why was Rachel so certain?

As I climbed the wind got stronger and stronger. I knew I had one last range to get over before a sharp descent into the Mumbai region. By mid-afternoon I had reached the top of the last big hill only to be hit in the face by wind that was similar to the winds of New Mexico. My pace dropped to 5 mph but I pushed on regardless and covered up my cycle computer again.

What followed was a big downhill day. I knew I had a 700 m drop and was excited. The wind was still strong but that didn't matter. Down and down I zoomed, undercutting trucks, overtaking tractors and flying past tuk-tuks to the amazement of many onlookers. Rachel and A.K. couldn't keep up. For miles I didn't even turn my legs. This was in fact the first proper downhill I had had since crossing the divide in Australia. Seeing my speedometer hit 40 mph was an incredible feeling and for the first time in a while I felt like a real cyclist again. Amazing such a small thing can make you feel so good.

That good feeling was swiftly taken away from me at my lunch stop when I saw something that will be engrained on my brain forever. I saw right behind the truck stop where I was eating a row of five men in a line evenly spaced a few metres apart from each other using their hands to wipe their arses. It was one of those things where you didn't really know whether it was actually happening, so just kept looking around to see if anyone else noticed, which no one did, and then looking back. I felt a little bit of vomit coming up. The technique was, while squatting they would have a bottle of water in one hand pouring it into their crotch area. The other hand was round the back cupping some of the water between their legs while washing said undercarriage. I wish I had never seen it and funnily enough I lost my appetite so gave the rest of my meal to a stray dog, who didn't seem to mind the spiciness of the curry.

\*

It was my last day cycling across India. It suddenly hit me that I had cycled across the whole of India, coast to coast. I hadn't managed to do that in America and this was a pretty good consolation prize. India had been a lot tougher than I had thought but all in all it was a great country. If you ignore that one-hour session on the loo, I hadn't really got properly ill either, which was a bonus, too. The short days meant I had put some healthy weight back on and was now a good 10.2 stone as opposed to the below 10 stone from Thailand days. The only last hurdle was to work out where the airport was and then navigate my way through the two million vehicles registered in Mumbai.

'Are you ready for your surprise?' Rachel shouted out the window.

'Really? I thought you were joking'

'Nope. We'll go ahead and get them, and wave you down.'

With that they zoomed ahead. I had no idea and spent the next five miles trying to guess. Them? It made no sense.

Eventually after about two miles I saw Rachel standing in the road with a camera filming me. I still didn't know what she had set up. Only when I got close did I see that there was a group of about twenty cyclists next to a café all cheering and waving at me. They were proper cyclists, too, judging by the fact they all wore helmets and were riding pretty nice racing bikes.

'What's this?' I asked, surprised at how embarrassed I was getting at all the attention considering all I got was attention all the way across India.

'These guys heard you were coming so I arranged for them to come and meet you to cycle to the airport.'

I was speechless. This was awesome. I had some cycling buddies for the last leg who certainly knew where the airport was.

I said hello and we all chatted for about an hour while I had some street food. I seemed to be the only one eating: a few said they weren't hungry and a few said they would never eat from street vendors. One of them even said they had never eaten a coconut from a street vendor. I couldn't believe it. Was it the caste system that deemed eating street food for the lower classes only or did they just have better food at home?

Navigating to the airport would have been damn near impossible and I was glad to have these guys with me. They were part of the Mumbai Cycle Club and met up every weekend to go for rides together. They also knew exactly how to deal with the bad drivers and were constantly shouting at people. You really need to push the confident/arrogant boundary when cycling through Mumbai. If drivers sense they might be able to push you out of the way, they would do so. If you are really arrogant and aggressive, drivers tend to give you more room as they aren't sure where you might go. Although hectic, we eventually reached the airport safe and sound. My flight out was in two days, which meant I had an entire day off, which I needed. We all sat at the airport for an hour waiting for Rachel and A.K. while eating, wait for it, pizza. Curry pizza obviously, but still pizza. Eventually Rachel appeared and it was time to say goodbye to A.K. He had never been to Mumbai but had a friend so was going to visit him for a few days before driving all the way back to Kolkata. I hadn't really had much time to chat to him other that a few minutes here and there at lunch stops, but Rachel had bonded with him and I knew he had enjoyed his adventure across India too.

It was time to say goodbye to my cycle buddies and head off to a friend of a friend's flat to stay for the night.

'This isn't goodbye Sean, we'll see you tomorrow.'

'Tomorrow?' I looked towards Rachel

'We have some things planned for tomorrow. Nothing big. But these guys will be there.'

My rest day turned out to be not so restful but good fun nonetheless. Rachel had organised for me to build my own traditional Indian bike, which I was then going to send back to London. I was going to get one on eBay but having one actually from India was amazing, and for the reasonable price of £40 was incredible. Rachel enlisted the help of Johann Daniels who was head of Mumbai Cycling. I was expecting to meet a Dutch fellow with a name like that, but Johann was as Indian as they come, except for the fact his English was impeccable, probably better than mine. He also owned a bike shop called Bike Shark, which is where I went to build my Indian bike. I say *I built*, but there seemed to be a scrum of people all helping out. I really had no idea how these bikes worked. You couldn't use ordinary tools, and things like the crank were basically smashed into the frame with a hammer. If you need a hammer to make a bike you can be sure it's pretty strong.

After building my lovely new bike which I had already named Meera – a Hindu goddess – Rachel said there was going to be a small gathering of cyclists who wanted to meet me in one of the parks, so we headed back into town. This small gathering turned out to be 100 keen cyclists and they had all arranged to do a midnight monsoon bike ride south towards the affluent area of Mumbai called Juhu. It certainly did look cool as we all weaved our way through the busy streets taking over the entire road. I really wanted to ride Meera but she had been too big to fit in the taxi to get to the park, so I cycled Maid Marian instead. Also I figured everyone would be interested to see Maid Marian as she had done me proud so far. I was roped into doing a quick impromptu speech, which landed up on YouTube in surprisingly quick fashion. Thereafter we spent a good hour taking over the streets of Mumbai to the annoyance of many motorists.

As I've already said, cycling is seen as a pretty lower-class activity in India and cyclists are the lowest on the list of hierarchy on the roads. Johann and the gang were keen to try and show that cycling was cool for everyone. In their hands, cycling is coming along nicely. There is even a Tour of India race which is growing fast. But as for me, my own tour of India was over. It was time to head back to Europe.

# 19

# HELLO EUROPE

As much as I loved the Asian leg of the trip, the constant attention and busyness had taken its toll on my mind. It was great to finally be in a country where no one gave me a second glance, or at least not for the same reasons. I had by now cultivated a pretty grotesque ginger beard that seemed to get people looking, pointing, and usually laughing, no matter where I was in the world.

My flight to Istanbul had been a daytime one, which meant there was less stress about having to get some sleep. I've never slept well on flights, but at least this was my last one. I'd never have to take Maid Marian apart ever again and although with each boxing and unboxing I got a little better, I was always nervous something would break or she would go missing again. I made my way to my hotel, where I had managed to download some maps, which made getting out of Istanbul a lot easier than it could have been.

My Turkish adventure started with something I'd almost forgotten about: a massively long hill to climb. Except for that one day in India and coming into Mount Isa in the outback, I hadn't seen a proper hill since the Rockies and my legs felt it. After a good fifteen-minute climb I made it to the top and down the other side only to be confronted with yet another climb. The going was slow but at least I had the downhills to recover. It was also great to have a huge hard shoulder that didn't have oncoming trucks on it. It meant I could actually listen to music again, which I hadn't done since Australia really. First on the list: Queen, 'Bicycle Race'. That always seemed to lift my pace while bringing a smile to my hairy face.

As the city disappeared behind me the coastal farmlands opened up ahead. Roads flanked by vibrant fields of sunflowers and the crystal blue ocean were a stark contrast to the overall brownness of middle India. My first stop for late breakfast was a kebab, coffee and Coke. I can't ever remember ever having a kebab for breakfast but it certainly hit the spot. I had also forgotten how much I missed coffee.

Istanbul was about 150 miles from the Greek border and I decided to try and push it all the way before nightfall. I had four weeks till I needed to get back to London with my Olympic Torch, which still meant averaging a good 130 miles per day through Greece, across to Italy on the ferry, around the French Riviera to miss the Alps and then up towards Calais. London here I come!

I had no idea if I'd be able to find a hotel near the border but thought I'd take a risk. I figured most borders have hotels. I stocked up 20 miles before and headed towards Greece helped along by a nice tailwind. Ah tailwinds. Where were you when I needed you most? It seemed an age since I last had one and I'd forgotten the jubilation and positivity you get bombing along at 18 mph without much effort. I was heading right into the sunset and although slightly blinding at times it was incredibly beautiful. The sunsets in India had been very orange because of the dust in the air. This sunset here was almost purple and a little crisper. It was as if I'd switched over to the HD channel. Everything seemed sharper.

About a mile from the border I came across a pretty rundown, yet still working, petrol station with a hotel attached. After I unpacked everything in my room I decided to go and get some food from the garage next door. I went outside still in Lycra but having taken off the bottom part of my tights. I walked around the wall towards the garage but it was closed. I'd been dreaming of Mediterranean salads, smoked ham and pasta for a while but I'd have to wait another day for that: dinner was a packet of nuts and a banana. I saw another man ahead of me and went over to ask him if there was anywhere I could get food. As soon as he saw me he started shouting something in Turkish, motioning for me to go back to the hotel. Again he shouted and looked even angrier. It was as if we were about to be attacked and I needed to take cover. Then he shouted again, pointed to my legs and then shook his finger at me. I knew right there that it was my stubbly calves that he had a problem with. I turned around and started to jog back to the hotel. They really do not like legs here. Even though this place was deserted and he was the only person around, it was still inappropriate.

The Turkish-Greek border crossing was pretty scary. I had only done two real land border crossings in the whole trip, which was Chile-Peru and Malaysia-Thailand (Singapore to Malaysia was just a bridge really and was like going to France. One quick check of the passport and you're off). There seemed to be a lot of military activity around and apparently it had been closed a few months back, which would have meant a 100-mile detour north. The man in the booth took his time looking through my passport which was pretty full with stamps, most of them smudged due to getting wet in Malaysia, but eventually, and with a suitably stern face that most border guards have, he waved me through. Hello Greece.

Within minutes you could tell I was in a predominantly Christian country. There were churches everywhere, all painted white with beautifully sculptured statues of Mary near the roadside. Some of the churches couldn't have held more than twenty people in them but still seemed in use. The plan was to head towards the coast. It'd be a shame to come all the way to Greece and not cycle along the crystal clear Mediterranean sea. The weather was good, the roads even better and after getting a map of Greece I finally knew where I was going.

From Singapore I had gotten rid of my small cycle bottles and had been carrying 1.5-litre standard water in each cage instead. This meant I was managing to carry over a litre more than before, which gave me around 90 minutes longer before needing to refill as I knew my sweat rate was about 500–800 ml per hour. The downside of using a normal water bottle was that every time I wanted to drink I had to unscrew the bottle top, hold the cap in my hand while holding the handlebars, and take a drink. I'd often drop the bottle top and then have to turn around and hope it hadn't fallen in a pile of cow shit or E.coli ridden puddles. So I was delighted when I looked at a sports drink bottle in a petrol station and realised the quick drink squirty lid would actually fit my 1.5

litre bottle. I could not believe it had taken me 13,000 miles to work this out. I bought two Lucozades, took their lids off and put them on my water bottles. I then stood back and gloated in my discovery. Oh, the simple things in life.

The days were warm but at only 30 degrees pretty cool in comparison to the last few months. The cloudless skies and fresh coastal air had an amazing way of lifting spirits as the miles rolled on. Being back in Europe in June meant the sun was setting pretty late and I had loads of daylight hours to cycle in. This meant that with 130-mile days I could easily afford a full hour's guilt-free lunch break. Even if it landed up being two hours that only meant I had to cycle through till 10 p.m., which was fine.

After reaching Kavala that first night, I continued along the coast to Thessaloniki. There was a direct road pretty much all the way along the coast. It seemed ideal except for a 15-mile section that was white on the map when all other roads were yellow. This suggested that the road might be gravel. My options were to either go quite far inland to miss this white section, which would add an extra hour to my day, or to give it a go. I figured that even if my pace dropped to 5 mph on the gravel it might still be quicker, and on the plus side, a lot more adventurous.

Turns out white roads do mean gravel and soon my lovely tar road ended. I had hoped for some good gravel but it was sandy and very bumpy and my pace dropped to around 3 mph – which is actually slower than walking pace. It was adventurous though and I pushed on enjoying my off-road adventure. The further I cycled the worse and worse the road became, until after about ten miles it came to a complete end.

My heart sank. No way! This couldn't be it. I couldn't go back. I was way past the point of no return. Ahead lay a small dirt path that headed down a rocky cliff. I looked ahead and saw the path continue up the other side about 100 m away. I figured it would be better to push Maid Marian than go all the way back and around again. I got off and started to walk through the rocks, occasionally having to pick Maid Marian up and lift her over various boulders. On and on I pushed, my shoes getting sand and rocks in them, battling the heat of the midday sun. Cycling shoes aren't the easiest to walk in at the best of times. Eventually the road seemed to kind of come back and the next few hours were a mixture of cycling and pushing my way through dry Mediterranean scrubland. It was hot and I ran out of water too, but knew that I wasn't too far from the next town, surely!

By 3 p.m. I was back on a main road and needed to stop, get the rock out my shoes and rehydrate. I headed for the nearest beach to find a restaurant. The first one was right on the cliffs overlooking the beach below. It was only once I had settled in and ordered a cheeky beer to celebrate my off-road adventure that I noticed something strange about everyone on the beach. They were all completely naked. Funny how just the day before, not that far from here, albeit in a different country, I was shouted at for showing my calves in public. You'd never catch me naked in a million years but good on these, mostly old, people, letting it all hang – and hang was the best word for it – out. It must feel liberating, I guess.

I carried on along the coast being distracted by naked people for the rest of the afternoon until reaching Thessaloniki. I found a café on the outskirts with Wi-Fi, so decided to check where and when the ferries go to Italy. Just north of where

I was were Macedonia, Kosovo, Bosnia and Montenegro. My mind started to race. What if I headed north? Could I even head north? Places like Kosovo and Bosnia were pretty dangerous countries to be in not that long ago. I had no visas, maps or anything. Also would I still be able to get back to London in time? I zoomed out even further to see the difference. It was a bit longer but in essence I'd be heading up in the same route running parallel to Italy. It would add about three days to my ride, but spread out over the next three weeks would only add about 15 miles per day extra. I really needed to make the decision now as I was already just past the road I'd need to take to head north. It was literally now or never. I normally love spontaneity but this seemed quite drastic. What if I got all the way to Kosovo and they didn't let me in and I had to turn around again?

'Come on Little Flying Cow, let's do this!' I said, fuelled by some Greek courage (Like Dutch courage but louder). I was excited again. Since America I hadn't really had much choice in my route really. Most of Australia was one road: Malaysia and Thailand similar along a thin peninsular, and India too. If I had been racing I probably wouldn't have made the decision to head into Kosovo. I'd been struggling with balancing pushing big miles (for nothing) and having an adventure ever since the accident. I think now, finally, I was coming to a happy compromise. I'd still need to do 140 miles per day to get to London in time but doing it through Kosovo, Bosnia and Albania made it a lot more interesting and fulfilling for me.

I jumped on Maid Marian and even gave a little 'Yeehaa' as I bombed a mile back to the road that would take me north. I went down into tri position and started taking my map out of the clear sleeve on my handlebars to move it to the next page. Another skill I'd become quite good at. In my excitement though, I wasn't concentrating on the road and all of a sudden hit a massive pothole, which sent me veering off into the road. I managed to stay on the bike but realised I had got a puncture. I was really annoyed at myself but it was my first puncture since that day in India when I'd had to change all my patches, so couldn't really complain. Something else was wrong though: her steering felt tight. There seemed to be a point, exactly when the wheel was facing forward, that the steering would click into position and stay there. I knew what had happened straight away. When I hit the pothole, one of the bearings in the steering column must have seized or broken or something. I tried wiggling it around but nothing. I decided to try carrying on cycling to see what it was like. Luckily it always clicked the wheel into straight position, so going in a straight line was easy. Taking corners was a little harder because I had to really force the handlebars to 'un-click' so that I could steer left or right. It wasn't hard but did mean I had to concentrate when turning and hope my wheel didn't click back into straight position halfway around a corner.

I headed north towards Macedonia along a pretty empty road. I passed a town off to the east called Kilkis. In my mind it was called Kill Kiss though, and would be the perfect place to film a James Bond movie. I was half-tempted to reroute into the town to see what it was like, but it would probably have been a disappointment and it was getting dark so I decided to push on. By seven I reached the road heading west towards the border. I was greeted with a lovely tailwind and headed on towards an amazing lake surrounded by forested mountains. It looked almost Austrian and a lot greener than the dry coastal route. There was a small hotel near the border, which I checked into with the plan of going through the border in the morning. If they let me in. I had no visa.

It turned out you don't need a visa to get into Macedonia, which was a relief. I went through with no problems at all. In fact they were the friendliest lot so far. Straight away I felt the sudden change in surroundings. I very much felt like I was in Eastern Europe now. Cars seemed older and rusty, architecture dilapidated or just dated, and there was no hard shoulder to cycle on. I was starving and suddenly realised they probably didn't use euros here and I had no cash. I needed to draw money but how much? What did things cost? What money do they use? I literally knew nothing about Macedonia except you didn't need a visa to enter it. As I was going through the border town I passed a small supermarket with a Coke poster in the window. 1 Coke = 50 ден. I figured if one Coke cost 50 ден then I could probably survive on 500 ден per day. I thought I'd be in Macedonia for at least two days, so needed 1000 ден. I went in search of a cashpoint, quite chuffed at my Sherlock Holmes-style skills of deduction.

Macedonia was incredible. My route started around a lake as the early morning mist danced on top of the mirror smooth water. I was surrounded by hills and soon left the lake to head inland to begin my Eastern Europe adventure. I climbed and climbed all day and even though I had probably the fifth-worst headwind of the entire trip it somehow didn't matter this time. I had found a small back road, which meant I didn't need to do the highway, and it was amazing. Up and up I climbed, taking in my new surroundings and getting smiles from people as I cycled past.

By lunchtime I looked at my map and I was already halfway across Macedonia. It felt weird that I could and probably would cycle across the entire country in one day. I stopped for lunch in a café and started chatting to the owner. The young chap, who was called Robert, seemed determined to tell me some history about Macedonia. He told me all about how Alexander the Great was in fact Macedonian and not Greek. He also said that the country isn't called Macedonia. It's called FYROM, which is actually even in brackets on Google maps. It was great to hear some of the history but I think Robert might have been trying to use me as a political weapon, as if I could do something about it. I guess he was proud of his country and wanted to tell every tourist who came in so that they got the story right and went away telling it. I liked that. We chatted for a good hour and he even found me on Facebook. We still keep in touch to this day.

I carried on skywards until reaching the summit and saw Skopje about 20 miles ahead in the valley below. I knew I'd have one of the best downhills of my life. For the next hour or so I barely peddled as I zoomed down the mountain. Was it worth the full day of climbing with headwinds? Hell, yes! I had a long ten-mile dead straight road as I headed for the centre of town to find a hotel. I was getting chased by a few dogs again, which meant only one thing, Chasing Dogs time. I had missed playing it and although a little rusty at first, I soon managed to get each barking dog a minimum of 200 m from where they started. I was happy with that.

I worked my way into the centre of town where there was a huge statue of Alexander the Great on a horse. Turns out café chap wasn't lying. It was 5 p.m. so I decided to park up outside a café, have a beer and people watch. Skopje city centre was very clean with loads of tourists and lined with al fresco cafes and bars surrounding the central statue of old Mr Great. People seemed well dressed, in a typical trendy Eastern European way. I sat for a few hours watching people as they stared back at me and smiled as they walked past the café.

I left Skopje early to head towards the Kosovo border. I was really nervous. Partly because if they didn't let me in, I had a long way back to go, and partly because I really had no idea if Kosovo was a safe place to cycle. My only knowledge of Kosovo involved pretty horrific images of tanks and warfare that I'd seen on TV as a kid. I know that was over a decade ago but I was still nervous.

I climbed and climbed all morning to get to the Kosovo border until eventually it lay in front of me. My heart started to race and I decided to join the back of the queue of cars instead of going to the front and trying to sneak in front of another driver like I normally do. The border guards seemed to be taking longer than normal to look at everyone's passports, which made me even more concerned. Eventually it was my turn and I went up to the window and gave the guy my passport. He looked at my picture, then at me, back at my picture and back at me. I'm completely clean shaven in my passport and now had a huge beard. He looked stern and then started flicking through all my smudged visa pages. Well this is it. He's looking for my visa and I don't have one. He stopped on each page and studied it closely. All thirty-two pages of them. I looked behind me to see an irritated van driver shaking his head.

The guard got to the last page, looked up at me again, got out his stamp, stamped my passport, gave it back to me and nodded. What? Was that it? Was I in? I guess so. I said thank you and tucked my passport into the bottom of my tights and raced off in case he changed his mind. My heart was still racing. Kosovo wasn't originally on my route and to be honest I'd never ever thought of visiting it in my life. I was here now though and was excited . . . kind of! More nervous, I guess.

My first impression of Kosovo was that it was even poorer than Macedonia. But the road heading inland was good and it followed a river. Although there were loads of trucks the drivers were pretty friendly. I kept thinking of war here in Kosovo and half-expected a tank to come round every corner. I didn't see any tanks but did see road signs for tanks. I obviously stopped to take a photo. Eventually I reached the plateau and headed towards Ferizaj. Up here it looked very *Sound of Music*: painted red tongue-and-groove wooden houses in fields surrounded by forested mountains. There seemed to be a lot of development too, which I guess is always a good sign for a country. I stopped for lunch and was surprised at the amount of pizza on the menu. I'm not sure what the traditional food of Kosovo is but I'm guessing it wasn't pizza.

I pushed on to the next major town, which is where I needed to start heading back down towards Albania. Again there seemed an uncharacteristic number of pizza restaurants. Had Kosovo only just discovered pizza? They were everywhere. Luckily pizza was quite good for me. It's high in fat, salt, protein and carbs, which I needed. My inquisitiveness needed to give a Kosovar pizza a go. I did and it wasn't anything special but fuelled me sufficiently.

I was disappointed to find myself leaving Kosovo so quickly. Although the people ate way too much pizza they were incredibly friendly and happy to see a tourist in their country. I didn't see one other tourist in my short ten hours in Kosovo. The one good thing is that I had an amazing downhill into Albania. On passing through the border, my route followed a lake and I stopped off at a random holiday park for a quick bite to eat before heading to the lakeside town of Kukës. On entering the town I passed some kids playing football; on seeing me they all stopped and two of them shouted, 'Money, money'. Seriously, I'm pretty sure they were wearing Puma trainers. I carried on into the centre of the city and found a cashpoint. Again, I had no idea how much money to draw so went with the middle figure on the screen as that was hopefully around £20. As I finished up I noticed an entire café looking at me and waving. I waved back and the all laughed. I carried on walking around the corner to try and find a hotel and two kids came running up to me.

'Where you from?' The older one spoke good English.

'I live in London,' I said still walking.

'I like football. Rooney yes.' He laughed and did an air goal kick. 'You need hotel. I show you cheap place.'

'Yes, please, that would be great.'

The kid started taking me down a street away from town. The buildings were pretty rundown but in a nice antique way. The hotel was pleasant and it only cost £5 for a room. I couldn't believe it. There might have been a hotel in Thailand that was £8 but I'm sure £5 was the cheapest I'd found in a while.

After heading out for dinner, I decided to walk back through the town to explore. I found a typical old man's bar filled with old Albanian men, playing cards and smoking around a dimly lit table. I liked it. There were a few tables on the pavement of a nice tree-lined street so I settled in for a cheeky beer. I sat there for a while as people carried on staring and pointing at me. A group of kids walked past me, all laughing and then at least one of them would run over, put his hand out and say, 'Money, money'. One of the old men in the pub would then tell them to bugger off and they'd run off laughing. It really didn't make sense at all. They were not poor in appearance by any means. It was a bit sad because other than that everyone seemed amazingly friendly, and beardless. I still hadn't seen one beard.

The next day I headed into the Albanian mountains. Bring on the hills. Within a few miles I turned off the main highway and was on a small farm road. It was incredible and I was greeted with a good few miles down to a small river before the first of many hills started. I still had to be careful on the downhills because of my sticky steering column, which still stuck in straight mode. I had kind of got used to it though, but still had to concentrate a lot on the corners.

The weather was good and I soon found myself in amongst Alpine-type forests with occasional abandoned and derelict buildings. The roads were almost empty and I barely saw any cars all morning. Although my legs were burning I felt strong. It wasn't too hot or too cold and the picture-postcard blue sky with green trees brought a calming effect to me, even with 150 bmp heart rate.

Up and down all morning until I came across my first town. I was starving so stopped and asked someone where I could get some food. The chap didn't speak English but understood. I was a bit early but he pointed at his watch and showed me ten fingers, which meant it was opening soon, ten minutes at an educated guess. I said thank you and sat at one of the tables outside in the sun while massaging my quads after a good morning of hills.

Rural Albania was amazing. Quaint village streets which often had an old man with his dog walking along with a stick, slightly hunched over, and wearing either grey or brown linen-type outfits. They didn't care much for this hairy ginger cyclist in a kind of wise and noble way. I was from a different world that they weren't particularly interested in.

While waiting for my meal three men came in for breakfast. They were all well dressed in suits and sat down chatting. Within a few minutes one of them waved the waitress over and shouted something. She turned around and got a bottle of vodka from the shelf and brought it to them. They poured each other a glass each and did a 'cheers' and knocked it back. Seriously. It was 9 a.m. It didn't stop at one. By the time my breakfast came, they had knocked back four pretty big shots. Amazing, all this before a day's work.

I carried on climbing all day and eventually reached the ski resort of Puka to restock some supplies. Today was by far the biggest climbing day since South America and my legs felt it. Although, unlike South America, my knees didn't hurt at all. I still can't believe such a small change in saddle height had fixed everything. I left Puka and started the best downhill of my life. Switchback after switchback, carefully making sure my steering didn't lock, all the way from 2000 m to nearly sea level. Time flies by when you are having fun. What an experience.

By early evening I headed towards the Montenegro border. There wasn't much in the way of hotels so I was surprised to see a Holiday Inn. I check it and turned out it was just called

Hotel Holiday and had nothing to do with the Holiday Inn. It was identical though, with the big green 'H' on a big sign outside, which was replicated on the room key rings too. It seemed a pretty recently-built hotel and I wondered how long it would take the real Holiday Inn to work it out and if there was in fact anything they could do about it.

I was quite excited about the following day as I'd be doing three countries in one day: Albania for breakfast, Montenegro for lunch and Bosnia for dinner. I hadn't used half the Albanian money I drew from the cash machine so decided to splash out on breakfast and use the leftover coins to buy three litres of Coke. Sugar wasn't a great energy source but I was feeling adventurous: I was looking forward to the sugar crash later; it was going to be huge.

Crossing into Montenegro was pretty seamless and again I noticed a change in poverty. Now there were donkeys pulling carts on the main roads as well as really incredible vintage tractors. It was a steady climb from the border into the countryside. There were a lot more cyclists too and we'd smile and wave at each other as I cycled past. At one point I saw an old man about 50 metres ahead of me trying to fix his bike on the side of the road. When I came up alongside him I saw that his chain had fallen off and he was trying to put it back on with a sickle to avoid getting his hands dirty.

'Hello', I said, embarrassed that I didn't even know what hello was in Montenegrin. 'I'll do it for you.'

My hands were already filthy from the bar tape on my handlebars, which now had five months of dirt and grime on them. He looked confused and just smiled at me. He obviously didn't understand what I said. I bent over, took the chain with my hand, put it along the bottom of the front cog and spun the pedal half a turn backwards to get it back on. By doing it this way you don't need to pick up your back wheel to pedal forwards. It took no more than three seconds. I looked up to see a still slightly confused look on the old man's face. I jumped back on Maid Marian and waved as I rode off. I looked around after about 50 metres to see the old man happily cycling along, still holding the sickle in his hand. My good deed for the day.

I guess karma does exist because I came to a T-junction in the road and was just turning left when a chap selling fruit next to the road beckoned me over. I wasn't in a rush so went to say hi. Unfortunately he didn't speak English but understood country names, so I pointed back and said 'Cycle Greece' and then pointed ahead and said 'Cycle to Bosnia'. He seemed really impressed and started loading loads of plums, apples and a pear into a bag. I really could have done with some fruit but I hadn't managed to find a cashpoint yet so had no money.

'I have no money, sorry!' I said apologetically.

'No money,' he said and thrust the fruit into my hands. I couldn't believe it. Maybe I need to do more random acts of kindness. I'd been craving fruit but not had enough as it's not very high in calories and took up a lot of room. This was a great treat though and I munched an apple and a pear even before leaving.

Montenegro is only about 100 miles wide but it is all uphill. It took me nine hours to do the 100 miles all the way up to 1000 m above sea level. It was incredibly beautiful and seemed pretty unpopulated. Where do they fit everyone or have they managed to keep a sustained population? Again I knew nothing about Montenegro except they usually have quite attractive Eurovision singers. I had tried to download maps on Google for Bosnia but there were literally five roads that Google decided to show: it was like they just decided to forget about it.

Like Kosovo I was nervous about cycling in Bosnia. I'd been warned about the fact that there were still loads of landmines all over the place and camping off the road was 'suicidal', as someone on Twitter kindly tweeted me. But after passing the border, I was greeted with the most incredible view I've seen in a long time. I was high on the top of a cliff overlooking wild forests below. I went to the edge of the road and looked down to the valley bottom. It was breathtaking. I'm not sure what I expected from Bosnia but not this. To add to the incredible view, I looked below to see a series of switchbacks heading all the way down to the bottom. This was without a doubt the best start to any country so far.

I zoomed down the hill weaving from left to right. I practically had the road to myself and it was hard to imagine this beautiful woodland might be swamped with unexploded landmines. By the time the road flattened out I was along the edge of a lake and heading towards Trebinje. I was quite early so decided to stop at the first restaurant to have a bite to eat. The waitress didn't know any English but the guy on the table next to me became her unofficial translator, a job he was quickly regretting being involved as the bombardment of questions ensued. Poor chap! The one bit of useful advice was that I needed to go into Trebinje. I probably would have stayed somewhere outside the city but was told it was incredibly beautiful and I needed to see it.

They weren't wrong; Trebinje was stunning. Very green, old stone buildings and a picturesque river running through the town. I worked my way into town and slightly fuelled by my huge beer from the restaurant, decided to stop at another bar. I settled in and a chap around my age came over to me and we started chatting. His name was Mikael and the conversation went in a similar way to the one with the guy in Macedonia, telling me about Alexander the Great. Mikael told me that this part of Bosnia was a bit boring and if I really wanted some amazing scenery I needed to head to the coast towards Dubrovnik. He showed me photos on his phone and it looked incredible: old seaside red buildings built into cliffs overlooking the Mediterranean. Maybe it was better than trawling through middle Bosnia. He also said it was pretty much all downhill to the coast. I guessed I would see how I felt in the morning.

How I felt in the morning was, well, rough as a badger's bottom. The last thing I could remember after five beers was having cars hoot at me as I walked back to my hotel in the dark. I really was a lightweight.

I was sad I wasn't getting to explore more of Bosnia, but once I reached the final summit and saw the glistening Mediterranean below, I knew I'd made the right decision. Mikael was right: the downhill to the coast was incredible. I soon found myself on the main road heading along the coast. This would be the road I would now use until I reached Italy. Although coastal, I was very wrong about it being flat. It was in fact incredibly hilly. This part of the Med is flanked by cliffs, and towns and villages are carved into the side. Annoyingly, the picturesque Dubrovnik that I saw on Mikael's phone was about 200 m below the main road and although I really wanted to see it I wasn't really in the mood to go all the way down and then back up again.

# 20

## POLISH POWER

The next big town on my journey was Split, which was 150 miles away. My route carried on along the coast just inland of Dubrovnik, back into a mile of Bosnia and then into Croatia again. I'm always fascinated at how a country's borders are decided. Usually through a series of horrible wars, I can imagine. Did Bosnia ask Croatia for a small section of coastline, because that's exactly what it looked like? Bosnia was inland but then for about a few miles the border cut straight down to the coast. Maybe it helped with importing things back in the day so that they didn't have to rely on other countries to get supplies. Who knows?

With the incredible coastline came the tourists, and with the tourists came inflated prices to match. I was shocked to be charged €7 for a cheese sandwich. I hadn't paid much more than a £5 for a meal since Australia, which meant for the first time in a while I needed to keep an eye on my budget. That morning I saw the first touring cyclist I had seen since Malaysia, when I'd met that couple with their twins. He was cycling 200 m ahead of me so I decided to catch up with him. I pushed hard expecting to catch him fast but found that he was pulling away from me. Wow, this guy was strong! He looked like he was on a race bike with a pannier rack attached to the seat post. My competitive side kicked in. I moved the Rohloff into fourteenth gear, or 'Bradley Wiggins Mode' as I liked to call it, slowly catching up with him.

The cyclist's name was Paul and he was from Poland. He was heading for Split as well, so we agreed to cycle there together. Paul looked to be in his early forties, slightly balding and about my height and weight. He was also really excitable. I fell back and we carried on at a nice pace along the coast. After about 20 minutes I went ahead and pulled Paul for a while. It was a good system. We carried on along the coast taking it in turns to pull each other along. It had been a little flat and we hadn't hit many hills. Paul was strong on the flats but his setup was by far heavier than mine, so I knew he would struggle on the hills.

We reached our first proper hill and just as I got up out the saddle Paul shouted at the top of his voice, 'Polish Powerrrr! Come on!' He got up out of the saddle and pushed it hard up the hill. I've always been good on the hills and although he put in a good effort, my lighter setup and 14,000 miles of training meant I overtook him halfway up, and in doing so shouted, 'Ginger Power!' He laughed and I saw him sit back in his saddle, almost giving up. I was about 50 m ahead by time I reached the top and stopped to wait for him. He came alongside me.

'Wow, you are strong? Where you cycle from?'

'I'm cycling around the world.'

'Whaaaat?' Paul was impressed. And hungry. 'I need food. Cream, cream, cream. Let's go!'

Did he just say cream? It was hard to tell with his accent. We pushed on to the next supermarket and went inside. I heard right. He went straight to the full-fat cream and took a 500 g tub of 30 per cent cream, which in doing some quick maths in my head was a total of about 1500 kcal. He then took a spoon out from his carrier bag and began devouring the cream all the while shouting, 'Cream, cream, cream is the best. Only fat, fat, fat good, only fat. Mmmmmmm!'

The guy was hilarious. I'd heard of fat-only diets before but this was extreme. I bought some chorizo, cheese and a flapjack while Paul turned up his nose at my carb-heavy meal and licked the inside of the carton. After our lunch break I was interested to see how Paul would cope energy-wise with only having fat for lunch. I was expecting him to be sluggish but in fact he was still very strong. We reached Split by dark and decided to go through and find a hotel on the other side of town. We hadn't really talked about it but I think we both just figured we'd share a hotel and then probably go our separate ways in the morning.

It turned out Paul used to be a professional bodybuilder and was Polish champion three years in a row. He called himself a monster and had dropped from 100 kg down to 63 kg, which was exactly the same weight as me. We were similar heights too, so he really must have been a 'monster' at 100 kg. I was also interested in his high-fat diet. He said fat was the best energy, increasing his cholesterol which then made his body produce testosterone, which in turn gave him more energy. It was pretty out-there thinking but he looked damn good for his age so there must be method in his madness.

I asked where he was cycling to and was happy to find out we were doing the same route all the way to Italy. I asked him if he fancied cycling together and he seemed genuinely excited. I was excited too.

Paul, as I might have guessed, had a very unique breakfast. He demanded a five-egg omelette and when it arrived went to the buffet table and took the entire bowl of butter blocks, the ones you get in hotels that are wrapped in paper. He then spent five minutes putting fifteen blocks of butter onto his omelette. Quick maths was that each block was about 100 kcal, so that was 1500 kcal of extra fat on his omelette. He then devoured the eggs and lifted his plate to drink the leftover melted fat. Then just when I thought I had seen it all, he began taking the empty butter wrappers and started rubbing them all over his skin.

'Fat is good for skin,' he said while rubbing them up his arms and all over his face. All I could think was, 'He is going to cook his skin when the sun comes out.'

We left the hotel and carried on along the coast. It was scenic and not too warm but the main entertainment was watching Paul. Every five minutes he'd shout 'Polska, Polska, Wooooo!' whenever he saw a car with a Polish number plate. Again his high-fat diet didn't seem to be affecting his performance at all. Every two hours he'd shout, 'Cream, cream, must have cream' and we'd stop for some full-fat cream.

I was interested to see if it worked so decided to try and copy Paul. I bought my tub of cream and ate it. It wasn't as bad tasting as I'd thought and I secretly loved that fact that I was getting 1500 kcal into my body in about four minutes. The next few hours were very strange. It took me a while to get used to it and there was a point when I was convinced I was having a heart attack because my chest was tight, but I soon felt a weird sense of energy. It was a calm type of energy. I had strength on the hills and didn't ever 'crash', as it were. I felt like I was cycling on a cloud and could see why Paul did this. I was lucky it worked so quickly because Paul told me that it can take the body three weeks to three months to train it to burn fat efficiently, but because I generally had high fat in my diet (along with carbs) my body was obviously good at using fat as an energy source. I decided to have more fat in my diet. I wasn't going to get rid of carbs though. I was still convinced you needed some carbs and protein for muscle repair throughout the day.

Instead of heading along mainland Croatia, Paul knew that we could go along a parallel peninsular and then onto Pag – an island. We could stay there for the night and then carry on and get a ferry back to the mainland further north. Getting off the busy main roads was a good idea because Paul loved to enforce the fact that cyclists are allowed in the main part of the road, even though there was a perfectly good hard shoulder he could use. He would get quite annoyed when cars drove to close to him. Now I appreciate that the rule says cyclists can use the main road, but it just seemed daft, and a bit suicidal, not to use the perfectly good hard shoulder. Getting run over has certainly made me look at roads differently. It's just not worth risking it. If there is a hard shoulder, use it. It might save your life.

The coastal road bent north and we carried on along a long narrow peninsular towards Pag. It got really dry and the landscape was covered in 10 cm sized white rocks. It was very barren, which gave me some sense of familiarity. I definitely preferred deserts to anything else. Paul continued to shout at

Polish drivers, try to pour water on his head and miss, and scream 'Polish Power' at every opportunity while I stayed behind him laughing the whole time. Miles seemed to fly by when I had front row seats to the best entertainment I'd seen in a while.

By early evening we were on Pag Island heading for the only town on the island, which was also called by the same name. It was a very picturesque old town on the seaside. It had been a good day on the bike.

The following day was another three-countries day: the plan was to have breakfast in Croatia, lunch in Slovakia or Slovenia – I wasn't sure which one – and then dinner in Italy. Paul needed to head back inland to get back to Poland for his mother's birthday so this would be our last full day together.

The first section of the day was a big climb where the main road followed the plateau of the island. It was surprisingly hilly for such a small island. We knew there was a ferry but had no idea how often it went and judging by the little traffic it couldn't have been too often. We arrived at the ferry to realise one was just leaving. The next one was in two hours. Result! Back on the mainland we were given a huge series of switchbacks to deal with as we climbed up. This part of Croatia was becoming more and more French Riviera like, as it got greener and greener. By lunchtime the crystal water was too much for Paul to resist and we stopped for a quick swim. I thought about it but it was a bit cold, so I decided just to have a beach shower instead. As I stood there, fully clothed, washing the salt off me, I suddenly realised that not that long ago I had opted for a swim in a lukewarm, bacteria-infested Indian river wishing I was on the Med. Now that I was here

I didn't feel like it. There must be something wrong with me. I turned around to head back to where Paul was swimming, to see him do a Daniel Craig James Bond coming out of the water scene. Other than the dodgy half-arm and half-leg cyclist tan, which always looks ridiculous, he could have been on the cover of any men's fitness magazine. There was a group of young girls in their early twenties checking him out. Well played Paul. I guess this fat-only diet thing must work.

We pushed in through Rijeka and along the flat Croatian Riviera. There were quite a few time-trial cyclists bombing along, which was nice to see. We then started our climb inland towards Slovenia, and into Italy. We hadn't quite reached the turning where Paul had to turn off, so found a small B&B for the night. It was run by an elderly German couple who were very friendly and even cooked us dinner. The rooms were simple but it was only when we went to bed that we realised there was no air-conditioning. It was still around 28 degrees at night and windless. Nevertheless, we both lay there half naked on the top of our sheets. I hadn't been there for more than a minute when a mosquito bit my arm. Within fifteen minutes, I had been bitten all over. I tried to go under the sheet but it was way too hot. The only thing I could think of was to put my entire winter cycle kit on, including socks, to stop them biting me. I did so but it was way too hot and I couldn't sleep. I needed to cool down and the only way I could think was to jump in the shower fully clothed. I did so and the cool water was incredible. I lay back down on the bed soaking wet and feeling cool. The mozzies stayed away. I repeated the process twice more in the night and although it was a broken sleep, it was at least some.

It was time for Paul and me to go our separate ways. It'd been really good fun to have a cycling buddy for a few days, even if to laugh at his craziness, which was always entertaining. We cycled to the top of the Trieste hill and said our goodbyes: he went inland and I went all the way down to the coast. Pasta, good roads and the famous Italian Riviera awaited me and I was looking forward to enjoying it.

# 21

## THE FINAL LEG

First on my Italian list was to have the biggest lasagne I could find. I loved lasagne and it was probably the best meal for cyclists due to the perfect balance of carbs, fat and protein. Naturally it wasn't hard to find and was made even better by adding six blocks of butter to it. Paul would be so proud. 'Fat is gooooood,' I found myself repeating and laughing out loud.

After Trieste the roads became almost completely flat again. It was a nice change from all the hills I'd been doing since Montenegro. There was also a noticeable change in both the quantity and quality of cyclists on the road. Up till now I was usually the one doing most of the overtaking around the world, but not here. Even seventy-year-old men were putting me to shame as they sped past on exquisitely crafted vintage steel bikes. Was every Italian a professional cyclist at one point in their life? It certainly seemed so.

I knew most of today would be flat as I worked my way round to Venice. The flat Italian farmlands and back roads were a pleasure to cycle on. I stopped again for another lasagne and then pushed all the way along the coast right to the last point of the headland that is opposite Venice. The last few hotels with Paul had been quite expensive, so to save some money I decided to find a campsite. There was one a mile down the road so I went there. It was pretty empty, and for €5, a bargain. I found a bush to set up my sleeping bag – I still didn't have a tent – and took off my cycle shirt but was still wearing the long-sleeved compression top underneath. I suddenly felt a bite on my back, and then another one on my arm. I looked down to see King Kong of the mosquito world taking a nice long gulp of my blood through my compression top. There was no way I'd be able to survive the night. I packed everything back up and left too embarrassed to try and explain why I was leaving. There was a hotel just down the way so I went there instead, a little depressed that I couldn't camp, and that I hadn't bought a tent, even after the accident.

I was hoping to take the ferry over to Venice and then carry on along the mainland and so was really disappointed to find out bicycles are not allowed in Venice. It was such a shame and I wasn't really keen on leaving Maid Marian chained up in the bike park at the ferry terminal. The only other option I had was to island hop the two islands that are opposite Venice. Each island is about six miles long and I'd have to take a ferry between each one.

The first island is called Lido and is incredibly beautiful, with pretty upmarket property. I don't know what Venice is like but it seemed this was where the wealthy lived and boated across to the mainland. I cycled the entire island in half an hour and waited for the ferry to the next island of Pellestrina. This island was far more rustic and had more of a fishing vibe.

I liked it! Again I had completed the island in half an hour, and so waited another half for the next ferry south while sitting on the edge of the jetty admiring all the old fishing boats and gondolas. I'd like to live on the water one day, I thought to myself. It seemed a simple life.

I carried on heading south along the coast taking in the incredible scenery, amazing quaint farmhouses and dead flat roads. Although I was almost going in the exact wrong direction to London I wanted to get a bit further down Italy to cross it, thus avoiding some of the hills in the north. By mid-afternoon I was just outside Ravenna and it was time to head inland and into the Italian mountains. I bypassed the centre of town and headed for Forli, which was slightly smaller and therefore quicker to get through. This would be my last major city before a couple of days of nothing but mountains and quaint Italian villages. I was really looking forward to it. Italian's steep history in cycling was something I really wanted to experience and the Italian mountains are famous for being both picturesque and brutal – a very rewarding combination.

I started to climb slowly and it wasn't long before it was just me and the road. It was only now that I realised how busy the Italian coastline was and how much I actually enjoyed being alone, not having to worry about cars and appreciating the sound of nothingness. Maybe I had become a hermit? How would this effect my life when I eventually returned home? Would I be able to sit in a crowded pub with my mates or would I opt out of all social activities and go for a cycle by myself instead? I was slightly worried that it might be the latter and I'd end up a lonely old man.

'Stop thinking about the end Sean,' I told myself, trying to focus on enjoying what I had left of the adventure.

I stopped for dinner and, because I was in Italy, a glass of wine in the tiny quaint village of Brisighella. The pastel coloured houses and cobbled streets were picture postcard stuff. I sat in the main square opposite what in any other country would be a pretty impressive cathedral but here was just another church. Scooters and Fiat 500s possibly, the only cars that would fit down the narrow streets leading off the main square, bombed past every few minutes. An hour after dinner I crossed the border into Tuscany, which is famous for its landscape and tradition. The villages were getting smaller and quainter the higher up I went. I eventually found a B&B that a lovely old lady owned. She gave me a bunch of fruit and a carafe of wine for bed. I love Italy!

My route was clearly a good cycle road judging by the number of cyclists overtaking me, most of whom were old enough to be retired, giving them the free time to go cycling on a week day. Like the day before, these old Italian cyclists had immaculate vintage steel frames bikes and rarely wore helmets in preference of a small cycle hat. They were very friendly as they zoomed past. Part of me knew they had lifted their pace to overtake me; we all do it. See a bike ahead of you and you're like, 'I'm going to have him.' I don't think I managed to overtake one cyclist all morning.

Tuscany was beautiful. The blue skies contrasted with the red buildings with wooden shutters, looking now as it had done decades, even centuries before. I wondered how expensive it would be to live here. It looked pricey but maybe it was normal because most of Italy looked like this. If living on water didn't work out for me then maybe a small cottage in Tuscany would do. One could dream.

After filling up my water bottles in a stream I reached the summit of the final mountain running down the middle of Italy. The climb had only taken me up to 900 m (3000 ft), which wasn't nearly as tough as I thought it might have been. I sat on the side of the road for five minutes taking in my surroundings preparing for what was most certainly going to be an amazing downhill into Florence. It didn't disappoint, not just for the fact I barely moved my legs for an hour, but the winding tree-lined, and mostly traffic-free, roads meant I could really make the most of it and enjoy whizzing past overhanging rocks a few feet from my head. It was so exhilarating and exciting I think I had a higher heart rate than on the uphill.

It was nice to be in the real Florence, which was a lot more picturesque than the American version – where I'd spilt my huge cup of coffee all over the pristine white tablecloth in that quaint café. As I sat down this time and ordered some pasta and a coffee I prayed that the same wouldn't happen. It was far less likely though, as Italy doesn't do cups of coffee the size of your head, making them a lot easier to handle.

The architecture of Florence, much like most of Italy, is breathtaking. As I wondered through on my bike I could easily imagine it looking very similar 1000 years ago, and pictured horse and carts with the occasion street-jousting match. Did that happen? Before the gun was invented did people challenge each other to a street jousting for trying it on with their wife or some such? For the rest of the afternoon cycling out of Florence, I was that jouster and every time a cyclist came towards me I was in battle again. Italy was definitely growing on me and giving my mind a good old creative workout.

As if my day couldn't get more exciting from a morning in the Tuscan mountains, and an afternoon jousting in

Florence, I saw that Pisa was just ahead of me towards the coast. Awesome. I had to go and do the cheesy 'Look I'm holding up the tower' photo. How I've judged those people in the past but when in Rome . . . um, Pisa!

Pisa was quite a big city but the old town, the part where the leaning tower was situated, was exactly on my route, which meant no detour at all. I worked my way through the old streets and soon enough came to the square surrounding the tower. My heart sank. It was rammed. There must have been a thousand people all standing on top of each other, on top of benches, climbing up lampposts, all trying get the classic Pisa photo. I started to feel a small sense of panic as I was engulfed by the crowds the further into the square I went, now walking with Maid Marian as cycling was not possible. On one side of the square was a row of street stalls selling typical tourist crap, plastic replicas and dodgy T-shirts. I hated it, took my quick photo with the Olympic Torch and left the mob as soon as possible.

My route north showed that I'd be able to cycle on the seafront for a good ten miles. It didn't disappointed either as I was given a long straight flat road which was teeming with time-trial cyclists and chain-gang groups out for their evening rides. I stopped for a quick pasta meal and heard the waiter go back to the kitchen saying 'Forrest Gump', to which they all looked at me and laughed. I had to laugh back. My beard was looking a bit like Forrest Gump's, or Chuck Noland's, Tom Hanks' other bearded character form the film *Cast Away*.

I finally stopped at a small B&B just outside Sarzana. The lovely lady who owned it said there was a supermarket open just down the road. I decided to walk there and for some strange reason I went barefoot. It was a good half-mile to the supermarket along the tar road, which was surprisingly painful on my now pretty-sensitive feet that had been in shoes constantly for the last five months. Annoyingly, it was closed. I looked up the road to see another area that might have something open, so walked there. It too was closed. I was now so far away from the B&B that heading back without food wasn't an option. Eventually I found a pizza restaurant and went inside to the stares of everyone. I was still in Lycra, dirty, hairy and barefoot. I wouldn't have let me in, but thankfully they did.

My feet were still painful the following morning. I looked at them to find two blisters, one on the heel of each foot and one on each big toe. I cursed myself at my stupidity as I struggled to put my shoes on.

I carried on through Sarzana and started to climb again. There were a few nerve-wracking moments when I had to cycle through an uphill tunnel. That may have been the slowest ten minutes of my life as the light at the end of the tunnel seemed to be getting further and further away from me. I wasn't even sure if cyclists were allowed in tunnels, which made the whole experience even more stressful. Italian police are probably quite scary.

The hills carried on along the coast but I didn't mind. It was stunning, sunny and I didn't need to plan much in the way of food and water. By mid-afternoon, I started to get saddle sores. I had been on the bike for just over 100 days and covered 15,000 miles or so and not once had I got saddle sores, but for some unknown reason, today I had them. My groin started to chafe really badly and after about an hour I couldn't even sit on my saddle anymore and had to cycle standing up. I tried to think why and the only explanation I had was that I hadn't washed my shorts in a few days and maybe there was a build-up of sweat and dirt. I decided to cut my day short and rest up. If the chafe broke through the skin I'd have a wound all the way to the end. The thought of that made me cringe. My arse really hurt.

My route the next day took me to Monaco. I was determined to cycle through the tunnel along the harbour that the Monaco Grand Prix takes. I don't follow Formula One but that seems to be the race that I always land up watching.

I wasn't sure if my road went through the tunnel and I didn't have a detailed map so just headed left until I hit the shoreline road and then turned right. I knew I'd get there eventually as long as the sea was on my left. As I navigated my way through Ferrari and Rolls-Royce lined streets it struck me how wealthy this place was. You always hear of it as being a place where millionaires go, but I had no idea it was this extravagant. The streets were pristine, houses were beyond comprehension and the super yachts way, way bigger than any house I've ever been in. Monaco is less than one square kilometre big and has a population of over 36,000, making it the most densely populated country in the world. I had no idea where these people were because it seemed pretty empty.

I eventually found my tunnel and zoomed through it making my own engine sound pretending I was Lewis Hamilton to the amusement of a few sailing types walking through. I stopped briefly to take a few photos before carrying on out the other side and back into France. Monaco isn't a place I'd ordinarily choose to go, but I was glad to have seen its utter ridiculousness.

My next stop was Nice, which I'd heard was, um, nice. I decided it was probably a good stop for late breakfast, or early lunch. It didn't really matter as I was going to have lasagne either way. Nice *was* nice and also full of topless women. I had forgotten France's casual views on boobs. It was funny to see women come down to the beach in their work clothes, looking very smart and professional, then strip half naked, sit in the sun for a while and then get back into work clothes and head back to the office. Casual lunch-hour naked tanning. I wondered if that changed office dynamics at all?

I pushed on south along the coast towards the famous Saint-Tropez, another place for the rich and famous to visit, and I wanted to see what all the fuss was about. I turned off the main road and followed the loop round along the coast. Within minutes I was cycling down pretty incredible residential streets flanked my huge multimillion euro cliff-side houses. I passed an estate agent and saw a villa for €32 million. I nearly fell off Maid Marian: €32 million euros for a villa. I kept saying it over and over again but no matter what accent I used, it still sounded ridiculous. Like Monaco, Saint-Tropez also seemed a little deserted. I guess it's because if you have that much money to spend on a house you probably are running a big business somewhere and this villa is probably a second home. It did have a pretty amazing beach though. I'd give it that.

I was now at one of the southernmost points along the Med and the next day I went round the corner, heading towards Marseille. This was going to be the point at which I would start heading home. I felt a bit sad. Up till then I was still having an adventure, but once I started heading north through France I really was done! Although I had managed, on the most part, not to think about going home, I now had to. My pace dropped as I thought of ways to somehow make the adventure live on. I really didn't feel like going home. I didn't feel like the questions, the sympathy, the failure, the meetings with sponsors and so forth. All I wanted to do was carry on cycling in the little bubble that I'd become accustomed too.

I was just coming into Marseille when I saw a sign for ferries to Tunis. I could get a ferry to Africa? My mind was all of a sudden searching for ideas, for excuses not to go home. I stopped on the side of the road looking across the vast ocean, imagining Africa just over the horizon and what potential adventures it could hold for me. I then thought about the old lady I met in the Rockies; I didn't even know her name, yet she had left an impact on me. Maybe that would be me in thirty years' time? Maybe I could just never go home? I could go over to Africa from here and then head south towards South Africa: that would add another year to my ride if I took it slowly. Then from there I could go to South America and head to Alaska. That would be another year or two. How long would it take to cycle everywhere in the world? However long it might take it still felt like it wouldn't be long enough for me to want to go home. There was no point needlessly dreaming though. I had no money left and had to go home. This was it. My journey was in its final stages. I turned north with a heavy heart.

It was a daunting feeling realising that it was nearly over. I felt sad. Life on the road was so simple. Cycle, eat, sleep, repeat. I loved it. I loved pushing myself. I loved trying to order food with sign language, five times a day, every single day. The thought of going back to normality, or whatever that meant, was scary. What was I going to do when I returned? On top of that I was also returning a failure. I had failed in my world-record attempt and the last thing I wanted was the sympathy pats on the head from my friends and family telling me how proud they were of me, still, and how I'd have totally beaten the record if I hadn't been run over. I didn't want any of that.

I don't remember much of that final stretch home. I was completely in autopilot mode. After a week or so I reached Caen and took the overnight ferry to Portsmouth. This was it. I was really now going home. I had a moment of reflection in the middle of the Channel. It was easy to get caught up in the whole travelling lifestyle but I'd had one incredibly life-changing journey and very grateful to have been able to do it. I was looking forward to seeing my friends and family. I figured I'd just ignore all accident-related questions and concentrate on the amazing stories, places and people I had met and seen.

I disembarked the ferry and was suddenly excited to have something I could have done with a lot more of on my journey – a Full English Breakfast. I cycled out of Portsmouth and stopped at the first café I could find. The waitress was very friendly and asked, 'Where've you come from and heading to, love?'

I smiled and replied, 'Portsmouth to London.'

'Wow, really! That's incredible.' She gasped and shouted back to her chef. 'This guy is cycling to London, give him extra beans.'

I'm glad I didn't say 'the world' as they probably didn't have enough beans for that.

It was a Sunday and I did a short cycle to Brighton to check into my final hotel for the trip. I had decided to officially finish my ride in a small pub in Camden, central London, on a weekday because I figured with it being a nice weekend all my friends would be away, but they'd all be back in London on the Monday and able to come to the pub after work. I had also managed to get a few friends and Twitter followers down to Brighton to ride the final leg back to London with me, which I was looking forward to.

I woke up early for my final day and went down to Brighton Pier, where I was going to meet my peloton. Being a typical British summer it was obviously pissing down with rain. I thought that no one would turn up, so was surprised to see a good eight people huddled by the coffee stand. There was Phil from my local bike shop, James Ketchell, a fellow adventurer friend, and even Ian who had helped me dodge the tornados in Oklahoma. I was honoured that people had made an effort to come all this way in the rain to see me. Rachel who filmed me in India was also there setting up GoPros on my bike and doing some filming. We were just getting ready when another cyclist came round the corner. I wiped the rain off my glasses and noticed who it was straight away. It was none other than previous world-record holder and the inspiration for the global bike race, Vin Cox. What an honour. Rachel had organised for him to come and cycle with me. It was good to be back and great to share similar stories with Vin from his cycle, the perfect companion for my last day in the saddle.

The route from Brighton to London is something I'd done a few times but mostly in reverse. Heading back to London felt annoyingly uphill but was in fact no different really. It was good to have people around me. The sense of familiarity and good old British humour was comforting for the last day. Also being in non-English-speaking countries for so long meant actually having a real unbroken conversation was a real highlight. We took it slow with Ian leading the peloton most of the way. He's pretty strong on the bike and even had me on the hills. I obviously blamed that on my fatigue. Yes, definitely my fatigue!

I had planned to get to the pub at around seven, which was enough time for all my mates to get there from work. It was slow progress working our way through the busy London streets, some of which I had cycled down on that first day nearly five months previously, not knowing at all what I was getting myself into.

I came around that last corner in Camden to a crowd of people all standing outside the pub looking in my direction. There was an eruption of cheers and whistles as I made my way towards them. It was all very overwhelming. All thoughts about the accident swept away as my friends and family all applauded as I headed towards them. A million things rushed through my mind in those last 100 metres. I'd just cycled 16,000 miles, through twenty-five countries in six continents in five months. I thought about the hills that killed my knees in South America, riding over a snake's tail in the Rockies, sharing a camp spot under a café with a few geese in Australia and being bitten by a rabid dog in the desert. All these memories came flooding back.

My ride was defined by so many factors that came in pairs. My two legs powered me around the world on two wheels. There were two of us: myself and Maid Marian, man and machine working in perfect harmony. I landed up having two completely different adventures with completely different goals: one before the accident, and one after the accident. All these were instrumental in my ride, but most of all I would not have been able to continue my ride both physically and mentally if it weren't for the power of two strangers – Martin and Missy Carey – who in their selfless kindness took care of me after the accident and made it possible for me to carry on with my adventure. The world needed more people like them and I'd never forget what they did for me.

As I cycled those last few metres to a wall of smiling and cheering faces in a small back-alley pub in London, I realised I didn't feel suffocated anymore. I had previously allowed London, through my own poor decisions, to drain me of all creativity and freedom. I could have let it define me but decided to cut free. Then sitting with my friends, laughing and chatting about my incredible adventure, I wasn't feeling claustrophobic and depressed by London anymore. I promised myself I'd never make the same mistakes again. I looked around and caught a glimpse of myself in the mirror above the bar. I had the biggest smile I had ever seen on my face. This was by far the happiest moment of my life!

Cycling around the world was something that I never thought I'd be able to do. Throughout my childhood I put it in the same category as going to the moon. It's just what 'other people' do, I thought. I made up excuses: I'll never have enough money; I'm not that good at sport; I can't ride a bike. All these excuses, I now realised, were complete nonsense. Everyone has the ability to save money (it's not as expensive as you think). Everyone has the ability to ride a bike. Everyone has the ability to get fit (a lot fitter than you think. Trust me. The human body is incredible). Unfortunately it took until I was thirty and miserable in life for me to really think about it. It was only then I realised that with baby steps, training and preparation, and most of all, the right attitude, that anything is possible. I only wish I had discovered it earlier on in life and had the confidence to go for it then.

Completing my round the world cycle not only set me up in a new 'career' as an adventurer but it has made me a lot more confident in my mental and physical ability. I am a lot happier and a lot more creative than I ever was. I've learned that we are all a lot more physically and mentally capable than we think we are.

So, I dare you to go out there and try something you thought was out of your league. I think you'll surprise yourself.

# APPENDIX: KIT LIST

## Bike Set-Up

Thorn Mercury Reynolds 853 steel frame
Rohloff 14-gear Speedhub
DT Swiss RR 465 wheels
Son Deluxe dynamo
BioLogic ReeCharge battery pack
Continental GP 4000s 25c tyres
Profile Design tri bars
Three bottle cages and bottles
Brooks Swallow Titanium saddle
Reynolds steel touring fork
Large stuff sack behind saddle
Triangular bar bag
Top tube bag
Stuff sack below tri bars
Dynamo front light

## Equipment

Super lightweight Yeti Passion One sleeping bag +15 comfort
Small Klymit X-Lite camping frame
Terra Nova super lightweight bivi
Standard bike tool
Three spare inner tubes
Spare brake pads
Six spare spokes
Spoke tool
Four tyre levers
Twenty-five self-stick puncture repairs
Four spare chain links
Maps
GoPro camera
Canon point and shoot camera
iPhone
SPOT tracker
Suunto Core watch
First aid kit
Factor 50+ sun cream

## Clothes

One pair of socks
One pair of gloves
One pair bib cycle shorts
Compression top
Cycle shirt
Cycle jersey
Rainproof overcoat
One pair winter leggings
One pair quad compression guards

Cap
Helmet
Neck warmer

You will notice a few things missing from my list:

A second pair of socks: socks reach dirt saturation pretty quickly and then just stink out your bag.

A tent: I figured I'd make a plan when it rained and stay in motels in cheap countries. The decision saved me over 1kg.

Casual clothing: seeing as all I was doing was cycling and sleeping, I didn't feel the need to take any casual clothes.

# THANK YOUS

Martin and Missy Carey. What can I say? Without your help and support I'd never have been able to carry on with the adventure that changed my life. I owe it all to you.

Everyone else from the White County hospital and the rest of Searcy who supported me in getting back on my bike again, physically and mentally.

The person who ran me over. Thank you for doing the right thing by stopping and calling 911. It was early and dark and you could easily have left me on the side of the road. I realise this was just an accident and please know I hold no grudges.

Spokes bike shop in Little Rock. Thanks for donating me new kit and helping me to carry on with my ride.

Mum, Dad and Kerry. Sorry for putting you through hell and thanks for understanding my reasons for carrying on after my accident.

Neil Hutchinson. Thank you for sponsoring me and allowing me to change my life. I don't think you realise just how desperate I was and who knows where I'd be if you hadn't taken a huge punt on me.

Caroline. Thanks for dumping my miserable ass and making me realise I really needed to change my life around.

James Carnegie. Mate. Thanks for being understanding and letting me leave the business we spent many years building together. I still have the framed £1 note on my wall.

Liz Marvin. Thanks for all your hard work in turning my round the world bike adventure into a story to share with the world. Turns out you can polish a turd.

www.seanconway.com

 @Conway_Sean

## Also by Sean Conway...

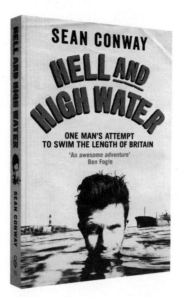

*'Rain pelted down on the back of my neck and saltwater rushed down my throat as I tried to breathe into a wave. A foghorn started booming from a lighthouse in the distance. For a moment I thought it was a rescue siren for me. Imagine if I got rescued on day two. That would be embarrassing.'*

Sean Conway set out from Land's End to be the first person ever to swim the length of Britain. On their tiny, leaky 26-foot-yacht, Sean and his three crew members faced bad weather, seasickness and the inevitable pressures of living in close proximity for months. He was stung repeatedly in the face by jellyfish and suffered a number of injuries, but he also experienced amazing night-time phosphorescence and saw the British coastline from a whole different perspective. As the trip wore on, Sean endured colder and colder water temperatures as he battled to make it to Scotland before winter.

This remarkable and funny story of an incredible 900-mile journey ultimately shows that you don't know what is possible until you truly put your mind to it.